Best Bike Rides
Connecticut

Help Us Keep This Guide Up to Date

Every effort has been made by the author and editors to make this guide as accurate and useful as possible. However, many things can change after a guide is published—roads are detoured, facilities come under new management, phone numbers change, and so forth.

We welcome your comments concerning your experiences with this guide and how you feel it could be improved and kept up to date. While we may not be able to respond to all comments and suggestions, we'll take them to heart, and we'll also make certain to share them with the author. Please send your comments and suggestions to the following address:

FalconGuides
Reader Response/Editorial Department
246 Goose Lane
Guilford, CT 06437

Or you may e-mail us at:
editorial@falcon.com

Thanks for your input, and happy riding!

BEST BIKE RIDES® SERIES

Best Bike Rides
Connecticut

The Greatest Recreational Rides in the State

DAVID STREEVER

FALCONGUIDES

GUILFORD, CONNECTICUT
HELENA, MONTANA

AN IMPRINT OF GLOBE PEQUOT PRESS

FALCONGUIDES®

An imprint of Rowman & Littlefield
Falcon and FalconGuides are registered trademarks and Make Adventure Your Story is a trademark of Rowman and Littlefield.

Distributed by NATIONAL BOOK NETWORK

Copyright © 2016 Rowman and Littlefield
All photos by David Streever, unless otherwise noted.
Maps by Alena Joy Pearce © Rowman and Littlefield.

British Library Cataloguing in Publication Information Available
Library of Congress Cataloging-in-Publication Data Available

ISBN 978-0-7627-8726-5 (paperback)
ISBN 978-1-4930-1428-6 (e-book)

∞™ The paper used in this publication meets the minimum requirements of American National Standard for Information Sciences—Permanence of Paper for Printed Library Materials, ANSI/NISO Z39.48-1992.

The author and Rowman and Littlefield assume no liability for accidents happening to, or injuries sustained by, readers who engage in the activities described in this book.

Contents

Acknowledgments viii

Introduction ix

How to Use This Guide xi

Ride Finder xv

Map Legend xvii

The Rides

Gold Coast and Fairfield County

1. Lordship Beach. 2

2. New Canaan: Arts and Nature 8

3. Wilton Hills and Reservoir 14

4. Sandy Hook Figure 8 21

5. Westport: Greens Farms 27

Hartford County

6. Case Mountain: Mountain Bike Ride 35

7. Case Mountain: Road Bike Loop 40

8. Glastonbury Orchards 46

9. Collinsville Trails and Reservoir. ℞ 52

10. Hartford City Parks 58

11. Hartford–West Hartford Loop 65

Northwest Hills

12. Barkhamsted Reservoir *2.2* 73

13. Torrington Loop . *18* 79

14. Winsted: Highland Lake . *11* 86

15. Litchfield Hills . *31* 92

16. Lakeville Lakes . *27* 99

17. West Cornwall Covered Bridge Ride. . *12* 106

18. Kent Hills . *23* 112

19. Macedonia Brook State Park . *15* 118

20. Lake Waramaug and Scenic Overlook . *12* 124

Overview

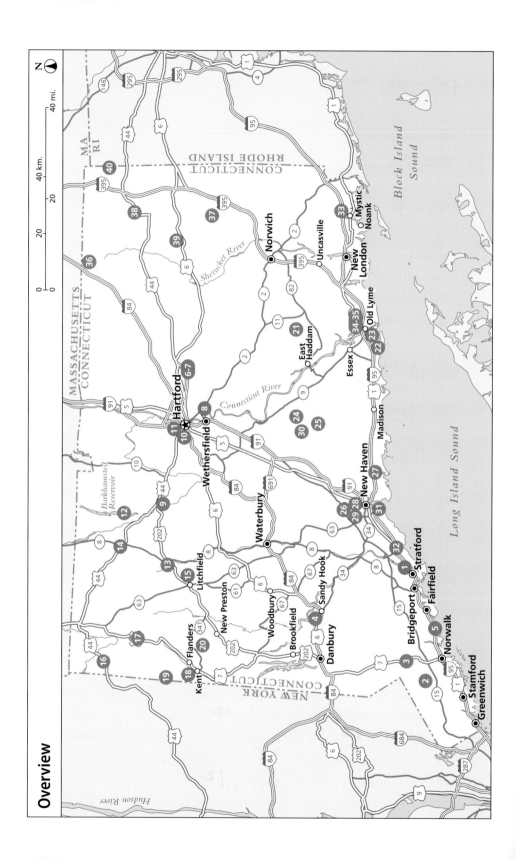

Connecticut River Valley

21. Devil's Hopyard and Johnsonville Ghost Town 131
22. Old Saybrook Beach Loop 138
23. River Valley Ferry Loop 145
24. Millers Pond State Park 152
25. Durham-Guilford Run 157

Shoreline and New Haven County

26. Back of the Giant 165
27. Branford Lakes and Stony Creek 172
28. New Haven to Lighthouse Point 179
29. New Haven Hills 186
30. Rockland Preserve State Park 193
31. West Haven Shoreline 198
32. Milford Beaches and Downtown Loop 205

New London County

33. Mystic-Stonington Loop 213
34. Old Lyme: Beach Trip 220
35. Old Lyme: Rogers Lake 227

The Quiet Corner

36. Bigelow Hollow and Yale Forest 234
37. Canterbury-Scotland Loop 240
38. Pomfret-Woodstock Loop 247
39. Natchaug State Forest Loop 253
40. Thompson: Quaddick Pond 260

References 267
About the Author 269

Key to icons used in this edition:

 Road Bike

 Mountain Bike

 Hybrid

Acknowledgments

This book was a community-driven effort that would not have been possible without the help and assistance of more people than I can possibly name. Fellow cyclists I met in small-town coffee shops sent me on wild hill hunts through the northwest; a kindly baker saw how exhausted I was and slipped me some packets of real maple syrup, which kept me going on a grueling day of exploration. The shared work of amateur historians and area cyclists proved invaluable in finding some of these rides, and the unique history and characteristics that contribute to the experiences. I also must thank the passionate cycling advocates who first made me consider riding a bike, including Elaine Lewinnek, Corinna Anderson, and Elm City Cycling of New Haven.

Matthew J. Feiner, owner of the Devil's Gear Bike Shop, got me into road bikes and on the specific one I rode. Rob Rocke, another friend from New Haven, suffered on a particularly unpleasant summer day over a hilly 80-mile route exploring potential routes suggested by our friend, Bill Tindill. Long-time friend Chris Valva, who lives near Hartford, helped plan routes and rode a number of them with me, including our hometown of East Haddam. William Kurtz, another friend in life and cycling, provided a place to stay in addition to years of assistance and help on the road. Lars Edeen sent me to Barkhamsted, and Christopher Mahoney gave me several routes through Wilton and New Canaan.

Most of this book was written in one of three locations: either at my home office in Richmond, or my co-working space, 804RVA, or at the Betty, our neighborhood bar. I'm grateful to the kind folks who made those spaces so welcoming.

My wife Hilary and I went on our first serious road ride together while planning the Lighthouse Point ride, on a lovely late-spring day. Special thanks to her for the invaluable support she provided throughout the traveling, planning, and writing of this book. Thanks to the many folks I couldn't name, who provided help even before I began this project, and the many, many folks I've ridden with over the years.

Introduction

Exploration and discovery are the best parts of cycling. No other mode of travel offers such direct contact with your surroundings. Driving a car insulates you from smells, sounds, weather, and even other humans; walking keeps you in touch, but only in a limited range. The bicycle allows for a rich experience of a large region in a timely fashion, establishing a middle path between fully human-powered and fully mechanical movement.

I've biked these roads for most of my life without realizing that the variety of terrain and conditions, all contained within a single small state, was so extraordinary. From any point in Connecticut, it's a fairly short trip to the ocean, the mountains, or the city, and the small towns are all charming in distinct ways. It was only in writing and researching this book that I reexamined my home state and learned to appreciate the wealth of historical, cultural, and natural attractions, fantastic riding, and memorable vacation destinations.

Likewise, exploration and discovery are the best parts of writing, too. Research involved thousands of miles of riding, sometimes on dead ends, or onto long-abandoned roadways that had become impassable wilderness. After one particularly confusing day, I learned what a "trap road" is; some atlases create a fake road or two in order to catch duplication of their maps. Some discoveries, like a European cafe in the middle of rustic farms, were fortunate; others, like an early sunset and dead lights on a long descent around a remote reservoir, were not. Research was also conducted off-bike, through conversations in coffee shops and bars, and countless phone calls to town historians, librarians, and city clerks. Town clerks, in particular, fielded my oddest questions and were always helpful. "Is there really a seaplane base in this lake? Is such-and-such road paved the whole way?"

The worst part was having to limit the book to forty rides. I found dozens of near-perfect routes, for all types of rides and riders. My guiding principle was to include a variety of routes to cover different interests and levels of ability, and I kept thinking of this as I discarded one route or restored another. While this guide represents an earnest attempt to share the best of the best in a number of categories, there is always an arbitrary or subjective aspect, and I may have discarded a route that you would have loved. I hope, then, that this guide serves as more than just a set of instructions, and that I can inspire you to do some exploration on your own, using my routes and notes as guidelines. I'd love to get feedback about routes and places I should have included that I missed.

This guide is heavy on road routes, but Connecticut also has an incredible array of off-road trails and mountain bike routes. These have mostly been omitted, because they are published on a plurality of websites and are easy to find and explore on your own. If you're in Connecticut and having a hard time finding people or places to ride, I encourage you to search for cycling advocacy or enthusiast groups in your area and get involved.

I've tried to represent Connecticut as the compelling place it is, and I hope that your own explorations and discoveries will bring you the same great joy mine have brought me!

How to Use This Guide

This guide is organized around six regions in Connecticut, loosely defined by county lines and geographic and cultural features. Connecticut eliminated county governments in the 1960s, but the borders still serve as useful shorthand to establish expectations for an area. The region introductions provide basic guidance on what to expect, both geographically and culturally, in each area.

This guide focuses on road routes, not because that is all Connecticut has to offer, but because the trails and mountain bike paths available are already well documented, both online and onsite. Connecticut has a limited but quickly growing number of off-road trails, carefully planned and well documented, and it seemed a waste to provide information so easily obtainable. Look to the References section to find a listing of websites for currently available trails in the state.

The roads of Connecticut are incredibly beautiful and often unpredictable; miles of country roads can suddenly give way to a four-lane highway. A ride can cover 20 miles of beautiful terrain, only to end up in a long stretch of suburbia or at a dead end. These routes have been prepared to minimize these unpleasant surprises, directing the user to less-traveled byways and back roads.

Routes have deliberately been kept on the shorter side, but they often intersect with or are near other routes; in these cases, instructions have been provided for forming longer trips. In addition, many areas are full of beautiful roads, and readers are encouraged to seek out alternatives and add-ons while riding.

Nearly every ride in this book takes place in a location that would make for a great weekend trip, with other rides nearby for the second and third days. Using the resources, routes, and maps, readers will be able to form short vacations that should appeal to cyclists and non-cyclists alike.

Connecticut is slowly embracing bicycling, thanks to the good work of many advocates and enthusiasts. If you're a local looking for more rides beyond the scope of this guide, consider reaching out to the groups working in your community; you can find them on social media and at municipal meetings on road issues. You may find routes and riding partners, and you may even end up working with your community to create new routes.

GPS

This guide was prepared with mileage from a dedicated GPS unit, passed through a computer mapping tool to correct and adjust calculations. Be aware of the limitations of whatever devices you decide to use, including battery power and accuracy, if you plan to follow mileage while riding these routes. Error-correcting phone apps can provide a high degree of accuracy for inexpensive phone-based GPS on roadways, but separate dedicated devices are slightly more accurate.

Cycling computers can also be used, but note that they work by measuring wheel rotations and are subject to different variables than GPS units. Testing and calibrating is important for any device. Mileage is given to the tenth of the mile and rounded up when between units.

Although Connecticut no longer has county governments, the county designations are still useful as geographic markers and rides were grouped by county when it made sense. Other rides were grouped by the more colorful region names used for state tourism efforts.

SAFETY

Biking carries inherent risks, and it is beyond the scope of this book to provide a comprehensive list of safety tips. Use the following general advice in conjunction with your own best judgment and always use caution.

Bike safety isn't always easy or intuitive. As a general guideline, stay in the road, riding with traffic; sidewalk riding and riding against traffic feel safe, but often present additional dangers. Adults ride bicycles too fast to travel on most sidewalks, and the risk of collision in intersections and at driveways is very high for sidewalk riders. In many communities, it is illegal to ride on the sidewalk; if the sidewalk does provide a safe and legal option, defer to pedestrians and ride with care around them.

Most of the rides in this book follow Connecticut's scenic roads, alongside automobile traffic, and bicyclists are expected to follow the same rules and regulations. Stop at stop signs and red lights, signal your turns, and in general, be a courteous road user. Make eye contact with motorists and be aware that they may not see you, even if you are wearing reflective clothing and using lights, which are requirements in bad weather and the dark.

I encourage you to ride without any audio accompaniment. Your safety depends on having access to all of your senses, and wearing headphones will limit your ability to hear other riders, voices, and vehicles.

On Off-Road Trails and Singletrack

Look for signage explaining local rules before taking any off-road rides. Hikers and horses always have priority; be aware of the other road users and prepared to stop for safety. Use a bell to alert other trail users before passing, and be courteous and polite in interactions. Stay to the right, pass on the left, and telegraph your actions to limit confusion.

Singletrack trails come with additional considerations. These are single-file trails that may also feature other users; dismount and let them take the entire trail to continue on their way. Follow the proper direction for trails (usually clockwise, except as indicated), and avoid "braiding" the trails by riding around obstacles. If you can't clear something, dismount and carry the bike without making grooves around the hazard. In general, stay off singletrack in inclement conditions or after wet weather, and don't clear leaves off the route or make other changes.

Weather

Weather can vary dramatically. Always be aware of conditions and try to carry at least a snack, plenty of water, and a small phone (silenced) for emergencies. Wear sunblock, even in the colder months, as long periods of time on the bike will expose you to more sun than you may realize. Wear layers, especially when it is cold, to adjust to temperatures as they change and as you warm or cool.

Equipment

While helmets aren't required for adults, they should be worn on any ride. On average, a cyclist crashes every 4,500 miles, and head injuries cause 75 percent of cycling-related deaths. While nearly every helmet meets the minimum safety requirements, the safest helmet will always be the one you wear; do not skimp on this purchase, and make sure to buy a comfortable well-fitting helmet that you will be happy wearing.

You should always have at minimum a front and rear LED light for visibility in case of weather changes or rides that go late. I didn't properly charge my bright night lights and was caught by an earlier than expected sunset while biking around the reservoir in Barkhamsted; it was a terrifying experience, but at least I had small blinkie LEDs so drivers had some idea where I was as I scrambled back to my car. Don't make my mistake; be over-prepared when it comes to lights.

Always be prepared to deal with a flat or minor repair issue. Some of these rides take place in remote areas, and you may not be able to get a cab or assistance. Bring a patch kit (check it routinely to make sure it's still good), a spare inner tube, and a hand pump or CO_2 system. A good multi-tool will let you deal with other minor issues that could otherwise end your ride.

Some riders use mirrors, a good idea, but be aware of their limitations. Do not assume you are safe to pull into traffic without looking in all directions first. Mirrors have blind spots, so you will want to look first.

Even minor crashes can injure hands and lead to deep cuts between the fingers. For this reason, half-finger gloves are recommended; the tough material will shield your skin. Wicking clothes and padded shorts will make for more comfortable rides, and are less likely to become embedded in the skin if you do crash.

A GPS device is recommended to follow the mileage in this guide. Dedicated devices are increasingly affordable and let you measure your distance without draining the battery on a cell phone you might need for an emergency. Finally, consider buying a lock, especially for rides that involve leaving your bike to eat inside or take a hike. Ask the folks at your local bike shop what they recommend.

How to Use This Guide

Ride Finder

BEST ROAD RIDES CONNECTICUT

3 Wilton Hills and Reservoir
4 Sandy Hook Figure 8
7 Case Mountain: Road Bike Loop
13 Torrington Loop
18 Kent Hills

21 Devil's Hopyard and Johnsonville Ghost Town
25 Durham-Guilford Run
26 Back of the Giant
29 New Haven Hills
35 Old Lyme: Rogers Lake
37 Canterbury-Scotland Loop

BEST MOUNTAIN BIKES RIDES

6 Case Mountain: Mountain Bike Ride

24 Millers Pond State Park
30 Rocklands Preserve State Park

BEST RIDES FOR SIGHTSEEING

8 Glastonbury Orchards
10 Hartford City Parks
20 Lake Waramaug and Scenic Overlook
22 Old Saybrook Beach Loop
23 River Valley Ferry Loop
27 Branford Lakes and Stony Creek

28 New Haven to Lighthouse Point
31 West Haven Shoreline
32 Milford Beaches and Downtown Loop
33 Mystic-Stonington Loop
34 Old Lyme: Beach Trip
38 Pomfret-Woodstock Loop

BEST RIDES FOR FAMILIES

1 Lordship Beach (using the sidewalks for children)
9 Collinsville Trails and Reservoir
10 Hartford City Parks
20 Lake Waramaug (Skip Scenic Overlook)
22 Old Saybrook Beach Loop
24 Millers Pond State Park

30 Rocklands Preserve State Park
31 West Haven Shoreline
32 Milford Beaches and Downtown Loop

BEST RIDES FOR SEEING BIRDS AND NATURE

2 New Canaan: Arts and Nature

5 Westport: Greens Farms

8 Glastonbury Orchards

12 Barkhamsted Reservoir

15 Litchfield Hills

19 Macedonia Brook State Park

BEST BACK AND OFF ROADS ROUTES

9 Collinsville Trails and Reservoir

12 Barkhamsted Reservoir

14 Winsted: Highland Lake

16 Lakeville Lakes

17 West Cornwall Covered Bridge
   Ride

19 Macedonia Brook State Park

36 Bigelow Hollow and Yale Forest

39 Natchaug State Forest Loop

40 Thompson: Quaddick Pond

Map Legend

═══⟨95⟩═══	Interstate Highway	✈	Airport
═══⟨1⟩═══	US Highway	⏜	Bridge
───⟨2⟩───	State Highway	■	Building/Point of Interest
═══⟨2⟩═══	Featured State/Local Road	✪	Capital
───────	Local Road	✝	Cemetery
▪▪▪▪▪▪▪▪▪	Featured Bike Route	🍴	Dining
■■■■■■■■■	Bike Route	◉	Large City
┼─┼─┼─┼	Railroad	17.1 ◆───	Mileage Marker
───────	Trail	🏛	Museum
─ ·· ─ ·· ─	State Line	🅿	Parking
～～～	Small River or Creek	▲	Peak/Summit
⬭	Body of Water	○	Small City/Town
▭	State Park/Forest/Wilderness/Preserve/Recreational Area	❶	Trailhead
▭	National Forest/Park	🚂	Train Station
		⟫	Waterfall

Gold Coast and Fairfield County

Fairfield County is an economic center along Long Island Sound, close to New York City where many residents work, and home to internationally known financial firms. This vibrant region is full of upscale restaurants and shopping boutiques, and is known colloquially as the "gold coast" for its combination of wealth and picturesque shore.

Some of the highlights in this section include the Weir Art Farm, the only national park dedicated to the arts, and the Glass House, a modernist home turned historic house museum, in New Canaan and Wilton respectively. All of the towns have water views, either along the shore or around reservoirs and rivers. There is also a mix of natural terrain and historic town centers.

The New Canaan and Wilton rides can be linked into a longer ride for distance cyclists, and both towns are full of quiet back roads suitable for exploration. The Westport ride was inspired by the Bloomin' Metric, an annual 65-mile ride sponsored by local advocacy group Sound Cyclists. Westport also has some built-up roads used heavily by New York commuters, so use caution when exploring off the mapped rides.

Sandy Hook is a quiet little community north of the other rides. The route originating there crosses the Housatonic River and explores some quiet, pretty back roads in nearby Southbury before heading back over the historic Silver Bridge.

Mass-transit users can access Wilton, New Canaan, Westport, and Stratford, where Lordship is located, on the Metro-North train line.

1

Lordship Beach

Lordship is a small coastal community on the southern peninsula of Stratford, surrounded by Long Island Sound on three sides and bordered by the Sikorsky Memorial Airport to the north. Lordship is a quiet suburb; residents primarily commute to office jobs in the rest of Fairfield County via Main Street or Lordship Boulevard, part of CT 113, the only road between Lordship and the rest of Stratford.

Start: American Shakespeare Theater grounds, on Elm Street

Length: 8.9 miles

Riding time: 40 to 60 minutes

Best bike: Hybrid or road bike

Terrain and trail surface: Asphalt, boardwalk

Traffic and hazards: CT 113 can be busy and slightly fast. Most streets are fairly low volume and slow.

Things to see: Lordship Beach, Short Beach, Stratford Point Lighthouse, "Point No Point," Long Beach, small aircraft at Igor Sikorsky Memorial Airport

Fees: None

Getting there: Elm Street is just off CT 130, near I-95. In either direction on I-95, take exit 32, then West Broad Street to a right turn onto Main Street. Turn left onto CT 130 and then right onto Elm Street. The park is just ahead.

GPS: 41.18538 / -73.12578

THE RIDE

This ride begins just outside of Lordship, at the grounds of the American Shakespeare Theater on Elm Street. This long defunct theater once hosted legendary stage and film actors. Ed Asner, Katharine Hepburn, Christopher Walken, Lynn Redgrave, and James Earl Jones are a few of those who performed during the theater's heyday.

The theater operated from the mid 1950s to the early 1980s and has sat vacant since; there are many proposals to repurpose the land, but it currently is owned by the town and put to no particular use. Parking is free, and the property is still lovely, covered in maple and elm trees for a shaded, scenic ride.

Bike out of the park and turn left onto Elm Street, a narrow, low-volume road with tree cover and single-family homes. After passing an office park on the left, you reach a stop sign and cross Birdseye Street, continuing along Elm to the signalized intersection with Main Street (CT 113).

The route turns left onto Main, a less pleasant street with more traffic, fast food chains, and large apartment buildings. Most of the road has a fairly wide shoulder to the right, but some sections are without much of a buffer; use caution and ride carefully, especially over the first half a mile. Cyclists with less road experience may be tempted to ride along the sidewalk, which is legal, but can be dangerous as well; keep a keen watch for turning vehicles that may not see you on the sidewalk.

The situation improves dramatically when you reach the Igor Sikorsky Memorial Airport, where the shoulder widens and remains consistent. The small airfield was once an important regional center for air travel, with connecting flights to major airports, but now mostly serves single-engine props, helicopter traffic to New York City, and enthusiast pilots with small planes. This makes for interesting scenery; expect to see historic planes and functional antiques parked on your right.

After the airfield, you pass marshy wetlands on the right, with more suburban housing on the left, up to a major intersection. Take a tight right onto Prospect Drive (still CT 113), and enter Lordship proper.

The surroundings mostly consist of suburban housing, and the road can be slightly fast, but the shoulder is wide and consistent right up to the traffic circle.

Carefully enter the traffic circle, exiting onto the second road, Oak Bluff Avenue, to continue following CT 113. This half-mile stretch of road is adjacent to scenic wetlands, to the right, and eventually reaches Long Beach Park, which you can explore as part of a detour. Long Beach is not an ideal biking spot; the undeveloped beach is more suited to walking exploration. The beach is a notable bird-nesting habitat and has neither food nor restrooms.

The mapped route continues on Ocean Avenue, a left off of Oak Bluff Avenue, with an immediate right-hand turn onto 5th Avenue. Running through a small neighborhood, 5th Avenue ends at a group of picturesque raised beach cottages directly overlooking the sound.

Take a left onto Shoreline Drive when 5th Avenue ends. This next section is a bit sandy, along tightly packed beach cottages and seasonal homes, with some views of the water on your right. At the end of the road, with 3rd Avenue on your left, ride past the barriers dead ahead and follow this closed road past Marnick's Restaurant onto Beach Drive.

You also pass curious "Point-No-Point." The name refers to an apparent spit of land jutting out from the shore, dwarfed by two longer points.

Beach Drive passes Lordship Beach for a truly gorgeous quarter-mile of coastal cycling. The view is distracting, but make sure to watch the pull-in parking on the right, which could prove dangerous. Ride along the sidewalk here to have an unobstructed view of the water and avoid being caught out by an inattentive driver.

The road curves along a wooded area behind the beach and intersects again with Ocean Avenue, where you turn right. This is a quiet neighborhood with a mix of beach cottages, saltbox homes, and larger, grander houses with ocean views.

In less than a quarter-mile, turn right onto Lordship Road, split in half by a grassy median. The road ends just ahead, around the 4.4-mile mark, at Lordship Beach, where you turn left onto Park Boulevard.

Park Boulevard provides a half-mile of unobstructed beach views on a quiet back road, ending at Cove Place, where you turn left to continue following the route until the road terminates in a T-junction with Prospect Drive.

Turn right onto Prospect Drive, through a slightly busier suburban neighborhood, and pass Riverdale Drive on the left, for a quick quarter-mile detour to the end of Stratford Point, with some nice water and marsh views.

When you reach the end, turn around, and ride Prospect Drive back, turning right onto Riverdale Drive. Riverdale is in a state of disrepair; the asphalt here is uneven and broken, but fine for a road bike. Watch for potholes and Wayne's Walk, a street sign over a narrow sidewalk behind a wooden fence, on the right. This path will take you to Short Beach, with nice views of the historic Stratford Point Lighthouse behind you.

The lighthouse has been automated and is still in operation by the Coast Guard, but it is closed to visitors. However, the view is quite nice and photogenic. Follow the sidewalk through Short Beach, being mindful of rough sandy patches, until passing restrooms and turning right onto Short Beach Drive,

View from the grounds of the American Shakespeare Theater.

the beach driveway. Follow this road until the left-hand turn on Dorne Drive, a fairly quiet and narrow stretch of road through marshland.

Turn right at the end of Dorne Drive, back onto Main Street (CT 113), and follow the route to the right-hand turn onto Elm Street, back to the Shakespeare Theater grounds, to finish the ride.

MILES AND DIRECTIONS

0.0 Start at American Shakespeare State Park

0.1 Left onto Elm Street

0.7 Left onto Main Street

1.8 Continue on Stratford Road

2.5 Right onto Prospect Drive

3.0 Enter traffic circle, exit on Oak Bluff Avenue

3.4 Left onto Ocean Avenue

3.5 Right onto 5th Avenue

3.7 Left onto Shoreline Drive

3.8 Straight to go off-road toward Beach Drive

3.9 Proceed onto Beach Drive

4.1 Continue on Jefferson Street

4.2 Right onto Ocean Avenue

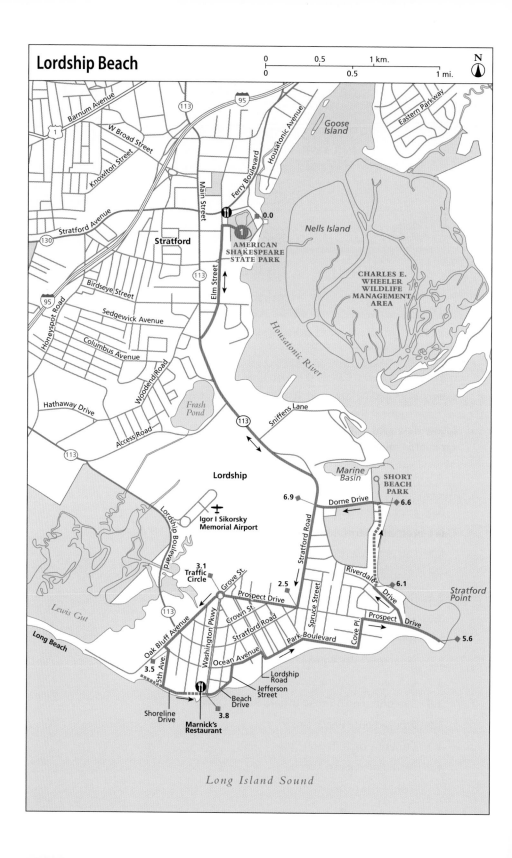

Lordship Beach

0   0.5   1 km.
0   0.5   1 mi.

N

Barnum Avenue

W Broad Street

Knowlton Street

Stratford Avenue

130

95

Honeyspot Road

Birdseye Street

Sedgewick Avenue

Columbus Avenue

Hathaway Drive

Access Road

113

1

113

95

Main Street

Elm Street

Ferry Boulevard

Housatonic Avenue

113

Stratford

Woodend Road

Frash Pond

113

Sniffens Lane

Goose Island

Nells Island

**CHARLES E.
WHEELER
WILDLIFE
MANAGEMENT
AREA**

Housatonic River

0.0

1

**AMERICAN
SHAKESPEARE
STATE PARK**

Lordship

Lordship Boulevard

Igor I Sikorsky
Memorial Airport

Lewis Gut

Long Beach

113

113

3.1
Traffic
Circle

Grove St.

Prospect Drive

Crown St.

Stratford Road

Oak Bluff Avenue

Washington Pkwy

5th Ave.

3.5

Ocean Avenue

Beach
Drive

3.8

Shoreline
Drive

**Marnick's
Restaurant**

Lordship
Road

Jefferson
Street

Park Boulevard

Spruce Street

Cove Pl.

Stratford Road

2.5

Stratford Road

Dorne Drive

6.9

Marine
Basin

**SHORT
BEACH
PARK**

6.6

Riverdale

6.1

Drive

Prospect   Drive

Stratford
Point

5.6

Long Island Sound

4.4 Right onto Lordship Road, then left onto Park Boulevard.

5.0 Left onto Cove Place

5.1 Right onto Prospect Drive

5.6 Make a U-turn

5.8 Right onto Riverdale Drive

6.1 Right onto off-road path, along beach

6.6 Left onto Dorne Drive

6.9 Right onto Stratford Road

7.1 Continue on Main Street

8.1 Right onto Elm Street

8.8 Right onto American Shakespeare State Park drive

8.9 Finish at park

RIDE INFORMATION

Bike Shops
Chris's Spoke and Wheel: 355 E Main St., Bridgeport; (203) 384-8779

Events and Attractions
Stratford Point Light: This historic lighthouse on the Housatonic River is maintained and staffed by the Coast Guard, on private property.

Restaurants
Lighthouse Deli: 348 Stratford Rd., Stratford; (203) 375-0303
Gaetano's Salumeria: 1886 Main St., Stratford; (203) 377-8860
Marnick's Restaurant: 10 Washington Pkwy., Stratford; (203) 377-6288; marnicks.com

Restrooms
4.4 Miles: Lordship Beach
6.6 Miles: Short Beach

New Canaan: Arts and Nature

New Canaan is a wealthy suburban town in southwest Connecticut, home to famous television personalities and writers, although many of the 20,000 residents commute to nearby Stamford and New York for financial sector jobs. New Canaan has been rendered in literature and film; the geography and architecture of the town served as the setting for the novel The Ice Storm, written in 1970 by Ang Lee, described as a work of "suburban angst" by film critic Roger Ebert.

Cyclists looking for a more challenging ride may combine this route with the 22-mile Wilton Hills loop. In that case, after riding through the reservoir, turn left onto Belden Hill Road instead of right, and follow it to Drum Hill Road, which ends at Ridgefield Road. Turn left onto Ridgefield Road and follow the Wilton instructions, staying on CT 106 (Wolfpit Road) for a very steep climb back to the last half of this route.

Start: Downtown New Canaan

Length: 15.9 miles

Riding time: 1 hour, 15 minutes

Best bike: Road bike

Terrain and trail surface: Asphalt

Traffic and hazards: Downtown New Canaan can be congested and busy. A short stretch on the return leg, on CT 123, can also be fast and a bit hectic.

Things to see: The reservoir, the Silvermine Arts Center, bustling downtown New Canaan, beautiful back roads, and quiet town parks

Fees: In downtown, the Morse Lot offers up to 3 hours free parking, but you probably want to park at the Locust Avenue lot or Railroad Station lot, where you can pay to park all day. Either of these lots is fairly close to the downtown start at the intersection of CT 106 and Main Street.

Getting there: New Canaan is highly accessible by train, with a Metro-North station in the town center. From I-95N, take exit 13 for US 1/Post Road and turn left. Turn right ahead onto W Norwalk Road. Continue onto White Oak Shade Road, then Main Street, and finally turn left onto Elm Street into downtown New Canaan. Follow signs for parking.

GPS: 41.14642 / -73.49197

THE RIDE

This 15.9-mile route starts in downtown New Canaan and travels along hilly, quiet roads through the surrounding area. It includes a scenic trip through a local reservoir and a visit to the Silvermine Arts Center.

From the start, you turn onto CT 106 or East Avenue, and head east on this slightly busy thoroughfare toward Mill Pond Park. Mill Pond Park is a town park situated around a beautiful pond, with benches and other seating areas, and walking trails along the Fivemile River.

Bear left past the pond to stay on 106, where East Avenue becomes Silvermine Road. Around the 2-mile mark, Silvermine Road turns right, leading to the Silvermine Arts Center, a great destination for arts tourists. This turn will be part of the return leg, but you bypass it for now. Turn left and then make an immediate right turn to stay on CT 106.

When you see the Connecticut Friends School, bear right again to stay on 106, avoiding the smaller road directly ahead. Near the 3.5-mile mark, turn left onto Old Boston Road, a quiet little road that curves and winds through the hills and forests of New Canaan. This area is quiet, scenic, and bordered by wildflowers and dense woods. The roads ahead are largely uphill, but the spectacular views of the reservoir up ahead are worth the effort.

Old Boston Road becomes Huckleberry Hill Road for a short stretch before you make a hard right onto Old Kingdom Road. Old Kingdom Road can be very steep, with some of the harder climbs on this route. Automobile traffic is rare, but use caution. The road is so narrow it's almost a single lane.

At the 5-mile mark the road turns left, becoming Reservoir Road, and then right onto Old Huckleberry Road. You ride down a quick little descent with an incredible view of the South Norwalk Reservoir on either side of you, which you cross on a narrow, low causeway.

Climb up one more short hill as you leave this scenic area, and take a right onto Belden Hill Road. Belden Hill Road can have moderate to high traffic, but is largely a quiet, rural street. Follow it for less than a mile and then turn right back onto CT 106. At the intersection of CT 106 and Silvermine Road, turn left this time, staying on Silvermine Road as it heads down toward Silvermine Avenue.

There is a possible food stop available at the Silvermine Market, a breakfast and lunch spot that offers gourmet food in a casual atmosphere and outdoor seating, and you can visit the Arts Center across the street on the right.

Once you've finished up here, take a left onto Silvermine Avenue and then a right to stay on it, and ride this quiet neighborhood street until it reaches busy CT 123, New Canaan Avenue.

Take a right onto this wide-shouldered but busy street, which passes numerous eateries and restaurants. You can stop now, or continue on into downtown New Canaan in just a few miles. CT 123 eventually intersects with CT 106 at Mill Pond Park; here turn left and finish your ride when you reach downtown at Main Street.

MILES AND DIRECTIONS

0.0 Start on Main Street and turn right onto CT 106

0.6 Continue on CT 106 (Silvermine Road)

2.1 Left to stay on CT 106

2.2 Right onto CT 106 (Wilton Road) then continue on CT 106 (New Canaan Road)

2.6 Right to stay on New Canaan Road

3.4 Left onto Old Boston Road

3.9 Continue on Huckleberry Hill Road

4.3 Right onto Old Kingdom Road

5.1 Continue on Old Huckleberry Road

6.2 Right onto Belden Hill Road

7.0 Right onto CT 106

9.0 Left to stay on CT 106

9.1 Continue on CT 106 (Silvermine Road)

10.1 Left onto Silvermine Avenue

12.1 Right onto CT 123

15.2 Left onto CT 106

15.8 Left onto Main Street

15.9 Arrive at finish

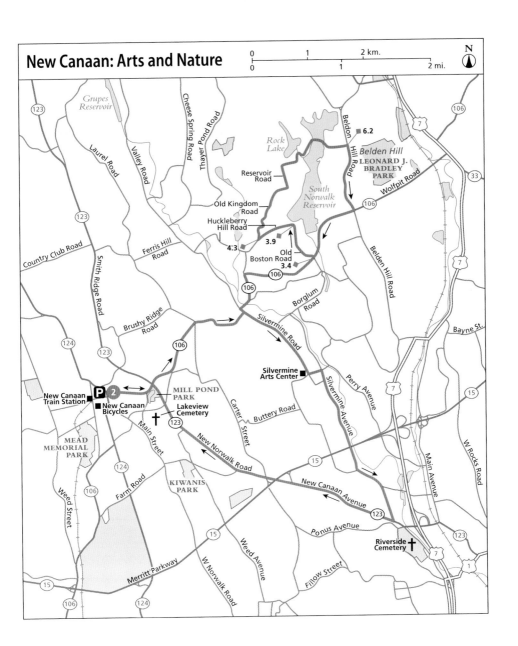

New Canaan: Arts and Nature

Views of the reservoir from the causeway.

RIDE INFORMATION

Bike Shops

New Canaan Bicycles: 24 Cherry St., New Canaan; (866) 629-2453; newcanaan bicycles.com

Outdoor Sports Center: 80 Danbury Rd., Wilton; (203) 762-8797; outdoor sports.com

Smart Cycles: 303 Strawberry Hill Ave., Westport; (203) 831-9144; smart cycles.com

Local Events and Attractions

Silvermine Arts Center: The center is considered the preeminent visual arts center in Fairfield County and is a great place to experience art in a beautiful natural environment. The center also hosts a variety of performing arts and has evening and weekend performances in addition to gallery tours and visual arts exhibits. One of the most popular exhibitions, Art of the Northeast (originally called "The New England Exhibition") has shown more than 6,000 works of art since it began in 1949. Some of the famous artists exhibited here include Louise Nevelson, Elaine de Kooning, and Milton Avery. Silvermine has a busy calendar of exhibitions and performances; check silvermineart.org in advance to plan your visit.

The New Canaan Nature Center: Less than a mile outside of downtown New Canaan, the nature center boasts seven aviaries in a birds of prey exhibit, seasonal programming, 2 miles of hiking trails, arboretums and greenhouses, and gift shops on 40 acres of preservation land.

The Glass House Tours

New Canaan was central to the modern design movement for roughly 20 years. Professors and students from the Harvard Graduate School of Design built homes here, as did Frank Lloyd Wright and many other modernist architects. In total eighty homes were built in the period; roughly sixty survive.

One of the most famous of these, the Glass House, was designed by Harvard School of Design graduate Philip Johnson, who lived here for 58 years until his death in 2005.

Johnson left the home and estate to the National Trust for Historic Preservation, and the group operates seasonal daily tours, which must be reserved in advance. The titular glass house, a Mies van der Rohe–inspired modernist home, is the main attraction, but the longest tours last close to 3 hours and include nearly a mile of walking through the 47-acre estate, with visits to the sculpture gallery and underground painting gallery, studio, guest house, and more.

Johnson worked on the space throughout his life, adding buildings not out of need for habitable space but to satisfy his creative impulses. One notable example is the Ghost House, a nonfunctional building he designed purely as an aesthetic curiosity. Bored by the view of forest from his studio space, Johnson had the idea to construct a nonfunctioning glass and steel home on top of the foundations of barns that had burned down before he purchased the property.

The Painting Gallery is built into a large grass-covered mound and houses important works of modern art from Cindy Sherman, Andy Warhol, Frank Stella, Julian Schnabel, and more. This berm house–style building was designed to echo the tombs of the ancient Greeks and to have minimal visual impact on the fields around the main house, hence the decision to raise up the earth around it. Views from the Glass House show a seemingly unobstructed view of rolling fields meeting the forest.

Capacity is very limited; subsequently, tours must be booked well in advance. If you're planning to visit, you want to reserve a spot on the website (http://theglasshouse.org/). Tour options range from the concise and structured (a short tour of just the titular home) to a free-ranging self-guided tour of the entire estate.

Restaurants

The Farmer's Table: 12 Forest St., New Canaan; (203) 594-7890

Elm Restaurant: 73 Elm St., New Canaan; (203) 920-4994; elmrestaurant.com

India: 62 Main St., New Canaan; (203) 972-8332; indianewcanaan.com

Locali: 32 Forest St., New Canaan; (203) 920-1440; localipizzabar.com

Wilton Hills and Reservoir

Wilton is a rural town in Fairfield County with roots stretching back to the early European settlers, who built the first homes here in 1651. The town has lovely historical character and natural beauty. Much of Wilton is located along a ridge, just south of a fairly mountainous area. This route explores some of the climbs, including a particularly gnarly descent down a rural back road, on the way to Georgetown, a neighborhood that overlaps Wilton and nearby Redding.

Cyclists looking for extra mileage could link this ride with the New Canaan ride, adding in a hilly climb around the reservoir for a few extra miles. On the return leg, instead of turning onto Horseshoe Road, follow Route 106 (Wolfpit Road) to Old Boston Road, and turn right onto it, following the reservoir section of the New Canaan directions, and then turning left onto Wolfpit Road and finishing the original route. This would add about 6 miles and 700 feet of climbing.

Start: Downtown Wilton

Length: 22 miles

Riding time: 1 hour, 45 minutes

Best bike: Road bike

Terrain and trail surface: Asphalt

Traffic and hazards: Downtown Wilton can be congested and busy. Watch for cars exiting and entering parking lots. Branch Brook Road is a highly technical descent on a poorly maintained road so use caution. CT 107 can be busy with large truck traffic.

Things to see: The Saugatuck Reservoir area and several nature preserves provide natural scenery. LaChat Town Farm, on Godfrey Road, is an interesting property maintained by the Nature Conservancy and the town of Weston. The grounds include a pre-Revolutionary homestead and a historically significant working farm.

Fees: None. There are several free parking lots.

Getting there: From I-95N, take exit 15 for US 7 North toward Norwalk/ Danbury. Turn left onto Grist Mill Road, then right onto Old Belden Hill Road. Turn right onto Range Road, and continue onto Horseshoe Road and then River Road, into downtown Wilton.

GPS: 41.19284 / -73.43096

THE RIDE

This 22-mile route starts on Old Ridgefield Road, a busy commercial street in Wilton Center. After passing by a number of commercial parking lots and driveways for the first quarter of a mile, turn left onto Ridgefield Road, a quieter road heading out of downtown toward the hillier parts of town.

At the 2-mile mark, turn right onto the very scenic and very brutal Nod Hill Road. In another half-mile, as the route passes Streets Pond on the right, it starts a 200-foot climb with grades up to 15 percent. The hilly ride continues until the route turns right onto Branch Brook Road, which has some of the fastest, trickiest descents in Connecticut.

The road is not as well maintained as it could be, but it's beautiful and incredibly technical; experienced descenders will love riding down these hills and sprinting up the next short climb.

There are three of these rather technical descents before the route turns left onto Mountain Road, which features a long, sustained climb that runs through a more populated but still quiet neighborhood. Near the end of this road, make a fast descent down to Danbury Road (US 7), and cross over onto School Street.

After crossing railroad tracks and the Norwalk River, School Street becomes CT 107 (Redding Road) and enters downtown Redding. This is a slightly built-up area, with commercial strips, heavy traffic, and large trucks. Food options are accessible along the right, on Main Street.

CT 107 heads northeast, mostly going uphill, gaining about 200 feet in elevation at the peak before a fast descent to a right-hand turn onto CT 53 at the 10.3-mile mark. Turn right to stay on CT 53 when the road reaches the Saugatuck Reservoir, passing over a small, historic bridge. CT 53 passes along nearly 5 miles of forestland, abutted by Devil's Den and the water company property around the reservoir.

At the 15-mile mark, turn right onto Godfrey Road, another quiet side road, for the next mile and a quarter. On the right, the route passes Lachat Town Farm. When the road ends in a T-junction, turn left onto the busier CT 57. CT 57 is a less-scenic road through suburban-style housing. The route follows

A quiet creek on the back roads.

CT 57 south for 1.2 miles, curving west and bearing right at a fork onto Old Mill Road. Old Mill Road bears left and becomes Cobbs Mill Road, ending in a T-junction with CT 53 (Cedar Road) just ahead. Turn right onto CT 53, then take a hairpin right just under 0.5 mile to stay on Cedar Road for a tiny stretch until it ends and the route turns right onto CT 106. Take a right and follow Cedar until it ends at CT 106, just a short stretch ahead.

CT 106 rolls through quieter neighborhoods, with more open spaces and woods on either side, for the next half-mile. Turn left to stay on CT 106, which continues mostly downhill with a very fast descent to US 7.

US 7 is busy and heavily trafficked. Use caution making the left-hand turn onto this main artery, and then take the first right turn to continue following CT 106. Turn right at Horseshoe Road, which becomes River Road, passing Schencks Island Park on your right, before the road returns to Old Ridgefield Road and finishes back in Wilton Center.

MILES AND DIRECTIONS

- **0.0** Start in Wilton Center on Old Ridgefield Road
- **0.3** Left onto Ridgefield Road
- **2.0** Right onto Nod Hill Road

Best Bike Rides Connecticut

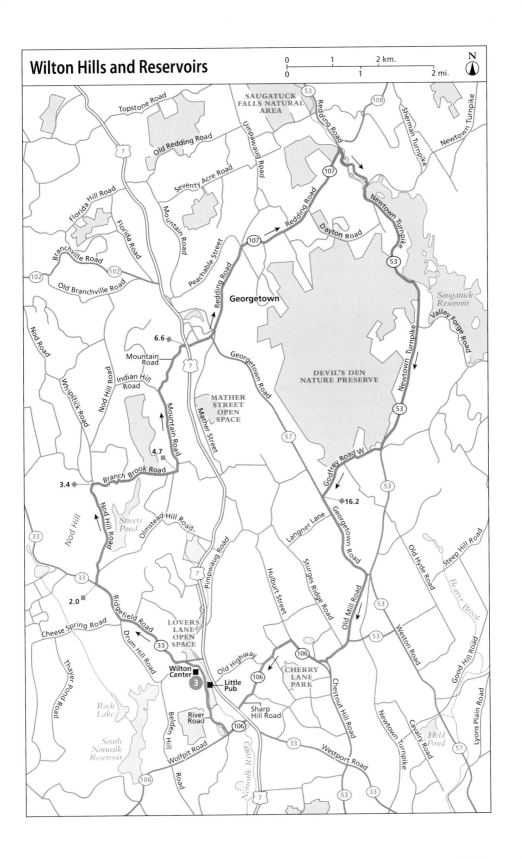

Wilton Hills and Reservoirs

Topstone Road

SAUGATUCK FALLS NATURAL AREA

Old Redding Road

Seventy Acre Road

Florida Hill Road

Mountain Road

Florida Road

Branchville Road

Old Branchville Road

Peachable Street

Redding Road

Umpawaug Road

Redding Road

Dayton Road

Sherman Turnpike

Newtown Turnpike

Newtown Turnpike

Saugatuck Reservoir

Valley Forge Road

Georgetown

6.6

Mountain Road

Indian Hill Road

Nod Road

Nod Hill Road

Whipstick Road

Mountain Road

Mather Street

Georgetown Road

MATHER STREET OPEN SPACE

DEVIL'S DEN NATURE PRESERVE

Newtown Turnpike

4.7

3.4

Branch Brook Road

Streets Pond

Olmstead Hill Road

Nod Hill Road

Nod Hill

57

Godfrey Road W

16.2

Langner Lane

Georgetown Road

Old Hyde Road

Steep Hill Road

Beaver Brook

2.0

Ridgefield Road

Cheese Spring Road

Drum Hill Road

LOVERS LANE OPEN SPACE

Pimpwaug Road

Hulburt Street

Sturges Ridge Road

Old Mill Road

Weston Road

Wilton Center

3

Little Pub

Old Highway

106

106

CHERRY LANE PARK

Sharp Hill Road

Chestnut Hill Road

Good Hill Road

Thayer Pond Road

Rock Lake

River Road

Belden Hill Road

Wolfpit Road

South Norwalk Reservoir

106

Norwalk River

Westport Road

Newtown Turnpike

Cavalry Road

Held Pond

Lyons Plain Road

57

N

0   1   2 km.
0   1   2 mi.

3.4 Right onto Branch Brook Road

4.7 Left onto Mountain Road

6.6 Right onto School Street to CT 107 (Redding Road)

10.3 Right onto CT 53

15.0 Right onto Godfrey Road

16.2 Left onto CT 57

17.4 Right onto Old Mill Road

18.1 Bear left and continue on Cobbs Mill Road

18.4 Right onto CT 53 (Cedar Road)

18.8 Right to stay on Cedar Road

18.9 Right onto CT 106

Weir Farm Art Center

Julian Alden Weir was an important figure in the development of American impressionism, and the namesake for the Weir Farm Art Center. Like the artists who founded the Lyme Colony, as a young man Weir traveled to Europe, where he drew inspiration from French artists and schools. Upon his return, he lived in New York, where he became an art buyer and collector; he taught drawing to supplement his income. One of his students brought a friend to a class, Anna Dwight Baker. She and Weir fell in love quickly, becoming engaged after a 3-week acquaintance.

As Weir began planning to marry, an art collector client of his, one Erwin Davis, made him a significant offer for one of the European paintings Weir had acquired; Davis proposed trading a 153-acre property in Connecticut and $10 for the painting.

Weir took the deal, and established a farm and retreat for himself and his new wife. The newlyweds headed to Europe for a lengthy honeymoon, and on their return, made the farm their permanent residence.

The farm provided an income and a happy home for the couple, who lived there for a decade, until Anna's death following the birth of their third daughter. Weir retreated and immersed himself in work for the World's Columbian Exposition in Chicago. During this time, Anna's sister Ella stayed on the farm, taking care of the Weir daughters. This led to a happy second marriage, with a courtship revealed in letters that are archived at the Weir Farm museum.

After marrying Ella, Weir grew in importance and formed an artists' group, "Ten American Painters"—or "The Ten"—with his friend Childe Hassam and seven other influential painters. Hassam was a prominent figure in the Lyme Colony at the same time, having influenced the work in Lyme away from Tonalism and into the developing American impressionist style.

Weir was later able to expand his farm with neighboring property, and his home became a destination for artists, who would travel to hunt, fish, paint, and enjoy Weir's hospitality.

Weir died in 1919, at 62, not long after receiving honorary degrees from Princeton and Yale, and declaring that it was time to pass the torch to younger artists like Marcel Duchamp and Pablo Picasso. The farm was inherited by his daughter, Dorothy Weir Young, who continued painting and living at the large estate with her husband, Mahonri Young. Dorothy died young from cancer, and the estate would have been lost with the death of her husband if not for his friends Sperry and Doris Andrews, who bought the property after his death in 1957.

Sperry and Doris were artists as well, and they kept the property relatively unchanged, realizing the historical importance of the site. It wasn't until the surrounding area started to change and modernize that they began their work as preservationists in earnest, inspired by Cora Weir Burlingham, the youngest daughter of Julian Weir. Cora had asked Doris if she couldn't save the pond her father had built with prize money from an early painting; Sperry and Doris were successful and soon expanded their efforts, leading to the preservation of 66 acres by the National Park Service.

The Andrews were given permanent residency for their efforts and lived on the premises for the rest of their lives. Doris passed in 2003 and Sperry in 2005, leaving behind a unique historical treasure.

19.4 Left onto CT 101 (Shap Hill Road)

20.6 Left onto US 7

20.8 Right onto CT 106

21.1 Right onto Horseshoe Road to River Road

22.0 Finish ride on Old Ridgefield Road

RIDE INFORMATION

Bike Shops
Outdoor Sports Center: 80 Danbury Rd., Wilton; (203) 762-8797; outdoor sports.com
New Canaan Bicycles: 24 Cherry St., New Canaan; (866) 629-2453; new canaanbicycles.com
Smart Cycles: 303 Strawberry Hill Ave., Westport; (203) 831-9144; smart cycles.com

Local Events and Attractions
Weir Farm Art Center: This unique national park is the only one dedicated to American art. The center was once an important artist community and played a role in the development of American impressionism. Three generations of American painters lived on the farm before it became a national park. The center holds tours, hosts artists-in-residence, and operates a visitor center and museum store. Admission is free. You can plan a trip on the National Park Service website: www.nps.gov/wefa/index.htm.
Wilton Library Association: This library is a community space where free events are held in partnership with the local arts community.
Saugatuck Reservoir: The Saugatuck Reservoir is a large, scenic, man-made body of water, which provides water to the surrounding towns. The reservoir is stocked with trout and is a popular fishing spot.
Lucius Pond Ordway and Devil's Den Preserve: The den and pond make up the largest tract of protected land in Fairfield County and the largest continuous preserve owned by the Connecticut Chapter of The Nature Conservancy. Recommended activities in Devil's Den are low-impact; hiking and bird watching are the two main attractions.
LaChat Town Farm: This property was donated to Weston by Leon Lachat on his passing. The grounds include a pre-Revolutionary homestead, dairy farm, community gardens, and historical exhibits. The town of Weston and The Nature Conservancy offer a number of programs and classes, including falconry, nature hikes, and history lectures. http://www.lachattownfarm.org/

Restaurants
The Village Market: 108 Old Ridgefield Rd., Wilton; (203) 762-7283; village marketwilton.com
Scoops Old Fashioned Ice Cream: 92 Old Ridgefield Rd., Wilton; (203) 834-1100
Little Pub: 26 Danbury Rd., Wilton; (203) 762-1122; littlepub.com
Uncle Leo's "Not Just Coffee and Doughnuts": 19 Main St., Redding

Sandy Hook Figure 8

Sandy Hook is a scenic village in Newtown, situated on the Housatonic River. The area is rich in preserves, sanctuaries, and waterways, making for excellent bike routes on long, low-volume roads. Originally settled by Stratford residents in the late 17th century, the town has a deep history and many notable residents, both past and present. Scrabble was invented here, and Olympic gold medalist Caitlyn Jenner (then known as Bruce) lived in Sandy Hook as a teenager. Current residents include Suzanne Collins, author of The Hunger Games *trilogy.*

Start: Village Perk Cafe on Glen Road

Length: 13.3 miles

Riding time: 1 hour

Best bike: Road bike

Terrain and trail surface: Asphalt

Traffic and hazards: Many of the roads are fairly narrow, without shoulders, and with moderate to high traffic speeds, but low traffic volumes. Use caution and position yourself where you can avoid hazards and be visible but still safe.

Things to see: Lake Zoar, wildlife preserves and sanctuaries, a historic steel truss bridge colloquially named the Silver Bridge

Fees: None

Getting there: The Village Perk Cafe is located very near exit 10 on I-84. Exit the highway and head toward CT 34 and downtown Sandy Hook, and turn left onto Glen Road just after the Foundry Kitchen and Tavern to arrive at the start of this ride.

GPS: 41.42088 / -73.28214

4

THE RIDE

This ride starts in the parking lot of the Village Perk Cafe, on Glen Road, in downtown Sandy Hook. The cafe is a charming little eatery with the usual breakfast and lunch staples, including a full espresso bar, locally baked pastries, sandwiches, wraps, paninis, and authentic Italian gelato. The cafe has scenic alfresco seating on a back deck overlooking the river and a cultivated garden. Parking in the lot should not be a problem, but if it's busy or packed, a number of other spots in the general area are available.

This is one of the hillier routes in this book, following roads that ascend and descend through this section of the Housatonic River valley. In 13 short miles, the total elevation gain is roughly 1,200 feet, although most of this is gained in one long segment near the middle of the ride.

Exit the parking lot by turning right onto Glen Road, and take the first left at the intersection ahead onto Riverside Road for a slight ascent on a narrow road with a fair volume of traffic. The road passes a small park area on the right, and then a historic cemetery on the left, before a fast downhill, where the character of the road becomes more quiet and rural.

Turn left near the 0.75-mile mark, and head uphill on Narragansett Trail, gaining nearly 100 feet of elevation on a country lane–like road. After reaching the peak, the road heads back downhill just before reaching Fairview Drive, where you turn left onto an even quieter and less traveled back road for a fast descent.

Near the 1.5-mile mark, Fairview Drive makes a 90-degree left-hand turn, which you take to continue on Fairview until you reach Glen Road, where you turn right, riding in a narrow shoulder.

A short distance ahead, the road crosses the historic Silver Bridge, named for the bright silver color it was painted. This is a historic truss bridge, built out of large steel triangular supports, which spans 308 feet across the Zoar Lake section of the Housatonic River.

After crossing the river, turn left onto River Road for one of the most scenic stretches of the ride. The next mile and a half will see the river on your left and the Bent River Sanctuary on your right. You pass forests, then a swampy marsh, and finally some open fields before turning right at a sprawling farmhouse onto Purchase Brook Road.

The farmlands belong to Mitchell Farm, a 500-acre family farm with sweet corn, squashes, potatoes, and a wide variety of other vegetables. The farm is one of the oldest in Connecticut and has been continuously operated for nearly 250 years; the current owners are the eighth generation to till the land. They operate a small market stand and welcome visitors.

A view from Silver Bridge in Sandy Hook.

Purchase Brook Road starts at an elevation of 109 feet, but you attain a max elevation of 466 feet on this heavily forested road before you turn right at the 5.5-mile mark onto West Flat Hill Road.

West Flat Hill Road continues climbing uphill, to a maximum of roughly 710 feet, where the road intersects with Peach Orchard Road. After the intersection, the road name becomes East Flat Hill Road, and the road descends quickly down a curvy, twisting road that passes the Audubon Center at Bent of the River.

This center was built on lands donated by the previous property owner, Althea Clark, who left a bequest for property maintenance and operation as an Audubon Center. The center opened in 2000 and has extensive, largely unmarked, hiking trails, as stipulated in Clark's will. Clark wanted visitors to have the same sense of exploration she experienced while walking the extensive property.

Shortly after passing the Audubon Center, at the 7.8-mile mark, the route reaches CT 172, South Britain Road. This is a busy and fast throughway with a fair shoulder to ride in. Immediately on your right is the South Britain Country Store, a classic general store with sandwiches, prepared foods, and restrooms.

This street passes some historic buildings, including the Old Town Hall Museum, a free attraction open every Wednesday for 2 hours from 10 a.m. to

12 p.m. The museum has a small permanent exhibit of maps, photographs, archives, and physical artifacts documenting the transition from a rural community to a suburban town.

Another highlight on this stretch is a small bridge crossing a scenic creek, near the 8.1-mile mark, just after the sign for a former farm.

Not far ahead, Daffodil Hill Growers provides an interesting detour; you see signs for the farm on your right, up Horse Fence Hill Road. The farm is a third-generation family farm specializing in interesting heirloom vegetables and expansive flower fields.

After passing this road the forest thins out, replaced with open meadowlands and distant hilltops. Near the 9-mile mark, CT 172 intersects with Main Street at a picturesque farmhouse. Turn right onto Main Street for more open views on the right, and continue along the generous shoulder, heading farther downhill.

Just before a pizza place on your right you pass a small plaza with a Dunkin Donuts, hidden behind a copse of trees on your left.

The road is fairly low-volume, paralleling the much busier I-84, which produces a lot of ambient noise. Main Street comes to an end near the 9.9-mile mark, where you turn left on the I-84 overpass, and continue on Ichabod Road, immediately turning right onto Fish Rock Road. Fish Rock Road is another low-volume road with very little housing and lots of trees. Continue on this for a half-mile or so, crossing back over I-84, and stay right as the road becomes River Road.

Around the 10.7-mile mark, River Road passes over the scenic Pomperaug River where it meets the larger Housatonic on a small, poorly maintained bridge with some rough sections of asphalt. The road continues along the Housatonic with more scenic river views on the left for the next mile, where you turn left to cross back over the Silver Bridge, continuing off onto Glen Road.

Follow Glen Road for the next mile and a half, enjoying views of Rocky Glen Scenic State Park on your right, until you reach your starting point in Sandy Hook and the end of the ride.

MILES AND DIRECTIONS

0.0 Start at the Village Perk on Glen Road, then take a left onto Riverside Road.

0.8 Left onto Narragansett Trail

1.3 Left onto Fairview Drive

1.6 Continue on Pootatuck Park Road

1.8 Right onto Glen Road and cross the Silver Bridge, then turn left on River Road

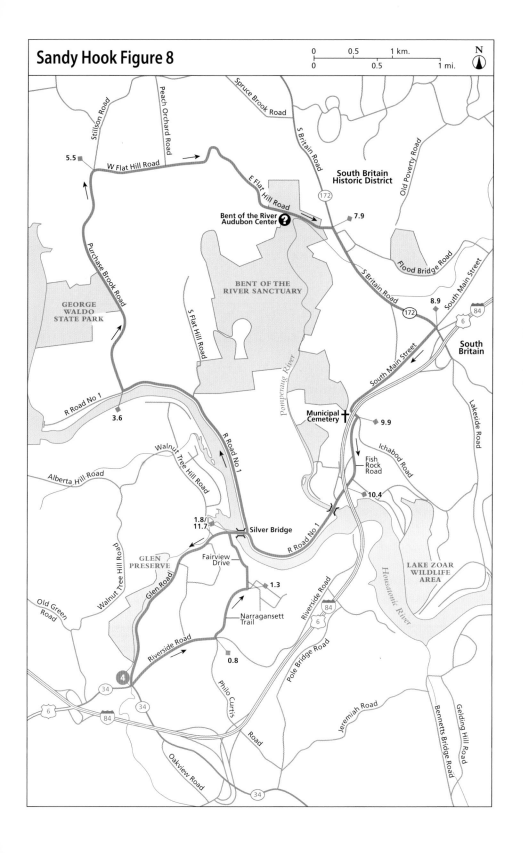

Sandy Hook Figure 8

0   0.5   1 km.
0   0.5   1 mi.

N

Stillson Road

Peach Orchard Road

Spruce Brook Road

S Britain Road

Old Poverty Road

5.5

W Flat Hill Road

E Flat Hill Road

South Britain
Historic District

172

Bent of the River
Audubon Center ?

7.9

Flood Bridge Road

S Britain Road

Purchase Brook Road

BENT OF THE
RIVER SANCTUARY

South Main Street

8.9

172

6

84

GEORGE
WALDO
STATE PARK

South
Britain

S Flat Hill Road

Pomperaug River

South Main Street

Lakeside Road

R Road No 1

Municipal
Cemetery ✝

9.9

3.6

Walnut Tree Hill Road

Ichabod Road

Alberta Hill Road

R Road No 1

Fish
Rock
Road

10.4

1.8/
11.7

Silver Bridge

R Road No 1

LAKE ZOAR
WILDLIFE
AREA

GLEN
PRESERVE

Fairview
Drive

Walnut Tree Hill Road

Housatonic River

Glen Road

1.3

Old Green
Road

Narragansett
Trail

Riverside Road

84

6

Riverside Road

0.8

Pole Bridge Road

4

34

Philo Curtis

6

84

34

Road

Jeremiah Road

Bennetts Bridge Road

Gelding Hill Road

Oakview Road

34

3.6 Continue on Purchase Brook Road

5.5 Right onto West Flat Hill Road

6.1 Continue on East Flat Hill Road

7.8 Right on South Britain Road

8.9 Right onto Main Street South

9.9 Continue on Ichabod Road, then right onto Fish Rock Road.

10.4 Continue on River Road

11.7 Left on River Road, cross the Silver Bridge, and continue on Glen Road

13.3 Finish at the Village Perk

RIDE INFORMATION

Bike Shops
Class Cycles: 77 Main St. N, Suite 105, Southbury; (203) 264-4708; class cycles.com

Local Events and Attractions
Lake Zoar: This artificial lake forms the borders of four towns. The lake is a calm, quiet place, surrounded by thick forests. The Newtown beach access is in Eichler's Cove.

Sticks and Stones Farm: This rural retreat offers hiking, yoga and other classes, and a tranquil escape. Check sticksandstonesfarm.com for calendar and more.

Town Players Little Theatre: This tiny little theatre has been a performance space for over 70 years. The Newtown Players perform a full season. See newtownplayers.org for tickets, schedule, and more.

Restaurants
Village Perk Cafe: 3 Glen Rd., Sandy Hook; (203) 364-9634; villageperk cafe.com

Foundry Kitchen and Tavern: 1 Glen Rd., Sandy Hook; (203) 491-2030; foundry kitchenandtavern.com

Figs Wood Fired Bistro: 105 Church Hill Rd., Sandy Hook; (203) 426-5503; figs woodfiredbistro.net

Westport: Greens Farms

Westport is a prosperous and wealthy coastal town in Fairfield County, named Machamux ("Beautiful Land") by the Pequot tribes who lived here before colonization. The first European settlers, a group of five families, arrived from neighboring Fairfield in 1648, settling the area now known as Greens Farms, in honor of one of the men. This ride begins in the small neighborhood that still bears this name.

Start: Machamux Park on Greens Farms Road

Length: 21.8 miles

Riding time: 1.75 hours

Best bike: Road bike

Terrain and trail surface: Asphalt

Traffic and hazards: Dangerous crossings at Route 1, and one tricky section passing the I-95 on-ramp.

Things to see: Bird sanctuaries, nature preserves, Southport Beach and Harbor, creeks and marshes

Fees: None

Getting there: Machamux Park is just around the corner from the Greens Farms Amtrak station, making for easy mass-transit access. Exit 18 on I-95 exits onto Sherwood Island Connector; from here, take a right onto Nyala Farms Road, then the next right onto Greens Farms Road, finally turning left to stay on Greens Farms Road and reaching the park.

GPS: 41.12199 / -73.32001

Westport is a culturally and economically significant town, as indicated by its many famous residents: Paul Newman, Martha Stewart, and even F. Scott Fitzgerald are just three examples from a very large list.

Beginning in Machamux Park, this 21.8-mile ride covers a few of the prime roads from the annual Bloomin' Metric ride, organized by local advocates and enthusiasts, Sound Cyclists. Take a left out of the park onto the low-volume suburban road and ride a short distance to the intersection.

Take the left onto Beachside Avenue, crossing over I-95 on a slightly deteriorated highway overpass bridge, before descending through scenic wetlands.

Beachside Avenue curves to the left when it reaches the coast, with some beautiful views over Long Island Sound to the right, before leading into a neighborhood of large estates, tasteful stone walls, hedges, and wrought-iron fences.

When the road narrows, stay right to continue onto Pequot Avenue through scenic Southport Beach and into a denser neighborhood with a mix of seasonal cottages, saltbox houses, and large, historic mansions.

After a quarter-mile, turn right onto Westway Road at a small four-way intersection. Follow Westway until the road ends in a T-junction with Harbor Road, and turn left, following the harbor.

Near the 3.25-mile point, Harbor Road curves to the right, at a very photogenic spot on a small bridge crossing the water; bear left onto narrower River Street toward downtown Southport.

River Street ends at busy Route 1, a high-speed four-lane road. Cautiously cross the street, turning left, and then right onto Pequot Avenue, riding up the small hill and past the shopping plaza.

At the top of the hill, turn right onto Mill Hill Road, and cross the bridge over the railroad tracks, immediately turning right onto Bronson Road.

Ahead use caution passing the I-95 on-ramp and follow the road beneath the I-95 overpass into a quiet residential neighborhood where the road narrows and traffic volumes drop off. Bronson Road follows a series of connected ponds and town parks, visible on the right, until it curves to the left, away from the water, to the intersection with Mill Hill Terrace, near the 4.3-mile mark.

Turn right on Mill Hill Terrace for a fast downhill ride that ends by a quaint stone bridge, then bear left onto Sturges Road.

Follow this quiet back road for a quarter of a mile through the Sturges Ponds Open Space, and turn right, back onto Bronson Road.

The next 0.8 mile has a very suburban feel, with houses built close to the road and each other, heading toward a small commercial district. When

An estuary near the Westport/Southport town line.

you see the gas station on the left, turn right onto Hillside Road, near the 5.5-mile mark.

This mild climb ends at a four-way intersection, where you turn right onto Hill Farm Road for a half-mile.

Shortly after crossing Duck Farm Road, Hill Farm Road ends; bear right onto Brookside Drive, a quiet rural road, for the next half-mile, until making a right turn onto Mill Plain Road.

Mill Plain Road is a fairly busy road with a wide shoulder. Turn left onto quieter Stillson Road in a quarter of a mile to continue circumnavigating the Springer Glen Open Space. The route ascends a fairly strenuous 100-foot climb, peaking and leveling out when you reach the intersection with North Benson Road, at the 7.5-mile mark.

Before the signalized intersection make a hairpin turn left onto North Benson, another quiet neighborhood road, which becomes Brookside Drive after a series of twists and turns, just before the 8-mile mark.

Brookside Drive leads to CT 58 and a heavily built-up commercial district, with a number of food and rest options. Continue on the mapped route and proceed cautiously on CT 58, or cut off the whole section by turning left onto Brookside and then left again onto Samp Mortar Drive if you'd rather avoid a busy area.

If you continue, a number of food options lie ahead, primarily chain eateries like Starbucks and Panera, and some diners and delis. After a quarter-mile on CT 58, take a careful left-hand turn onto Samp Mortar Drive.

Samp Mortar Drive is a comparatively quiet neighborhood street, with a fast descent, and some scenic views of the eponymous reservoir on the right. When you see a creek on the left, continue straight over the small bridge, back onto Brookside Drive.

Follow Brookside Drive for 0.6 mile to the earlier intersection with Mill Plain Road; this time, turn right onto Burr Street, for a challenging climb of nearly 300 feet over 1.25 miles, leveling out somewhat as you reach Congress Street.

Turn left onto Congress Street for another 40 to 50 feet of climbing before a fast 100-foot descent, heading down to the overpass of Route 15 (Merritt Parkway). This part of the road passes along Larsen Sanctuary, a Connecticut Audubon Society property that has boardwalks for hiking the picturesque marsh and wetlands.

Shortly after passing the Audubon Center, climb another big hill and turn left just after it levels out, onto Longmeadow Road, near the 13-mile mark.

This rural back road ends in a half-mile, after a fast descent, at a T-junction with Redding Road. Turn left onto Redding Road for 0.2 mile. When you see a nursery on your left, turn right onto Catamount Road.

Catamount Road heads downhill for nearly a mile and a half, with a little climbing before you turn left onto slightly busier Sturges Highway. Follow Sturges Highway for 1.4 miles until it ends at Cross Highway, where you turn right.

Cross Highway is another scenic road with homes on large setbacks and rural stone walls. Ride under a highway overpass, below Route 15 (Merritt Parkway), and then bear right at the fork to stay on Cross Highway for another 0.1 mile, to a four-way intersection with Bayberry Lane.

Turn left onto Bayberry for a long mile-and-a-half stretch through another quiet neighborhood with a marked shoulder. At the 18.7-mile mark, turn left onto Long Lots Road, and then immediately right onto Maple Avenue North.

Maple Avenue North heads slightly uphill before descending into a denser, sprawling section of Westport, along busy Route 1. This is a major intersection; cross carefully with the light, and ride another half-mile to the intersection with Clapboard Hill Road.

Turn right for the last mile onto Clapboard Hill Road, through a suburban neighborhood of large homes with smaller setbacks. This road features

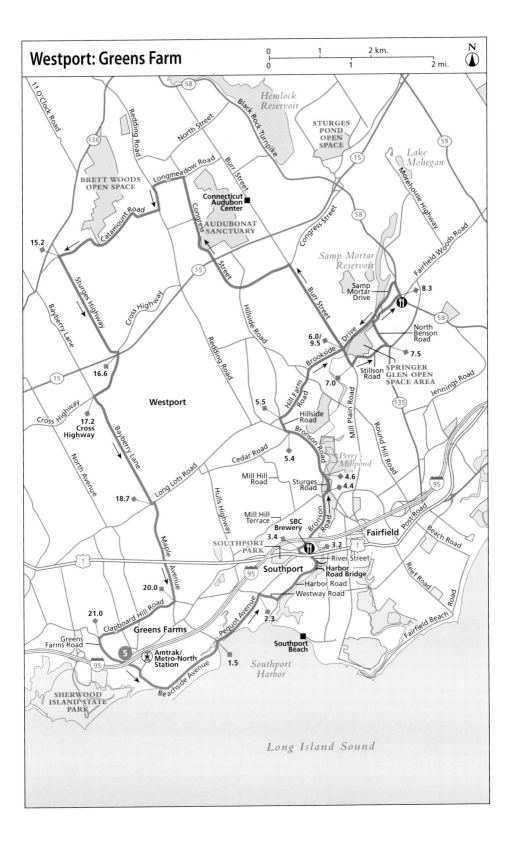

Westport: Greens Farm

0   1   2 km.
0   1   2 mi.

N

11 O'Clock Road

Hemlock
Reservoir

58

STURGES
POND
OPEN
SPACE

Black Rock Turnpike

North Street

Redding Road

136

BRETT WOODS
OPEN SPACE

Longmeadow Road

Burr Street

Congress Street

Connecticut
Audubon
Center

AUDUBONAT
SANCTUARY

15

Lake
Mohegan

59

Morehouse Highway

Catamount Road

Congress Street

Samp Mortar
Reservoir

58

Fairfield Woods Road

15.2

Sturges Highway

Cross Highway

Street

15

Burr Street

Samp
Mortar
Drive

Drive

8.3

North
Benson
Road

58

Hillside Road

Baybery Lane

16.6

Cross Highway

15

Hill Farm Road

Brookside

6.0/
9.5

7.5

7.0

Stillson
Road

SPRINGER
GLEN OPEN
SPACE AREA

135

Jennings Road

Cross Highway

17.2
Cross
Highway

Westport

Redding Road

5.5

Hillside
Road

Mill Plain Road

Round Hill Road

95

North Avenue

Bayberry Lane

Cedar Road

Bronson Road

5.4

Perry's
Millpond

4.6

4.4

Long Lots Road

Hulls Highway

Mill Hill
Road

Sturges
Road

Bronson Road

18.7

Mill Hill
Terrace

SBC
Brewery

3.4

3.2

Fairfield

Post Road

Beach Road

1

SOUTHPORT
PARK

River Street

Harbor
Road Bridge

Reef Road

95

Southport

Harbor Road

Westway Road

Maple Avenue

20.0

Clapboard Hill Road

21.0

Greens Farms

Pequot Avenue

2.3

Fairfield Beach Road

1

Greens
Farms Road

5

Amtrak/
Metro-North
Station

1.5

Southport
Beach

Southport
Harbor

95

Beachside Avenue

SHERWOOD
ISLAND STATE
PARK

Long Island Sound

the last climb, a fairly steep 60-foot hill, before a fast descent down to Greens Farms Road. Bear right around the grass triangle, and then turn left onto Greens Farms Road, past a lovely open field on the right.

After a half-mile, turn left again to stay on Greens Farms Road. You will see Machamux Park just ahead on your right to finish the ride.

MILES AND DIRECTIONS

0.0 Start at Machamux Park on Greens Farms Road, then take a left onto Beachside Avenue.

1.5 Continue on Pequot Avenue

2.1 Proceed onto Pequot Avenue

2.3 Right onto Westway Road

2.6 Left onto Harbor Road

3.2 Continue on River Street

3.4 Left onto Post Road to cross to continue on River Street and stay right to continue on Pequot Road

3.5 Right onto Mill Hill Road then right onto Bronson Road

4.3 Continue on Mill Hill Terrace

4.4 Bear left on Sturges Road

4.6 Continue on Bronson Road

5.4 Right onto Hillside Road

5.5 Right onto Hill Farm Road

6.2 Right onto Brookside Drive

6.7 Right onto Mill Plain Road

6.9 Left onto Stillson Road

7.5 Left onto North Benson Road

7.9 Continue on Brookside Drive

8.3 Left onto CT 58 (Black Rock Turnpike)

8.5 Left onto Swamp Mortar Drive

8.9 Continue on Brookside Drive

9.5 Right onto Burr Street

10.7 Left onto Congress Street

13.0 Left onto Longmeadow Road

13.4 Left onto Redding Road

13.6 Right onto Catamount Road

15.2 Left onto Sturges Highway

16.6 Right onto Cross Highway

17.2 Left onto Bayberry Lane

18.7 Left onto Long Lots Road, then a quick right onto Maple Avenue North.

19.9 Right onto Clapboard Hill Road

21.0 Left onto Greens Farms Road to finish

21.8 Finish at Machamux Park

RIDE INFORMATION

Bike Shops
Cycle Dynamics: 971 Post Rd. E, Westport; (203) 226-3790; cycledynamics.com
Smart Cycles: 303 Strawberry Hill Ave., Norwalk; (203) 831-9144; smart cycles.com

Local Events and Attractions
Bloomin' Metric: This is the most popular supported ride in the state, drawing thousands of cyclists in late May or early June, during the peak flowering season for the numerous azaleas and dogwoods. Sound Cyclists uses the event as a fundraiser for their club efforts to improve cycling throughout the region.
Sherwood Island State Park: This state park, the first in Connecticut, hosts the start and finish of the Bloomin' Metric each year. The park includes a beach on the Long Island Sound, observation decks in the marshes, and tranquil picnic grounds.

Restaurants
Coffee an' Donuts: 343 Main St., Westport; (203) 227-3808
Steam Coffee Bar: 2 Post Office Ln., Westport; (203) 349-5164; steamcoffee bar.com

Restrooms
0.0 Miles: Around the corner from the start, at the Greens Farms train station

Hartford County

Hartford County, in the center of the upper half of the state, is home to the state capitol and government. Two rides start in the principal city of Hartford, one of them following the popular Discover Hartford Bike Tour through off-road parks, and the other featuring some of the nicest roads out into West Hartford.

Rides in this region also include Collinsville, an incredibly cute former mill town near the border with Litchfield County, and several in Manchester and Glastonbury to the east. The Collinsville route features beautiful dirt roads and trails around a major reservoir and would be an ideal ride for a hybrid or hardy road biker. While principally commuter suburbs of the capital, Manchester and Glastonbury also have a high number of orchards, farms, and quiet, scenic roads. Two rides feature the mountain biker favorite Case Mountain, a massive state property ringed by low-volume roads with generous shoulders.

Hartford is full of culture, boasting the first public art museum in the nation in the Wadsworth Atheneum and a heavy concentration of iconic buildings and the Hartford Symphony Orchestra. The city also has an extensive park along the Connecticut River, full of sculptural works and river views.

While it isn't included in any of these routes, one of the two historic ferries in Connecticut crosses the river between Glastonbury and Rocky Hill. There is some nice riding in Rocky Hill; check out the Two Ferry Ride, a popular annual event hosted by Cycling Concepts in Glastonbury, crossing the river twice, over the Hadlyme-Chester and Rocky Hill-Glastonbury ferries.

Case Mountain: Mountain Bike Ride

Glastonbury's Case Mountain may be the state's best-kept secret from a mountain bike perspective. This 640-acre recreational area and the neighboring forest set aside by Manchester's water department provide exciting, highly technical riding on club-maintained trails. Bicycling *magazine listed it as the number one spot in Connecticut in 2012. Following this mention, the popularity of the park almost proved to be its undoing, but recent efforts have restored a 12.6-mile loop connecting the many access points.*

Start: Case Mountain parking lot on Birch Mountain Road

Length: 13.6 miles

Riding time: 2 hours

Best bike: Mountain bike

Terrain and trail surface: Dirt singletrack

Traffic and hazards: There is no traffic. Use caution around hikers, who have right of way. Only ride this route clockwise, and make sure that the trails are dry. Do not ride singletrack trails after rain or in wet conditions. Make sure to bring water, snacks, and a cell phone in case of problems. When approaching a hazard or challenge beyond your ability, dismount and carry your bicycle, to avoid adding to braided trails running around the challenge.

Things to see: Vernal ponds appear throughout the park. Look for one after the Case Mountain Summit on the return leg along the carriage path. The Case Mountain Summit provides excellent views, as does the ridge and summit of Birch Mountain in the southeast portion. Near the end, look for a tranquil sight at Case Pond. Other views include a mountain laurel grove, within a mile or so of the trail start, and many lovely natural scenes throughout.

Fees: None

THE RIDE

This is not a ride for beginners. The trails feature several brutally steep climbs, white-knuckle downhills, rocky ledges, and intimidating corners. There are numerous areas that novice riders may need to dismount to pass, both for safety and for preserving the integrity and quality of the trail. Novices may prefer entering on the fire roads from Coop Road and following those for an easy, self-explanatory ride. The staff at nearby Bicycles East is an excellent local resource. The bike shop experts host a weekly ride through the property and are longtime supporters of the park.

Case Mountain Lot can fill up quickly. For another entrance, try the fire road off of Coop Road, in the southwest. From here, ride the fairly easy 1-mile fire road to a small trail. This trail heads north a short distance and then curves to the right, following a windy path eastward to a long fire road. Turn right and then immediately left onto this loop, noting the entrance point, and follow the directions below, starting after the technical descent at the 6-mile mark.

The entrance for this ride is easy to spot on the southern side of the Case Mountain Lot. Once inside, the carriage path heads rather steeply uphill and is briefly joined by a blue line hiking trail, from the left, for a quarter-mile or so, diverging near the peak of the climb.

The route levels out and at the 2-mile mark heads into a mile-long downhill section, ending where the blue line trail rejoins. The two trails continue together, for less than a half-mile, up a fairly steep climb, before the single-track trail enters a section of quick cutbacks and turns, continuing uphill.

The trail peaks for a brief respite just before the 4-mile mark, followed by a somewhat technical section over a quarter-mile, then continues up another steep ridge.

Once at the top of the slope, the trail turns right and continues following the ridge up and down over a rolling section. This area should afford several excellent views out over the surrounding region.

A technical descent awaits around the 6-mile mark, with a series of nearly a dozen quick little switchbacks, followed by a final short climb and a beautiful mile-long descent over a less challenging segment. Near the bottom of the descent, pass through Roaring Brook and into a 2-mile segment over less steep climbs on a route that nearly describes an oval.

The route curves back to the north near the 10-mile mark, meandering up a gentle hill to a section back along the blue-blaze trail. Near the 12-mile mark, after the blue-blaze trail diverges, you near the summit of Case Mountain, with its scenic views of Hartford in the distance.

After the summit, the ride heads mostly downhill toward Case Pond, a tranquil spot approaching the 13-mile mark, before rejoining the outgoing trail right at the trailhead and parking lot.

MILES AND DIRECTION

0.0 Start on white-blazed trail at Case Pond Lot

0.7 Continue on white-blazed trail over intersection with blue-dot trail

Waterfall at the pond parking lot for Case Mountain Park.

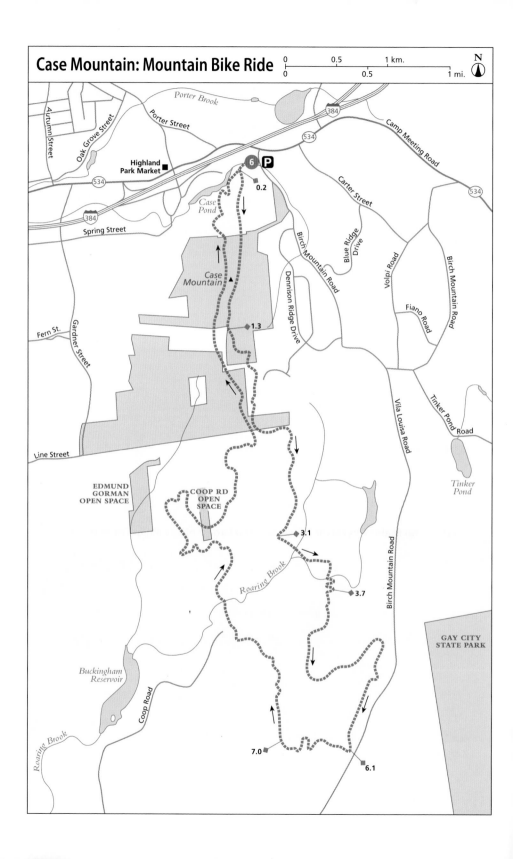

Case Mountain: Mountain Bike Ride

0   0.5   1 km.
0   0.5   1 mi.

N

Porter Brook

Autumn Street

Oak Grove Street

Porter Street

384

534

Camp Meeting Road

Highland Park Market

6 P

0.2

534

534

384

Spring Street

Case Pond

Case Mountain

Carter Street

Blue Ridge Drive

Volpi Road

Birch Mountain Road

Fiano Road

Birch Mountain Road

Fern St.

Gardner Street

1.3

Dennison Ridge Drive

Birch Mountain Road

Line Street

EDMUND GORMAN OPEN SPACE

COOP RD OPEN SPACE

Vila Louisa Road

Tinker Pond Road

Tinker Pond

3.1

3.7

Roaring Brook

Buckingham Reservoir

Coop Road

GAY CITY STATE PARK

7.0

6.1

Roaring Brook

1.1 Turn left onto blue-dot trail where white-blazed trail reaches a summit point and curves right

1.9 Turn left to stay on trail

2.6 Turn left onto Coop Road (fire road) then right back onto trail

4.5 Turn left to stay on blue trail

5.8 Turn right, away from parking area and Birch Mountain Road, to continue on blue trail

6.5 Turn right onto Fern Trail

7.8 Cross Coop Road and continue on blue trail

9.0 Turn right onto yellow trail and continue

10.4 Turn left onto blue trail

11.3 Turn left onto white-blazed trail

11.9 Turn right toward Case Pond

13.6 Finish at Case Pond Lot

RIDE INFORMATION

Bike Shops
Cycling Concepts: 2343 Main St., Glastonbury; (860) 633-3444; cyclingconcepts.com
Bicycles East: 331 New London Turnpike, Glastonbury; (860) 659-0114; bicycleseast.com

Events and Attractions
Crusin' on Main: This classic car show is the largest of its kind in Connecticut, held annually in August (cruisinonmainstreet.org).
Wickham Park: This 250-acre park contains gardens, open fields, woodlands, ponds, and other attractions. Admission is charged.

Restaurants
Cosmic Omelet: 485 Hartford Rd., Manchester; (860) 645-1864; cosmicomelet.com
Lucky Taco Cantina and Tap Room: 829 Main St., Manchester; (860) 432-2274; luckytacoct.com
Corey's Catsup and Mustard: 623 Main St., Manchester; (860) 432-7755; catsupandmustard.com

Case Mountain: Road Bike Loop

Manchester is a great town for Hartford-area cyclists seeking rural, naturally scenic riding routes. This ride provides an alternative take on Case Mountain, previously detailed as a prime mountain biking destination in Ride 6, to showcase the long, well-maintained local roads that are popular with area road cyclists.

Start: Case Mountain parking lot on Birch Mountain Road

Length: 13.6 miles

Riding time: 1 hour

Best bike: Road bike

Terrain and trail surface: Asphalt

Traffic and hazards: With some exceptions, all of these roads are wide, with generous shoulders. Traffic speeds can be fast, particularly near the 7.5-mile mark, near the intersection of CT 83 and CT 94.

Things to see: Case Mountain Park, Full Circle Farm, a wide-open view of a pond and wetlands on the descent down Hebron Avenue, forests, and natural surroundings

Fees: None

Getting there: Exit 4 on I-384 provides convenient access to the area. From the east, take the exit and turn right onto CT 534 (Highland Street) and follow to Birch Mountain Road and the parking lot. From the west, take the exit to Glen Road, and turn left onto Wyllys Road, then right onto Highland Street to Birch Mountain Road and the lot.

GPS: 41.7669 / -72.48006

THE RIDE

This route approaches the Glastonbury Orchards ride near the intersection of CT 94 and CT 83. Cyclists looking to add more than 20 miles, for a 34-mile figure-eight, should take a left onto CT 83 and then a right onto Brook Street, and follow the maps from Glastonbury Orchards (Ride 8).

This 13.6-mile ride starts off with a long stretch of climbing, comprising the majority of more than 1,000 feet of elevation gain. After the first 4.5 miles of climbing, the rest of the ride is comfortably rolling, downhill, or flat.

Start the route in the Case Mountain parking lot and take a right onto Birch Mountain Road for the next mile and a half. Birch Mountain Road follows a hard left turn and then continues, bearing left, where it meets Villa Louisa Road in a T-junction, near Full Circle Farm and Birch Mountain Day School, a private preschool and kindergarten program.

Full Circle Farm is a lovely equestrian center, on a gorgeous hilltop with scenic overlooks of the surrounding countryside, that offers boarding and training. You see part of their property on the left as you approach the right turn onto Villa Louisa Road ahead.

Villa Louisa is another scenic road, with sparse housing and development. On the left, you pass a catering and special event venue, which hosts weddings, corporate events, and important milestones in a fairy-tale setting. Most of the magic is behind the building facade, but the landscaping and natural environment provide a scenic view.

After passing Villa Louisa the road curves slightly and continues into another forested area, named Birch Mountain Road again. This beautiful and hilly stretch of road travels directly through the Case Mountain forest and past a number of hiking and biking trails in a peaceful area with almost no buildings or development.

Just as the road starts to head downhill, it ends in a T-junction with Hebron Avenue, a higher-speed throughway for travel to and from Hartford and the eastern edge of the county. Take a right here into the generous shoulder for a long, at times steep, 2-mile descent over 400 feet of elevation. The road is minimally developed with some single-family homes and a small suburban development but is mostly bordered by trees and grassy fields.

Before a last steep descent near the 6-mile mark, a particularly scenic view awaits of a pond and wetlands, which are part of the Vinnick Open Space. After passing this view, the route continues past the subdivision, leveling out for a half-mile, with a small rise and drop, ending at the intersection with CT 83, near the 7.5-mile mark.

Turn right onto CT 83, Manchester Road, noting the shopping plaza to the right. Highland Park Market, a family-owned grocery chain, operates one of their five local markets here. The small grocery offers restrooms, a deli, and a wide selection of prepared foods.

The route continues north along Manchester Road, past modern suburban homes on the right and a church on the left, in a short rural section, bordered on the left by the Buckingham Recreation Area, a small municipal park with hiking trails and sports fields.

The next half-mile is slightly more built up. Suburban homes adjoin without bordering greenways, but the wide shoulder and quiet neighborhood still feel rural and pleasant by bike.

Manchester Road turns right up ahead, passing the Minnechaug Golf Course on the left, an expansive, carefully manicured expanse of grass along a slightly busy road. This section of Manchester is a popular commuter route, so use caution if riding it near rush hour.

After the golf course, with Mountain Road straight ahead, follow Manchester Road as it curves to the left. The next quarter-mile passes tasteful subdivisions on a slightly busy but slower stretch of road.

Take the first right onto Line Street, a narrow road without a shoulder starting in a quiet neighborhood. This is the last serious climb, with a gradual hill heading straight up a 100-foot span of Line Street.

The road continues past the Manchester Country Club on the left and then back into Case Mountain Park territory for a long stretch of quiet, heavily wooded road. Line Street turns left near the 10.6-mile mark, becoming Gardner Street.

Gardner Street continues slightly uphill past a parking area for Case Mountain on the right and a Girl Scout camp on the left, exiting the park into another quiet neighborhood with expansive lawns and sidewalks.

After roughly a mile more, the road widens and gains a shoulder and the route reaches the intersection with Spring Street.

Turn right onto Spring Street, near the 12-mile mark, and ride through the rest of the neighborhood, until the road narrows, curves, and passes over a charming stone bridge with views of the creek below. A small waterfall from Case Pond, crossed by a lovely stone bridge, is visible to the right. You might stop and explore this area after turning the next corner and passing Glen Road on the left.

Follow Spring Street past the extension road, bearing left onto Wyllys Road for a short stretch up to Highland Street.

Another Highland Market is here, to the left, as is the off-road multi-use Charter Greenway.

For a detour to the west end of Manchester, turn left onto the Charter Greenway for a marked off-road route about 4 miles long. The route provides bike access to several eateries in Manchester, including popular breakfast spot Cosmic Omelet and many scenic views of waterways.

A low-slung barn over marshy fields.

To continue the route, turn right onto the last spur of the Charter Greenway and follow it to the northeast. Follow this trail for the next third of a mile, exiting it through the parking lot, and turning right onto Camp Meeting Road when it ends.

Camp Meeting Road travels through the highway overpass bridges with a generous shoulder. Take the first right turn, onto Birch Mountain Road, and then turn right into the Case Mountain State Park to finish the ride.

MILES AND DIRECTIONS

0.0 Start at Case Mountain State Park parking lot on Birch Mountain Road

1.5 Right onto Villa Louisa Road

2.3 Continue on Birch Mountain Road

4.6 Right onto Hebron Avenue

7.5 Right onto Manchester Road

9.5 Proceed onto Manchester Road

9.7 Right onto Line Street

10.6 Continue on Gardner Street

11.9 Right onto Spring Street

12.8 Continue on Wyllys Road

13.0 Right onto Highland Street

13.3 Continue on Camp Meeting Road

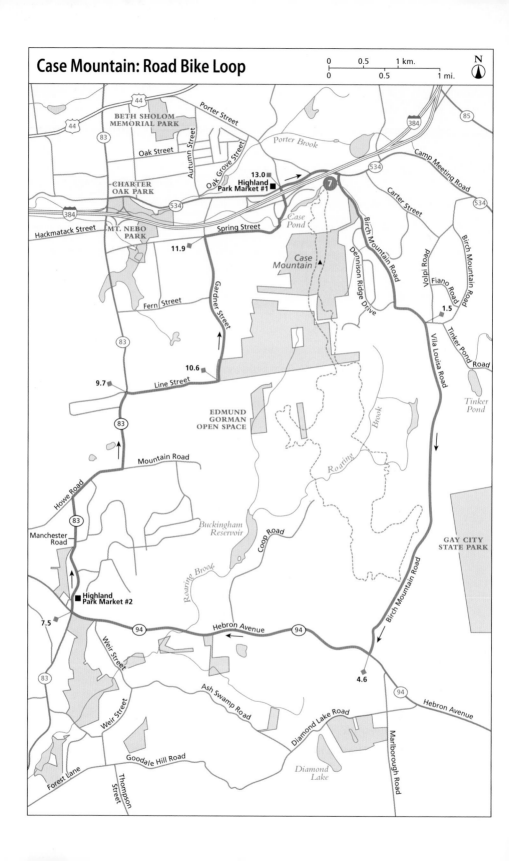

Case Mountain: Road Bike Loop

0   0.5   1 km.
0   0.5   1 mi.

N

A lovely granite home, covered in ivy, on Hebron Avenue.

13.5   Right onto Birch Mountain Road

13.6   Finish at parking lot

RIDE INFORMATION

Bike Shops
Cycling Concepts: 2343 Main St., Glastonbury; (860) 633-3444; cycling concepts.com
Bicycles East: 331 New London Turnpike, Glastonbury; (860) 659-0114; bicycleseast.com

Events and Attractions
Crusin' on Main: This classic car show is the largest of its kind in Connecticut, held annually in August (cruisinonmainstreet.org).
Wickham Park: This 250-acre park contains gardens, open fields, woodlands, ponds, and other attractions. Admission is charged.

Restaurants
Cosmic Omelet: 485 Hartford Rd., Manchester; (860) 645-1864; cosmic omelet.com
Lucky Taco Cantina and Tap Room: 829 Main St., Manchester; (860) 432-2274; luckytacoct.com
Corey's Catsup and Mustard: 623 Main St., Manchester; (860) 432-7755; catsupandmustard.com

Glastonbury Orchards

Settled in 1636 on the banks of the Connecticut River, Glastonbury is one of the oldest municipalities in the state. Glastonbury is a modern town with a charming, historic feel, and a carefully preserved natural environment. This ride starts in the downtown area and follows the river valley before some big climbs on quiet, winding roads through picturesque orchards and farms. The orchards operate seasonally, and riders should check ahead for current hours and offerings.

Start: Main Street by the Glastonbury Green

Length: 18.8 miles

Riding time: 1.5 hours

Best bike: Road bike

Terrain and trail surface: Asphalt

Traffic and hazards: Downtown has nose-first parking, so watch for cars backing up. Main Street in general can be a bit busy, but the rest of the roads are quiet back roads with low traffic volumes.

Fees: None

Things to see: The many orchards and farms this route passes are the primary attractions. One particularly beautiful stretch occurs along Coldbrook Road, where the road abuts a bucolic creek with young-growth forest bordering both sides.

Getting there: Hebron Avenue is the main road connecting to Main Street, right near the ride start at the green. Take CT 2 to Hebron Avenue (exit 8) and then drive into downtown Glastonbury. CT 2 can be reached directly from I-84 or with a CT 3 connection from I-91.

GPS: 41.71206 / -72.60852

THE RIDE

This ride starts in downtown Glastonbury on the Center Green, by Daybreak Coffee Roasters. Daybreak is a long, narrow cafe with healthy, hip fare, baked goods, and an espresso bar. On the same block is a bike shop, Cycling Concepts, and a few blocks away in a shopping plaza on the New London Turnpike is a second shop, Bicycles East.

To extend this ride, refer to the previous route, Case Mountain: Road Bike Loop (Ride 7) for details on making a 34-mile figure-eight route.

Ride south on Main Street along the charming Glastonbury Green, past local retail boutiques and a number of restaurants, watching carefully for cars leaving the nose-in parking spots. After 2 miles, turn right to stay on Main Street, leaving the denser downtown area. The road narrows and traffic speeds increase slightly over the next mile and a quarter.

Just ahead on your right, you pass the local Audubon Society Center. Shortly after the center, you pass the Old Cider Mill, a once-operational mill in a historic building now used as a seasonal farmers' market.

Near the 3.25-mile mark, just after the Glastonbury Historical Society building on your left, the route turns left onto Hopewell Road. A short detour past the turn, down the little hill ahead, are two popular local spots. The first on the left, Harpo's Bakery and Coffee Shop, is a local institution popular for pastries, cakes, and other baked goods. They also offer pizzas, deli sandwiches, breakfast, and drip coffee. The second shop, in the small plaza on the left, is So G, a specialty coffee roaster. In a cozy little sitting room So G serves espresso drinks, drip coffee and teas, and a small selection of soups, baked goods, and sandwiches.

Following the route, Hopewell offers the first tough climb of the ride, with grades around 10 percent and a 100-foot ascent. This is a winding, low-volume road, passing through quiet wooded areas and suburban housing separated by greenways.

Just after the climb levels out, you pass the Joseph Preli Farm and Vineyard on your right. After the vineyard, the road passes by the Cotton Hollow Nature Preserve on the right, curving along the scenic forest, also on the right. At the stop sign, head right onto Matson Hill Road for a long but more gradual climb of 250 feet. Halfway up the climb, at the 5.1-mile mark, Matson Hill Road curves around Rose's Berry Farm on the left, with the entrance just ahead up the next section of hill.

Matson Hill Road evens out in a half-mile or so and curves to the left as the route approaches Belltown Hill Orchards, a fourth-generation family owned and operated orchard. In just over a half-mile, stay left, as the road becomes Woodland Street and starts to descend quickly through picturesque

Historic mill and industrial site near Rose's Berry Farm.

farmland and meadows. Near the 6.6-mile mark you pass Dondero Orchards, another fourth-generation family operation, on your left.

A mile and a quarter or so after the orchard, make a nearly 180-degree right turn onto Coldbrook Road. This particularly scenic road passes through water company property and a dense young forest on one of the calmest stretches of this route.

When the road forks, navigate around the grassy median and turn left onto Country Club Road. This road covers a half-mile before ending at a T-junction with slightly busier Wassuc Road.

Turn right onto Wassuc Road and then bear left at the fork to stay on Wassuc Road. Cross over CT 2 on the highway overpass and bear right to continue onto Toll Gate Road.

Take the first left just ahead onto Thompson Street. Thompson is a long, quiet, neighborhood street that heads uphill, reaching a peak elevation of around 615 feet.

Thompson Street ends in a T-junction with Goodale Hill Road; make a left turn and then an immediate right onto Weir Street, a quiet little neighborhood street.

In a third of a mile turn left onto Shoddy Mill Road, another short connecting road, then turn right at the end onto slightly busier Manchester Road.

Cautiously take the first left onto Brook Street for a fast descent through another calm neighborhood. Manchester Road ends at a stop sign but there becomes Neipsic Road, so continue straight ahead.

One of the many orchards visited on this ride.

Neipsic is a long and narrow suburban road; it passes single-family homes, a school, and a number of municipal parks and open spaces. It isn't the most scenic road of the route; depending on foliage and season you may have some nice views of the Nipsic Pond on your left before the 15-mile mark.

At the intersection with the New London Turnpike, very carefully cross over the turnpike onto Hubbard Street. Follow Hubbard beneath a highway overpass and then past the Glastonbury Green Cemetery, on the right, reaching Main Street in just under a mile.

Turn right onto Main Street and follow it the last 0.8 mile up to the start point to finish the ride.

MILES AND DIRECTIONS

0.0 Start on Main Street by the Glastonbury Center Green

2.0 Right to stay on Main Street

3.2 Left onto Hopewell Road

3.6 Proceed onto Hopewell Road

4.5 Right onto Matson Hill Road

6.3 Left onto Woodland Street

7.8 Right onto Coldbrook Road

9.5 Left onto Country Club Road

Glastonbury Orchards

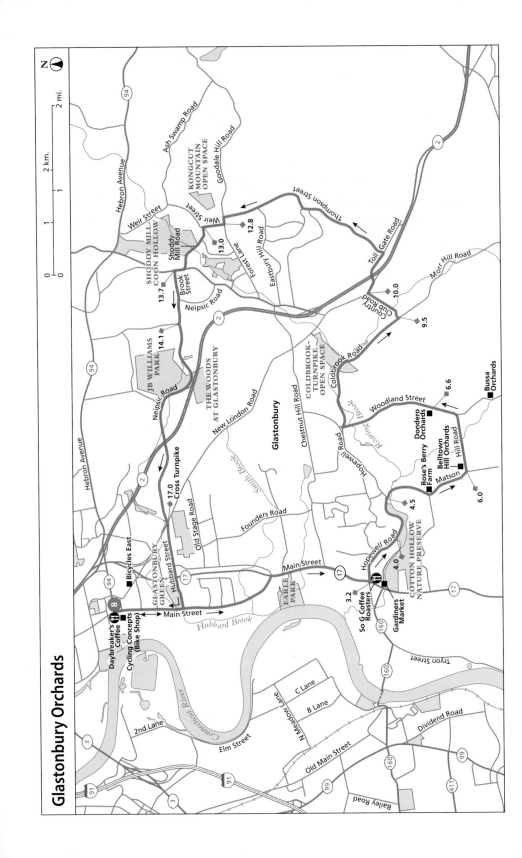

10.0 Right onto Wassuc Road

10.2 Continue on Toll Gate Road

10.5 Left onto Thompson Street

12.8 Left onto Goodale Hill Road and right onto Weir Street

13.1 Left onto Shoddy Mill Road

13.7 Right onto Manchester Road and then left onto Brook Street

14.2 Continue on Neipsic Road

17.1 Continue on Hubbard Street

18.0 Right onto Main Street

18.8 Finish on Main Street

RIDE INFORMATION

Bike Shops
Cycling Concepts: 2343 Main St., Glastonbury; (860) 633-3444; cyclingconcepts.com
Bicycles East: 331 New London Turnpike, Glastonbury; (860) 659-0114; bicycleseast.com

Events and Attractions
Center at Glastonbury Connecticut Audubon Society: This center has indoor exhibits, family-friendly events, and a small wildlife garden; visitors interested in hiking are encouraged to use the public park next door.
Joseph Preli Farm and Vineyard: This vineyard is open seasonally for wine and cider tastings, and operates a small farm stand out front.
Rose's Berry Farm: Rose's is a pick-your-own berry farm with other produce, pies, and food, open seasonally.
Belltown Hill Orchards: This orchard is known in particular for their hot apple fritters and apple cider doughnuts.
Dondero Orchards: The Dondero family offers seasonal picking, a farm stand, and a popular alfresco dinner series right on the farm. Diners eat on the lawn, picnic style, throughout the summer.

Restaurants
Daybreak Coffee Roasters: 2377 Main St., Glastonbury; (860) 657-4466; daybreakcoffee.com
So G Coffee Roasters: 882 Main St., South Glastonbury; (860) 633-8500
Harpo's Bakery and Coffee Shop: 908 Main St., South Glastonbury; (860) 657-4111; harposbakery.com

Collinsville Trails and Reservoir

Collinsville is a village of just under 4,000 residents in Canton, best known for the historic downtown district. This Hartford County town is well situated on the Farmington River and has great access to rails-to-trails projects and national acclaim as a tourist destination. Collinsville was voted one of the "coolest" small towns in America by Budget Travel magazine. This ride also visits the Nepaug Reservoir in neighboring Burlington, once the largest artificial lake in Connecticut. The trails around Nepaug have easy connections to the trails around Collinsville, creating the 12-mile loop that this route follows.

Start: Downtown Collinsville

Length: 11.8 miles

Riding time: 1 hour

Best bike: Hybrid bike

Terrain and trail surface: Asphalt and hard-packed dirt

Traffic and hazards: The dirt road sections may be treacherous for skinny tires. Most of the roads are quiet and low-volume, except the short section after leaving the trails around the reservoir.

Things to see: Nepaug dam and reservoir, scenic water views, a historic pedestrian/cyclist bridge, historic Collinsville, lovely off-road trails

Fees: None

Getting there: From I-84W, take exit 39, Farmington, for CT 4W. Signs lead to CT 179 and 4; follow this road to the bridge in Collinsville and then take a right onto Main Street and find parking. From I-84E, take exit 20 onto CT 8N/Torrington. From 8N, take exit 42 onto CT 118, Harwinton. Take a right onto CT 118 and CT 4E through Burlington, followed by a left onto CT 179. CT 179 leads to Bridge Street, where you turn right, then right again onto Main Street to parking.

From I-91N, take exit 22N-22S, and merge onto CT 9N toward New Britain. Then, take exit 32 for I-84W toward Waterbury, exiting onto CT 4/Farmington. Follow CT 508 to CT 4W to Huckleberry Hill Road, which turns into Center Street, before reaching downtown Collinsville.

GPS: 41.81076 / -72.9215

THE RIDE

Starting on Main Street in downtown Collinsville, this 11.8-mile ride covers nearly 900 feet of elevation, making it more challenging than it may appear. Most of the climbs are not very steep, with only one or two sections approaching grades of 10 percent.

From Main Street, cross the road onto the Farmington River Trail, turning right and then left onto Bridge Street. The route abuts the historic Collins Axe Factory Building on the left, which you ride around as you approach and cross a bridge with scenic views of the Farmington River below.

Turn right onto Torrington Avenue, a fairly quiet road heading uphill on probably the most challenging leg of the ride, directly into the reservoir property, where it levels out.

At the 1.9-mile mark follow the road as it curves left and becomes Nepaug Dam, a half-mile stretch of off-road trail that ends when it meets Litchfield Turnpike (US 202).

Litchfield Turnpike is fast, and traffic has no stops here; use caution to cross the road and turn left, following the turnpike through a scenic area surrounded by woods for 1.8 miles until a left-hand turn onto South East Road.

South East Road is another quiet side road. Like Torrington Avenue, it also heads uphill, and it will be the second challenging section. This road continues for nearly 2 miles, flattening out, then becoming Covey Road.

The route follows Covey Road for 1.5 miles before turning left onto Hotchkiss Road, at the New Britain Fresh Air Camp. Hotchkiss Road leads into a fairly rough section of dirt road and an incredibly scenic ride through quiet forests along the southern shore of the reservoir.

Turn left after a half-mile on Hotchkiss Road onto Cold Brook Road for roughly 2 miles of dirt and pavement; the road ends at well-paved Barnes Hill Road, where you make another left, and then ride onto Claire Hill Road in a quarter-mile.

A cyclist rides over the trestle bridge near Collinsville.

Take the first right onto Sand Bank Hill Road, a tiny curvy section of pavement that ends at Canton Road, where you take a right and then an immediate left onto Burlington Avenue. Burlington Avenue is another twisty little path; bear right onto Arch Street and continue until you reach the off-road path for the Farmington River Trail (not to be confused with the Farmington Canal Trail).

Turn right onto the trail and ride over the historic bridge, crossing the Farmington River. Exit back in downtown Collinsville, behind the shops and restaurants you passed when you started the ride, finally turning right onto Main Street to finish the route.

MILES AND DIRECTIONS

0.0 Start on Main Street

0.1 Right onto Farmington River Trail and then left onto Bridge Street

0.2 Right onto Torrington Avenue

History of Collinsville

Proximity to the river makes the town a popular spot for outdoor recreation, just as it once drew the industrialists who created the industry that the town was founded around. In 1826 Samuel Collins and his younger brother built a mill here where they made axes and other edged tools. The Collinsville Company closed in 1966, after 140 years in business. The remaining factory buildings have been converted to mixed-use developments with retail boutiques, antiques stores, and artisans.

Historian Diana Muir, originally of Old Lyme, believes that die-casting was invented here by Elisha Root, inventor and machinist, while he worked for the Collins brothers. Root would later work for Samuel Colt in his firearms factory and make many contributions to manufacturing. After Colt's death, Root took over as president of Colt Firearms until he died in 1865.

Muir documents her claim in *Reflections in Bullough's Pond*, a fascinating history of the ecosystem and economy of New England. Her book explores the overlaps and intersections between the natural world and the Industrial Revolution that occurred in New England when settlers made the transition from agriculture to manufacturing.

1.9 Continue on Nepaug Dam

2.4 Left onto Litchfield Turnpike

4.2 Left onto South East Road

6.1 Continue on Covey Road

7.7 Left onto Hotchkiss Road

8.2 Left onto Cold Brook Road

10.3 Left onto Barnes Hill Road

10.5 Continue on Claire Hill Road

10.7 Right onto Sand Bank Hill Road

10.9 Right onto Canton Road and then left onto Burlington Avenue

11.0 Right onto Arch Street

11.4 Continue on Farmington River Trail

11.7 Right onto Main Street

11.8 Finish on Main Street

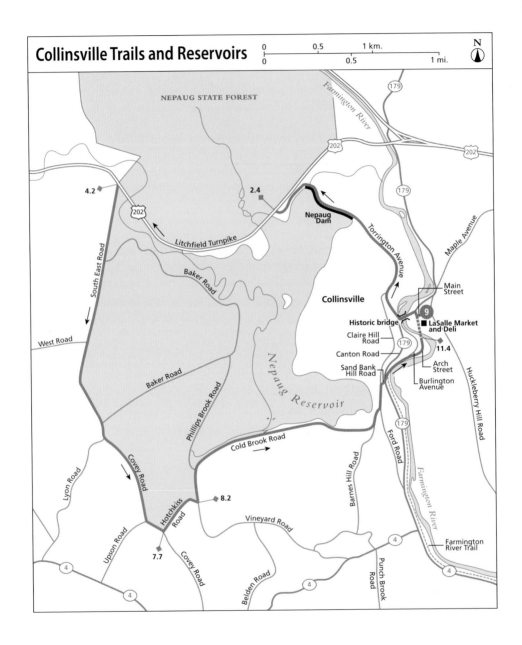

Collinsville Trails and Reservoirs

0   0.5   1 km.
0   0.5   1 mi.

N

NEPAUG STATE FOREST

Farmington River

179

202

202

179

4.2

202

2.4

Nepaug Dam

179

Litchfield Turnpike

Torrington Avenue

Maple Avenue

South East Road

Baker Road

Collinsville

Main Street

West Road

Baker Road

Phillips Brook Road

Nepaug Reservoir

Historic bridge

Claire Hill Road

Canton Road

Sand Bank Hill Road

9

LaSalle Market and Deli

11.4

179

Arch Street

Burlington Avenue

Huckleberry Hill Road

Cold Brook Road

Lyon Road

Covey Road

Hotchkiss Road

8.2

Vineyard Road

Barnes Hill Road

Ford Road

179

Farmington River

Upson Road

7.7

Covey Road

Belden Road

4

4

Punch Brook Road

4

Farmington River Trail

4

4

Bike Shops

Benidorm Bikes: 247 Albany Turnpike, Canton; (860) 693-8891; benidorm bikes.com

The Bicycle Cellar: 532 Hopmeadow St., Simsbury; (860) 658-1311; bloomfield bike.com

Bikers Edge Avon: 16 Ensign Dr., Avon; (860) 678-7770; bikersedge.com

Local Events and Attractions

Collinsville Farmers' Market: This seasonal market operates weekly from June to September, every Sunday.

Canton Historical Museum: This museum in downtown Collinsville exhibits dioramas, rooms, and industrial artifacts to recreate the early years of the community.

Farmington River: Collinsville Canoe and Kayak operates river tours on rental boats and provides classes and instruction. The outfit also offers a well-stocked selection of new kayaks and canoes for sale. The river can be easily explored on foot or by bike, via the Farmington Valley Greenway, a rails-to-trails project that this route partially covers.

Nepaug Dam and Reservoir: This scenic body of water is popular with birders and hikers. The dam is orbited by off-road trails that are suitable for hardy cycling and walking. This man-made lake was controversial when it was first planned and required the removal of roughly three dozen homes. The controversy around the construction, combined with superstitions about the graveyards over which the dam was built, have led to local speculation that the dam is a nexus of supernatural activity. There is, of course, no verifiable data to support the claims of UFO sightings, ghosts, and general bad luck in the area, but the legends make for fun lore.

Bridge Street Live: This entertainment venue books comedy, music, and other performance acts.

Restaurants

LaSalle Market and Deli: 104 Main St., Collinsville; (860) 693-8010; lasalle market.com

Crown and Hammer Restaurant and Pub: 3 Depot St., Collinsville; (860) 693-9199; crownandhammer.com

Francesca's Wine Bar and Bistro: 105 Main St., Canton; (860) 352-8157; francescaswinebar.com

Bridge Street Restaurant: 41 Bridge St., Collinsville; (860) 693-9762; 41bridge street.com

Hartford City Parks

Once one of the richest cities in the nation, Hartford grew rapidly during the Industrial Revolution, doubling in population over the course of a decade. To ameliorate overcrowding and other urban woes, the Reverend Horace Bushnell proposed building a city park in an area occupied by tanneries, pigsties, and a garbage dump. Through an at-times contentious process, the area previously described by Bushnell as "hell without the fire" became the first public park in the nation. Named after the man who first imagined it, Bushnell Park is home of the state capitol building and also hosts a number of events each year, including the Discover Hartford Bike Tour, which inspired this route.

Start: Bushnell Park near Lily Pond and the carousel

Length: 11.5 miles

Riding time: 1 hour

Best bike: Road bike or hybrid

Terrain and trail surface: Asphalt

Traffic and hazards: Downtown Hartford can be a challenge, so use caution and be aware of the traffic around you. The parks are peaceful and car-free. If you are nervous riding on busy city streets, you may wish to walk the short distance from the park to Charter Oak Avenue, to avoid riding on Main Street and the intersection of Jewell and Trumbull. Also use caution after Riverside Park on the connecting streets to the Keney Park area; they are short, but can be busy with weekday traffic.

Things to see: In Bushnell Park, the Capitol, the carousel, and Lily Pond. This ride also passes the Wadsworth Atheneum Museum of Art, the Connecticut River, a sculpture walk in Riverside Park, Keney Park, and a number of important historic landmarks and buildings.

Fees: None

Getting there: From I-91, take exit 29A for the Capitol Area onto Whitehead Highway. Take the second exit from the traffic circle onto Elm Street to the park directly ahead. From I-84E, take exit 48 for Capitol Avenue and turn left onto Capitol Avenue to the park. For I-84W, take exit 48 for Asylum Avenue, and turn left onto Asylum Avenue to the park.

GPS: 41.76536 / -72.67858

THE RIDE

This route starts on Jewell Street, on the north side of Bushnell Park. Nearby landmarks include the carousel, added in 1974, and a lovely pond with water fountains and sculptures.

Follow either the park path or Jewell Street to the intersection with Trumbull Street; turn right, and then very carefully cross the oncoming lanes onto Gold Street.

The Stone Field sculpture garden is on the left. Just beyond the field and the church is the Ancient Burying Ground, Hartford's oldest historic location. This graveyard dates back to 1644.

As you approach the intersection with Main Street, the iconic Travelers Insurance building is visible on the left. Turn right and use caution on this busy block. The Wadsworth Atheneum Museum of Art is on the left in the iconic Gothic Revival building, followed by the Burr Mall, with an enormous abstract stegosaurus sculpture by Alexander Calder, and lastly, Hartford City Hall.

Continuing on Main Street, the route passes a few other notable buildings, including the Butler-McCook House and Garden.

Approaching the intersection with Charter Oak Avenue, near the half-mile mark, take a careful left turn. Charter Oak Avenue heads slightly downhill and has the first on-street bike path of the route. Follow Charter Oak Avenue until it becomes Van Dyke Avenue and then take a hairpin turn, beneath the highway and over an old railroad line, for trail access to the Riverside.

Take a left, keeping the river to your right, and follow the path north for nearly a half-mile, heading back under the highway overpass, into the Sculpture Walk at Riverside Park.

Meander through the park along the Riverwalk, which heads under another highway overpass up ahead, before exiting onto the Riverside Parkway. At the end of this quiet road, carefully turn left across four lanes onto Weston Street, turning right in 0.3 mile to follow Weston. Weston Street here is fairly built up and busy; be attentive and watch the driveways.

Bushnell Park pond.

At a major intersection, turn left onto Boce Barlow Way, an elevated road-way crossing the railroad below. The mapped route shows a zigzag here, turning right onto Windsor, then left onto Main Street, but it's easier and safer to cross with the crosswalk and cut through the parking lot directly ahead of you onto Kensington Street.

Kensington Street is a quieter, single-lane neighborhood street with a comfortable shoulder. At the first intersection, turn right onto Hampton Street, a similar neighborhood street, and follow it for nearly a half-mile, until it ends in a T-junction with Tower Avenue.

Turn left onto Tower Avenue and ride to the Keney Park entrance at the intersection with Barbour Street. Turn right to enter the park and follow posted signs to the road through the park, past the golf course, cricket fields, and basketball and tennis courts.

Nearly 700 acres, Keney Park is the largest park in Hartford, built out of three connected sections; this first part is the Barbour portion. After completing the loop, exit onto Barbour Street, heading south.

After passing the Wish School on the left, turn right onto Charlotte Street for a quarter of a mile, turning left on Waverly Street, and then take the next right onto Love Lane.

Love Lane is a quiet, narrow road that passes through the second portion of Keney Park (Waverly), ending in a T-junction with Vine Street.

Carefully cross Vine Street into the park, and turn left, to follow the park road south. This section of the route is roughly a mile, passing a number of

A view of sculptural works overlooking the Connecticut River from Riverside Park.

sports and recreation sites, with a tennis court right before the park entrance at Greenfield Street.

After exiting, cross Greenfield onto Woodland Street, a fairly low-volume road that starts off in an area with old, underutilized buildings, before reaching the more vibrant section ahead. After a mile on Woodland, turn left heading east onto Niles Street, a narrow, low-volume city street. As you near the end of the street you see the bright brick edifice of Trinity Episcopal Church. Trinity has the distinction of being the first "free" church in the city of Hartford; when it was built, other city churches charged a "pew fee" to parishioners.

Turn right onto busy Sigourney Street, taking the first left onto Farmington Avenue. Farmington Avenue is a pretty side street between the Aetna buildings and the towering Cathedral of St. Joseph, home to a dozen carillon bells, each weighing as much as 3,850 pounds.

At the end of this block, turn right onto Flower Street, which passes beneath the last of the Aetna buildings and then I-84, before turning left at the major intersection with Capitol Avenue.

The capitol dome should be visible ahead and to the left. Carefully ride the 0.4 mile on this busy street until you see the Bushnell Performing Arts Center and Hartford Symphony Orchestra buildings ahead. Turn left here onto Trinity Street, keeping the capitol building and park on your left.

Ride to Jewell Street and turn right to finish the ride, arriving back at Lily Pond.

MILES AND DIRECTIONS

0.0   Start at park on Jewell Street

0.1   Cross Wells onto Gold Street

0.2   Right onto Main Street

0.5   Left onto Charter Oak Avenue

1.0   Continue on Van Dyke Avenue

1.1   Left for trail access

2.5   Proceed onto Riverside Parkway

3.2   Left onto Weston Street

3.5   Right to stay on Weston Street

3.7   Left onto Boce Barlow Way

4.1   Right onto Windsor Street

4.2   Left onto Main Street, then right onto Kensington Street.

4.4   Right onto Hampton Street

4.8   Left onto Tower Avenue

5.1   Right into park, follow park road/trail loop back to start

6.8   Cross Tower Avenue onto Barbour Street

7.2   Right onto Charlotte Street

7.4   Left onto Waverly Street

7.5   Right onto Love Lane

7.8   Cross Vine Street into park, follow park road to exit

8.7   Cross Greenfield Street on Woodland Street

9.7   Left onto Niles Street

10.1   Right onto Sigourney Street

10.2   Left onto Farmington Avenue

10.5   Right onto Flower Street

10.8   Left onto Capitol Avenue

11.2   Left onto Trinity Street

11.4   Right onto Jewell Street

11.5   Finish at park

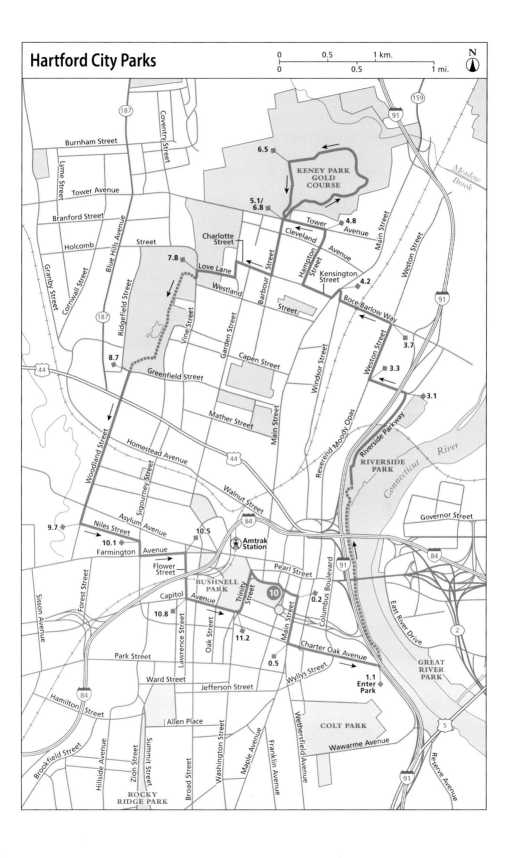

Hartford City Parks

0   0.5   1 km.

0   0.5   1 mi.

N

187

Burnham Street

Coventry Street

Lyme Street

Tower Avenue

Branford Street

Holcomb   Street

Blue Hills Avenue

Granby Street

Cornwall Street

Ridgefield Street

187

44

6.5

KENEY PARK
GOLD
COURSE

91

159

Meadow
Brook

5.1/
6.8

Tower   Avenue   4.8

Cleveland   Avenue

Main Street

Weston Street

Charlotte
Street

7.8

Love Lane

Westland

Barbour   Street

Street

Hampton
Street

Kensington
Street

4.2

Boce Barlow Way

91

Vine Street

Garden Street

Capen Street

Windsor Street

Weston Street

3.7

3.3

8.7

Greenfield Street

Mather Street

Main Street

Reverend Moody Opes

3.1

Riverside Parkway

RIVERSIDE
PARK

Connecticut   River

Woodland Street

Homestead Avenue

44

Walnut Street

Governor Street

84

Sigourney Street

Asylum Avenue

9.7

Niles Street

10.1

10.5

Farmington   Avenue

Amtrak
Station

Pearl Street

91

84

2

Flower
Street

Forest Street

BUSHNELL
PARK

Capitol

Avenue

10.8

Lawrence Street

Oak Street

Trinity Street

10

Main Street

Columbus Boulevard

0.2

East River Drive

Sisson Avenue

11.2

0.5

Charter Oak Avenue

Wyllys Street

GREAT
RIVER
PARK

Park Street

Ward Street

Jefferson Street

1.1
Enter
Park

84

Hamilton   Street

Allen Place

Hillside Avenue

Zion Street

Summit Street

Washington Street

Maple Avenue

Franklin Avenue

Wethersfield Avenue

COLT PARK

Wawarme Avenue

5

Brookfield Street

Broad Street

ROCKY
RIDGE PARK

91

Reserve Avenue

RIDE INFORMATION

Bike Shops
Ray Taskar Bicycles: 93 Franklin Ave., Hartford; (860) 247-0191
Newington Bicycle and Repair Shop: 1030 Main St., Newington; (860) 667-0857; newingtonbike.com
Cycling Concepts: 2343 Main St., Glastonbury; (860) 633-3444; cyclingconcepts.com
Bicycles East: 331 New London Turnpike, Glastonbury; (860) 659-0114; bicycleseast.com

Local Events and Attractions
Discover Hartford Bike Tour: State advocacy group Bike Walk CT hosts an annual ride throughout Hartford. Learn more on their site, bikewalkct.org.
Butler-McCook House and Garden: One of twelve historic house museums operated by CT Landmarks.
Wadsworth Atheneum Museum of Art: The Wadsworth was the first public art museum in America. The prestigious collection includes European Baroque art, French and American impressionist paintings, Hudson River school landscapes, and modernist and contemporary works.
Connecticut State Capitol: The State Capitol offers tours through this imposing Eastlake Style domed building.

Restaurants
Salute Eatery: 100 Trumbull St., Hartford; (860) 899-1350; salutect.com
Vito's By the Park: 26 Trumbull St., Hartford; (860) 244-2200; vitosct.com

Restrooms
0.0 Miles: Port-a-johns in Bushnell Park
2.6 Miles: Port-a-johns in Riverside Park

Hartford–West Hartford Loop

Hartford is full of historic buildings, iconic landmarks, and beautiful parks, but it's also a car-centric urban environment that can be challenging to bike. This route was adapted from local cyclists' training routes to provide a 15-mile loop on long stretches of calmer roads, past scenic parks, into neighboring West Hartford.

Start: Garden Street

Length: 15.1 miles

Riding time: 1.5 hours

Best bike: Road bike

Terrain and trail surface: Asphalt

Traffic and hazards: Farmington Avenue can be hectic, as is the intersection with CT 128, and a short section of the return loop on Albany and Bloomfield Avenues.

Things to see: Elizabeth Park in Hartford, a charming foot bridge over Trout Brook and, with a short detour, the urbanist Blue Back Square development in West Hartford.

Fees: None. The Liam E. McGee Memorial Park does not allow parking, but free curbside parking is in ample supply on the side streets.

Getting there: The ride starts on Garden Street, just off exit 48 on I-84W. From I-84E, take exit 48A to Asylum Avenue, then turn right onto Garden Street.

GPS: 41.77122 / -72.68646

THE RIDE

The state capital was once a wealthier, more prosperous, city, but it is still an important employer in the insurance industry. This ride begins behind the corporate headquarters of insurance giant The Hartford, by the Liam E. McGee Memorial Park, named in honor of the popular CEO who led the company through a turnaround following the 2008 financial crisis.

This ride starts on Garden Street, in front of a private park owned by The Hartford. Riding westward, turn left ahead onto Collins Street, a fairly low-volume urban street with shade trees, apartments, and small offices.

The route follows Collins for a half-mile, passing through the Saint Francis Hospital campus, before turning left onto Woodland Street. Follow Woodland for one block, about 0.1 mile, and then turn right onto Asylum Avenue.

Asylum became a pleasant and bike-friendly street following a massive redevelopment plan that added a busway and was designed for safer pedestrian and cyclist access. After crossing a picturesque bridge with brick and wrought-iron fencing, bear right to stay on Asylum, continuing until the intersection with Whitney Street at Elizabeth Park.

For a leisurely detour, ride to the park entrance on Prospect Avenue, about 0.1 mile off the route, farther up Asylum.

The mapped route turns left onto Whitney Street, with a narrow bike lane over the next quarter-mile and views of the park to the right. Cross Elizabeth Street and take the next right, onto Fern Street.

Fern is a quiet neighborhood street bordered by single-family homes. Turn left at the first turn, onto Oxford Street, which starts off in a quiet neighborhood before reaching busy Farmington Avenue in a third of a mile.

Turn right for a short stretch on Farmington Avenue, a busy, multi-lane road with dedicated turning lanes, curbside parking, and large commercial properties. In 0.2 mile, carefully turn left onto quiet South Highland Street for just under a half-mile.

Turn right onto Boulevard, a safer, lower-volume parallel of Farmington Avenue, for the next half-mile, until reaching Quaker Lane South. Turn left and follow this narrow neighborhood road for 0.2 mile, turning right at the gas station onto Park Road, toward downtown West Hartford.

In two blocks you reach Trout Brook and the small park built around it (note the attractive foot bridge on the right) and see signs for Blue Back Square, West Hartford's much-touted new urbanist development. The property features major retailers, restaurants, and mixed-use buildings, all built at an attractive, pedestrian-friendly scale. If you're interested in visiting the plaza, don't follow the signs at Trout Brook Drive; instead, continue forward,

Scenic city overlook from Elizabeth Park.

and turn right onto Raymond Road, a narrower, slower street leading into the development.

The mapped route continues along Park Road, crossing South Main Street at the 4.6-mile mark, becoming Sedgwick Road, where it narrows and a comfortable shoulder opens for cycling.

Follow Sedgwick Road for the next quarter-mile, and turn right onto Four Mile Road, a narrow neighborhood road with no center lane mark.

In a half-mile, turn left onto Farmington Avenue and then take the second right onto Arlington Road, another quiet suburban neighborhood street.

At the end of Arlington Road, bear left at the fork onto scenic and quiet Whitman Road. Whitman is a narrow tree-lined street bordered by small single-family homes on the left and picturesque Fairview Cemetery on the right.

After the park, Whitman becomes Braeburn Road for a third of a mile, ending in a T-junction with Mountain Road at the 6.2-mile mark.

Turn right onto Mountain Road for a 3.5-mile stretch, with nearly 200 feet of climbing, over a set of mostly gently rolling hills. Traffic lights are infrequent; the only two major intersections are with Fern Street and US 44.

Near the end of Mountain Road, take a right turn onto Watkins Road, along an open field adjoining a church on the right. Watkins is a short stretch of road that ends just ahead, at Simsbury Road, where you turn right and ride through the Tumble Brook Country Club property.

Simsbury Road is a slightly fast road with a generous shoulder, modest suburban homes, and a narrow buffer of trees. The road is largely a pleasant

11

diversion from city riding, but do use caution crossing the built-up intersection with CT 218.

Just after the Hartford Golf Club property, Simsbury Road curves right, turning onto CT 189. Continue along this busier street, passing the University of Hartford on your left, until the road ends at a T-junction with Albany Avenue (US 44).

Use caution and turn left with the traffic light, following this even busier street for the next half-mile. After riding an elevated section of road over railroad tracks below, turn right onto Homestead Avenue.

Homestead Avenue is a four-lane road through a busy, car-centric commercial section with some attractive former industrial buildings in view on the left. Follow Homestead for nearly a quarter-mile before turning right onto Woodland Street.

Take the second left onto Ashley Street, riding along the other side of the St. Francis Hospital campus, for 0.4 mile. The route passes Sigourney Square Park on the left and then turns right onto Sigourney Street for one block.

Take the first left back onto Collins Street and finish your ride in a third of a mile, turning right onto Garden Street.

MILES AND DIRECTIONS

0.0 Start at Liam E. McGee Park on Garden Street
0.2 Left onto Collins Street
0.7 Left onto Woodland Street
0.8 Right onto Asylum Avenue
1.4 Left onto Whitney Street
1.9 Right onto Fern Street
2.0 Left onto Oxford Street
2.3 Right onto Farmington Avenue
2.5 Left onto South Highland Street
2.9 Right onto Boulevard
3.4 Left onto Quaker Lane South
3.6 Right onto Park Road
4.4 Continue on Sedgwick Road
4.6 Right onto Four Mile Road
5.1 Left onto Farmington Avenue
5.2 Right onto Arlington Road

Hartford—West Hartford Loop

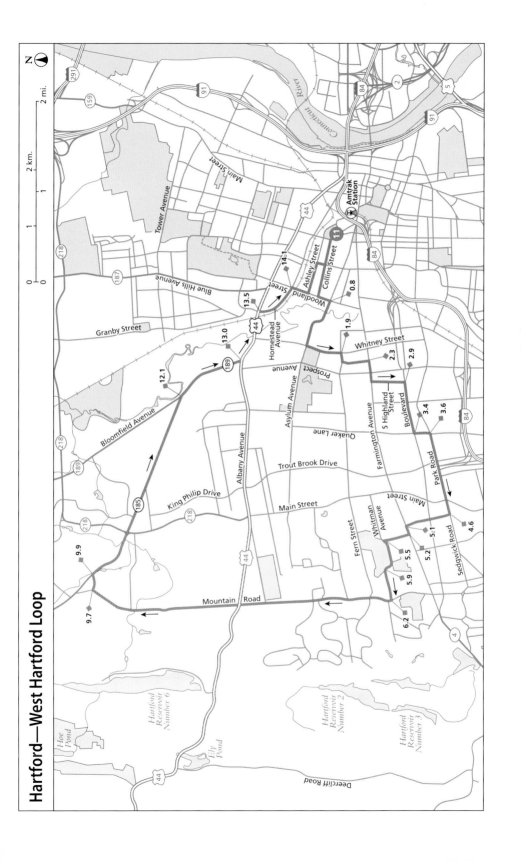

5.5 Left onto Whitman Avenue

5.9 Continue on Braeburn Road

6.2 Right onto Mountain Road

9.7 Right onto Watkins Road

9.9 Continue on Simsbury Road

12.1 Continue on Bloomfield Avenue

13.0 Left onto Albany Avenue

13.5 Right onto Homestead Avenue

14.0 Right onto Woodland Street

14.2 Left onto Ashley Street

14.6 Right onto Sigourney Street

14.7 Left onto Collins Street

15.0 Right onto Garden Street

15.1 Finish ride at Liam E. McGee Memorial Park

RIDE INFORMATION

Bike Shops
Ray Taskar Bicycles: 93 Franklin Ave., Hartford; (860) 247-0191
Newington Bicycle and Repair Shop: 1030 Main St., Newington; (860) 667-0857; newingtonbike.com
Cycling Concepts: 2343 Main St., Glastonbury; (860) 633-3444; cycling concepts.com
Bicycles East: 331 New London Turnpike, Glastonbury; (860) 659-0114; bicycleseast.com

Local Events and Attractions
Elizabeth Park: This 100-acre property includes a public rose garden, a fine dining restaurant, ponds, greenhouses, and large, open lawns for picnics and sunbathing. Many consider it the most beautiful park in the city.
Discover Hartford Bike Tour: State advocacy group Bike Walk CT hosts an annual ride throughout Hartford. Learn more on their site: bikewalkct.org.
Connecticut State Capitol: The State Capitol offers tours through this imposing Eastlake Style domed building.
Blue Back Square: A New Urban development, Blue Back Square has a variety of eateries and boutique shopping.

Stately gabled home near the park.

Restaurants

Pond House Cafe: 1555 Asylum Ave., West Hartford (Elizabeth Park); (860) 231-8823; pondhousecafe.com

Delicacy Market and Catering: 774 Farmington Ave., West Hartford; (860) 236-7100; delicacymarket.com

Max Burger: 124 LaSalle Rd., West Hartford; (860) 232-3300; maxrestaurant group.com

Restrooms

1.5 Miles: Elizabeth Park

Northwest Hills

Litchfield County encompasses the Northwest Hills, a geographic region characterized by the Berkshire Mountains range, rolling farmland, and scenic valleys. Much of the region was bypassed by the Industrial Revolution, preserving the natural beauty and charm of its New England forests and mountains.

The town of Litchfield stands out because of its pre-revolutionary–style green and its architecture, mostly built during the Colonial Revival period of the late 19th century. Litchfield is in the center of many of the rides, and offers a mix of upscale dining, local shopping, and high culture, all in a vibrant village setting.

Many of the rides pass through Kent, a versatile community along the Hudson River Valley in New York and the Housatonic River in Connecticut. The area has a healthy agricultural economy and is a tourist destination for shopping and natural attractions, including Macedonia Brook State Park, the waterfalls at Kent Falls State Park, and the Appalachian Trail. On the New York border, motorists detour to drive over Bull's Bridge, one of two historic covered bridges still open to automobiles in the state.

Upriver a bit, the village of Cornwall is home to the West Cornwall Covered Bridge, the second of the two bridges. The short and hilly ride in this region can easily be extended with a ride along scenic roads west, toward Sharon, and then finished by looping back east.

Don't miss Great Falls, a potentially spectacular waterfall located near Falls Village, just off the Lakeville Lakes route (Ride 16). After heavy rains, this waterfall provides an incredible sight to visitors. Kayaking up the Housatonic to see it from below is highly recommended.

12

Barkhamsted Reservoir

This ride can be easily combined with Kent Hills (Ride 18), which joins US 7 2 miles south of a section of this route in the Cornwall Bridge area. This added loop would add 4 miles via a short stretch on US 7 to pick up the Kent Hills path. Long-distance cyclists could also take US 7 north from West Cornwall to the 27.4 mile Lakeville Lakes ride (Ride 16) (7-mile detour, one-way), or a longer, more scenic route on West Cornwall Road west to White Hollow Road, with a right onto Lime Rock Road and then a left onto Dugway Road to connect to the Lakeville Loops, adding 12 miles one-way.

Barkhamsted is a far northern town along the border with Massachusetts. This small Litchfield County town is primarily made up of state forests and water company land surrounding the Barkhamsted Reservoir. The town itself is made up of two villages: Pleasant Valley and Riverton, both to the west of the reservoir. Pleasant Valley is the town center, with municipal buildings, a school, and the post office, in a scenic location along the Farmington River. North of Pleasant Valley, along River Road, is the village of Riverton, a small commercial center at the confluence of the Still and Farmington Rivers.

Start: Saville Dam parking area

Length: 22.2 miles

Riding time: 1 hour 45 minutes

Best bike: Road bike

Terrain and trail surface: Asphalt

Traffic and hazards: This is a remote area with sometimes fast traffic, but very little of it. Bear and moose sightings are not unheard of.

Things to see: The Saville Dam, Barkhamsted Reservoir, a scenic overlook near the end of the first half of the ride, and a historic schoolhouse

THE RIDE

This hilly 22.2-mile ride contains more than 2,200 feet of climbing. The first half of the ride is the hardest, with a large hill right at the start after you turn onto Beach Rock Road. You reach the peak elevation fairly early and have a series of rolling hills before a big descent and a second long climb, followed by another set of rolling hills, and a final descent back down to the dam.

This ride starts at the Saville Dam, with a small parking area, and street-side parking just off the dam. Once you've parked, you can take advantage of the photo opportunities over by the small tower rising out of the water, and then head west on Saville Dam Road for a half-mile, taking the first right onto Beach Rock Road. This is also the first steep climb of the ride, gaining nearly 200 feet in a short distance with double-digit grades in some sections.

As the road descends away from the peak you pass historic Barkhamsted Center Cemetery on your right; stay right as the road turns on Center Hill Road. Center Hill Road passes the Old School House Museum, a Historical Society property, just before a multi-road intersection at the 1.4-mile mark. Take Boettner Road, a steep climb up a quiet side street that runs parallel to the busier Center Hill Road before rejoining it just after 2 miles.

The scenery on the left will be less populated now, as you pass along People's State Forest. At the 6.2-mile mark, continue straight, onto CT 20.The route follows CT 20 for the next 9 miles or so, but local road names are used to help with wayfinding. This first segment is Center Street, running through Hartland, a tiny town on the far western edge of Hartford County, home to less than 2,000 residents.

The hills are less steep and less frequent here, but you have another nearly 200-foot climb between you and Booth Hill, starting around the seventh mile and finally ending a quarter of a mile past the 8-mile mark, where the road name changes to Morrison Hill Road. The road passes through Tunxis State Forest, a large state park home to bear and moose; sightings are not uncommon, so keep an eye out for wildlife as you careen through the corners.

This interesting building juts out from the Saville Dam.

Morrison Hill Road curves and twists, skirting the hill it's named after, before a fast, winding, 500-foot descent over nearly 3 miles of road that take you around the northernmost edge of the dam. At the 11.2-mile mark, stay right as the road becomes North Hollow Road, heading east and then south, toward East Hartland.

The second big climb of the ride starts at the 12-mile mark, with another 500 feet of elevation gain, before leveling off on a curving road. Take a right turn onto CT 179 in East Hartland, a sleepy little town with beautiful scenery, then an immediate left to stay on CT 179, South Road.

CT 179 has a generous shoulder and mostly passes through forest, with the occasional modern home. The road is a slightly busier street than the previous ones, but still quite safe to bike on, and mostly flat compared to the earlier route.

CT 179 meets CT 219 at the 19.3-mile mark. Continue straight, onto CT 219, East Hartland Road, and climb the last small hill of the route, gaining about 100 feet, before the final descent to the dam.

Rolling hills and a pastoral stone wall.

The descent starts right around the 20-mile mark and continues down through a fork in the road; bear right onto CT 318, Saville Dam Road, at the 21.8-mile mark, and follow the road to where you parked to complete this ride.

MILES AND DIRECTIONS

0.0   Start on CT 318

0.4   Right onto Beach Rock Road

1.4   Continue on Boettner Road

2.0   Continue on CT 181

6.2   Continue on CT 20

15.3   Right and then left on CT 179

19.8   Continue onto CT 219

21.8   Right onto CT 318

22.2   Finish ride at parking lot

RIDE INFORMATION

Bike Shops

Benidorm Bikes: 247 Albany Turnpike, Canton; (860) 693-8891; benidorm bikes.com

The Bicycle Cellar: 532 Hopmeadow St., Simsbury; (860) 658-1311; bloomfield bike.com

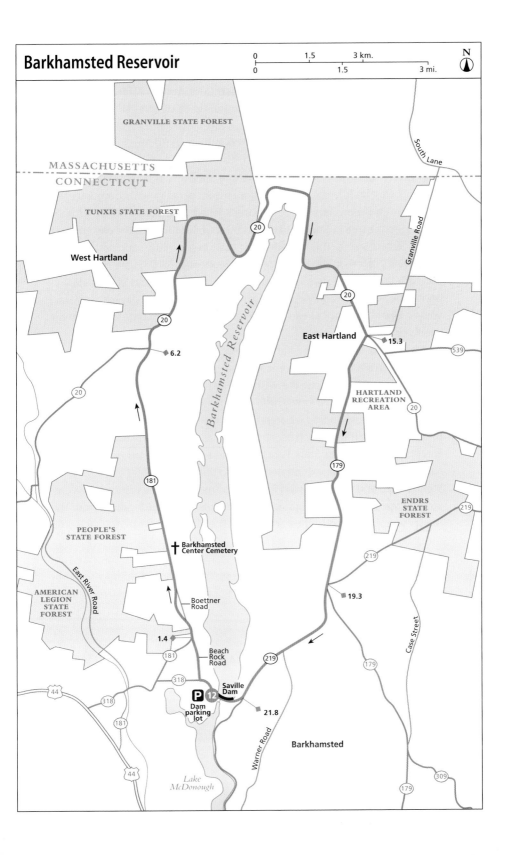

Barkhamsted Reservoir

0   1.5   3 km.
0   1.5   3 mi.

N

GRANVILLE STATE FOREST

South Lane

MASSACHUSETTS
CONNECTICUT

TUNXIS STATE FOREST

Granville Road

West Hartland

20

20

20

◆ 6.2

East Hartland

◆ 15.3

539

20

**HARTLAND
RECREATION
AREA**

Barkhamsted Reservoir

20

181

179

**PEOPLE'S
STATE FOREST**

**ENDRS
STATE
FOREST**

219

East River Road

† **Barkhamsted
Center Cemetery**

219

**AMERICAN
LEGION
STATE
FOREST**

219

■ 19.3

Boettner
Road

Case Street

1.4 ◆

Beach
Rock
Road

181

219

179

318

44

**Saville
Dam**

P 12

Dam
parking
lot

318

181

■ 21.8

Warner Road

Barkhamsted

44

*Lake
McDonough*

179

309

Events and Attractions

American Legion/People's State Forest: Just north of Pleasant Valley, between the reservoir and Riverton, are hundreds of acres of woods criss-crossed with hiking trails and a camping site. Cross-country skiing, canoeing, and kayaking are permitted, along with hunting and fishing, seasonally, and by permit.

The Nature Museum: Formerly "The Stone Museum," this charming historic building was built from local fieldstones and paneled with gorgeous red American Chestnut, harvested from trees felled by the blight that virtually eradicated the tree in Connecticut and throughout much of the eastern part of the United States. The museum was built in the 1930s, and sat dormant for 50 years before it was renovated and reopened. Exhibits are nature-centric, with taxidermied fauna and interactive tracking displays of animal paw-prints. The museum is only open seasonally, from Memorial Day to Labor Day; you may want to check ahead at www.psfnaturemuseum.org/ to see current events or exhibitions.

Barkhamsted Lighthouse: Barkhamsted was the name of a community started when a Wethersfield woman of European descent married a local man from a native tribe against the wishes of her father. The two struck out on their own, settling into a lonely little cabin far into the wilderness. They were joined by others, including laborers from a nearby soapstone quarry, and the brightly lit cabin they lived in became known as the Barkhamsted Lighthouse. Trails from the People's State Forest provide access to the property, and the Nature Museum has an exhibit dedicated to the lighthouse.

Saville Dam and Barkhamsted Reservoir: This man-made reservoir was created by the Saville Dam, built in 1940, and filled over an 8-year period. The new reservoir flooded homes and farms. The surviving properties make up the Barkhamsted Center Historic District.

Squire's Tavern: The Barkhamsted Historical Society operates this museum near the entrance into the People's Forest. The historic building was renovated and turned into a permanent exhibit of early settlement life. The society keeps regular hours and also holds special events for holidays.

Restaurants

Sweet Pea's Restaurant: 6 Riverton Rd., Riverton; (860) 379-7020; sweetpeas restaurant.com

The Catnip Mouse Tea Room: 15 Riverton Rd., Riverton; (860) 379-3745

The Coach Stop: 6 Hartland Blvd., Hartland; (860) 413-3545

Torrington Loop

Torrington is a charming little city in Litchfield County. Despite a catastrophic flood in 1955, the historic downtown is still home to the largest concentration of art deco buildings in the state. One of the best examples of this architecture, the Warner Theater, is a magnificent building with an iconic illuminated marquee and vertical sign. It was built in the construction boom of the 1930s and is still in operation. Downtown boasts a healthy Main Street–style economy with a small-town feel.

Start: Coe Memorial Park in downtown Torrington

Length: 18 miles

Riding time: 1.75 hours

Best bike: Road bike

Terrain and trail surface: Asphalt

Traffic and hazards: Some of the roads can be slightly busy; Torrington is at the center of several regional transportation routes. Most of the riding is on pleasant, lower-volume roads, with one exception near the end of the ride where Winsted Road approaches the edge of downtown and a built-up, car-centric commercial area.

Things to see: The Warner Theater, other historic art deco buildings downtown, the Naugatuck River, Coe Memorial Park, Stillwater Pond State Park, Burr Pond, and the Still River Greenway.

Fees: None. Coe Memorial Park offers free parking. If the small lot is crowded, ample street-side parking is available.

Getting there: CT 4 is recommended from Hartford and other points east. Exit and turn right onto Birge Park Road to New Harwinton Road, and then take a slight left onto East Main Street to downtown

Torrington. From New Haven, New York City, or other points south, take CT 8 to exit 44 for US 202 toward downtown, and turn left onto East Main Street to the ride start.

GPS: 41.79993 /-73.12164

THE RIDE

This 18-mile route is fairly hilly, with a total elevation gain of 1,333 feet, primarily in the first half. After reaching the 9-mile mark, and peak elevation on Taylor Brook Road, the last half is a fast descent back into downtown Torrington.

The ride starts near the scenic Naugatuck River and the confluence of Main Street and Litchfield Street, in Coe Memorial Park. Exit the park and turn right onto Litchfield Street, passing the public library on the left and then carefully crossing the busy intersection, bearing left over the bridge.

Note the scenic view of the Naugatuck River below, on the right, and turn left at the intersection ahead onto Water Street past a row of businesses in a long, lovely brick building with detailed embellishments and curved windows.

Near the half-mile mark, turn left onto Church Street, a narrow connecting road with a few homes and businesses. After the traffic signal, turn right onto Riverside, a more suburban-feeling road with occasional views of the Naugatuck River on the right. This narrow road doesn't have much of a shoulder, but low-traffic volumes, sidewalks, and multi-family housing make it feel pleasant and safe.

Riverside is a little more built up approaching the intersection with CT 4, after which it becomes Norfolk Road (CT 272). This 2.5-mile stretch has less dense housing, more river views, and a comfortable shoulder.

Traffic speeds pick up after the 3-mile point as the route approaches Stillwater Pond, where development drops off, providing lovely views of the water on the right and the forested backyard of the University of Connecticut's Torrington campus.

After the end of the pond, turn right for a quick little descent on Marshall Lake Road, over less well-maintained asphalt, before beginning the major climb of the day.

The route follows Marshall Road for a half-mile; in the middle of a climb, turn left onto Weingold Road, a quiet, rolling country road with meadow views on the left and thickly forested woods on the right. After a particularly steep section, the road passes the bucolic Weingold Dairy Farm, which maintains an antique operational barn, on the right.

One of many historic homes in Torrington.

After the farm, Weingold Road is largely undeveloped, making for a scenic, quiet ride through a beautiful natural forest full of birch and mixed hardwoods. The road surface gets a bit rougher in a short section near the end, where it becomes Blue Street; keep an eye out for a rustic barn conversion on the right.

Blue Street climbs up and around Park Pond, with a scenic overlook on the right at the peak of the climb. After the vista, expect a rocky descent for almost a half-mile, with a quick, short climb after a tranquil spot on the shore of the pond.

After the little climb, turn right onto Ashley Road (CT 263) for a short ascent and some rolling sections of pretty road. Keep right to stay on Ashley Road past beautiful old farms and large country homes until the road reaches the tiny historic green in Windsor Center.

Bear right onto South Road, another quiet country road, and through the next intersection for a ride past Hurlbut Pond on the left and a picturesque barn. The route passes through a historic cemetery, fenced in with a

Magnificent estate with four fireplaces on route.

less-attractive chain-link fence, before turning left at the forking intersection onto Platt Hill Road.

Head downhill for a short section of Platt Hill Road, and take a quick right at "The Little Red Schoolhouse" onto Taylor Brook Road for a fast downhill before three tiny momentum-driven climbing sections.

Peck Road, on the left, is part of Ride 14, the Winsted: Highland Lake ride. A detour for extra mileage is possible by turning left here and following the Winsted directions in reverse, eventually rejoining this route on Winsted Road. The only downside is missing the amazing descent ahead, past scenic Burr Pond.

The road becomes Burr Mountain Road after passing Peck Road, and starts to descend gradually until Burr Pond on the right. Ahead, the average grade is 9 percent, for a fast, technical descent down to the intersection with Winsted Road.

The route turns right here, either on Winsted Road, or on the Still River Greenway directly across the street. Winsted Road is pleasant enough, but the greenway is recommended for the beautiful marsh views.

The greenway is not yet completed and currently isn't very long; it exits after only a mile, where the route turns left onto Winsted Road. Winsted Road has a comfortable shoulder and feels relaxed despite the fast traffic.

The road gets slightly built up on the outskirts of downtown Torrington, with a busy light-industrial section, but still has beautiful natural views of ridges and forest on the left.

Near the 16.7-mile mark, the route turns left onto Main Street, in the heart of Torrington's historic art deco district. Of particular note is the Warner Theater, on the left, just before reaching the bridge and turn on Litchfield Street to Coe Park.

Post-ride, Torrington offers a number of small restaurants and eateries in the downtown area, many of them reflecting the heritage of a large Italian-American population, descended from a major immigration during the construction and manufacturing boom of the early 20th century.

MILES & DIRECTIONS

0.0 Start at Coe Park on Litchfield Street

0.0 Continue on South Main Street

0.0 Continue on Main Street

0.0 Left onto Water Street

0.4 Left onto Church Street

0.7 Continue on Riverside Avenue

1.9 Continue on Norfolk Road

4.5 Right onto Marshall Lake Road

5.0 Left onto Weigold Road

6.8 Continue on Blue Street

8.0 Right onto Ashley Road

8.6 Right onto West Road

9.1 Right onto Newfield Road

9.2 Left onto South Road

10.0 Left onto Platt Hill Road

10.2 Right onto Taylor Brook Road

11.4 Continue on Burr Mountain Road

12.7 Right onto Winsted Road

16.7 Left onto Main Street

18.0 Continue on South Main Street

18.0 Right onto Litchfield Street to finish

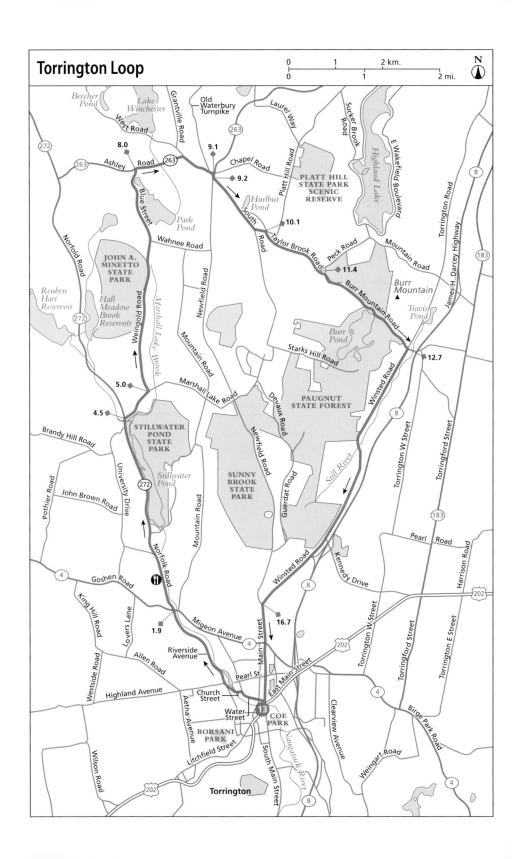

Torrington Loop

0   1   2 km.
0   1   2 mi.

N

Beecher Pond
Lake Winchester
Grantville Road
Old Waterbury Turnpike
West Road
272
8.0
263
Ashley Road
263
263
9.1
Chapel Road
9.2
Laurel Way
Sucker Brook Road
E Wakefield Road
Highland Lake
8
Norfold Road
Blue Street
Park Pond
Wahnee Road
South Road
Hurlbut Pond
Platt Hill Road
PLATT HILL STATE PARK SCENIC RESERVE
10.1
Taylor Brook Road
Peck Road
Mountain Road
Torrington Road
183
Reuben Hart Reservoir
272
JOHN A. MINETTO STATE PARK
Hall Meadow Brook Reservoir
Weingold Road
Marshall Lake Brook
Newfield Road
Mountain Road
11.4
Burr Mountain
Burr Mountain Road
Travis Pond
James H. Darcey Highway
Brandy Hill Road
5.0
Marshall Lake Road
Starks Hill Road
Burr Pond
Winsted Road
12.7
4.5
STILLWATER POND STATE PARK
Devaux Road
PAUGNUT STATE FOREST
8
Torrington W Street
Torringford Street
Pothier Road
University Drive
Stillwater Pond
272
John Brown Road
Mountain Road
SUNNY BROOK STATE PARK
Newfield Road
Guerdat Road
Still River
183
Pearl Road
Harrison Road
4
Goshen Road
Norfolk Road
Winsted Road
8
Kennedy Drive
202
Torrington W Street
Torringford Street
Torrington E Street
King Hill Road
Lovers Lane
1.9
Migeon Avenue
Main Street
16.7
202
4
Clearview Avenue
Birge Park Road
Westside Road
Allen Road
Riverside Avenue
Pearl St.
East Main Street
Weingart Road
Highland Avenue
Church Street
Aetna Avenue
Water Street
13
COE PARK
Naugatuck River
Wilson Road
BORSANI PARK
Litchfield Street
South Main Street
202
8
4

Torrington

RIDE INFORMATION

Bike Shops
Bikers Edge 2: 427 Winsted Rd., Torrington; (860) 496-7770

Events and Attractions
Burr Pond: This park has an interesting history as an industrial site; it was the first place where milk was condensed and evaporated for preservation. The park has bathrooms, a boat launch, and a small picnic area with beautiful views of the man-made pond.

Warner Theater: This theater hosts a wide variety of live performances from musicals to stage productions, ranging in tone from time-worn classics to provocative and daring modern works.

Nutmeg Conservatory: This dance academy is a nationally-recognized leader in ballet training.

Coe Memorial: This municipal park functions as the town green. It was a gift of the Coe siblings, in memory of their mother and father, the president of the Coe Brass Company.

Restaurants
Vientiane Thai Cuisine: 231 High St., Torrington; (860) 489-0758; torringtonthaicuisine.com

Backstage: 84 Main St., Torrington; (860) 489-8900; backstageeatdrinklive.com

Alfredo's Italian Eatery & Cafe: 168 Water St., Torrington; (860) 482-1888; alfredoseatery.com

Noujaim's Food & Catering: 2936 Winsted Rd., Torrington; (860) 618-5733; noujaims.com

Restrooms
0.0 Miles: Coe Memorial Park
12.5 Miles: Burr Pond Park

14

Winsted: Highland Lake

The city of Winsted, part of the town of Winchester, was one of the earliest mill towns in Connecticut and an important manufacturing center. The historic architecture of the downtown district is particularly notable, containing examples from a wide range of styles and periods: ecclesiastical, Victorian, neoclassical, Greek Revival, Queen Anne, and Colonial Revival are all represented in this unique community.

Start: East End Park in downtown Winsted

Length: 10.9 miles

Riding time: 45 to 60 minutes

Best bike: Road bike

Terrain and trail surface: Asphalt

Traffic and hazards: The very start of the ride can be slightly rocky. The road here is built up and has a number of car-centric businesses with large parking lots. Near the 1-mile mark the road widens and crossing can be difficult depending on traffic volume. Nervous riders may wish to dismount and use the pedestrian crossings to navigate to Lake Street, where traffic thins out, before the next 10 miles of mostly quiet road and greenway riding.

Things to see: Highland Lake, historic architecture, Burr Pond, the Still River Greenway, and lovely, relatively untraveled back roads.

Fees: None

Getting there: Winsted is near the end of CT 8, which exits onto US 44. Take a left from CT 8 and follow US 44 to Park Place. Parking should be plentiful, both around the green and on neighboring side streets, but pay attention to signage and posted limits.

GPS: 41.92102 / -73.06085

THE RIDE

This ride starts on Main Street, by the East End Park and town green. The route covers nearly 11 miles, starting with a ride through the scenic downtown, and then climbing up to nearby Highland Lake for a fairly level section along the length of the recreation area.

Highland Lake is over 3 miles long, making it one of the largest lakes in the state. It is also one of the cleanest, thanks to a high elevation and plentiful underground sources of fast, fresh water. The road around Highland Lake incorrectly registers as flat on GPS apps; combined with the ascent up Burr Mountain Road, the total elevation for this short ride will top 700 feet.

The route starts in a run-of-the-mill commercial section on Main Street, just before a series of restaurants and eateries in small, connected buildings. The local cinema, Gilson Cafe and Cinema, is a popular date night choice that offers specials on dinner and a movie.

The road narrows and beautifies in this more pedestrian-friendly section, with a narrow grass median separating the two lanes before the more architecturally diverse section that features a number of former industrial buildings.

Near the 1-mile mark, the road opens up into a faster and more car-centric section. Carefully take a left turn with the light onto Lake Street, over a nondescript bridge, and bear left ahead for a seriously steep climb up a twisting road that ends in a T-junction with West Lake Street and an incredible view over the water below.

Take a right onto West Lake Street, where an often-flooded short section of road crosses a small waterfall from the lake. If the water is deep or uncomfortable to cross on bike, take the elevated walkway next to it to pass over this short section.

The route passes a boat launch and then turns left onto West Wakefield Boulevard past a popular local beach. This section of Highland Lake, First Bay, is one of two smaller bays before the wider, larger, Third Bay. First Bay has very little development along the water, except private boat launches, with large, year-round housing built along hills on the right.

GPS apps will show the rest of this road as mostly flat, but it actually rolls quite a bit, with small, quick little climbs following the natural contours of the shoreline. The route continues along West Wakefield, past the First Narrows and along Second Bay, which has more housing on the left that obscures the view at times.

Leaving Second Bay, still on West Wakefield, you may see the Wheeler Point property across the water on the left. This is home to a beautiful and

A historic green on a side road in Winsted.

private Tudor mansion, once owned by a family who operated a private sea-plane base, named Seavair's Landing, in the middle of Third Bay.

Third Bay is also built up with development along the water but has some spectacular views in the south, before Bristol Cove. West Wakefield ends in a curve around one small inlet, with a short climb to a stop sign; turn right onto Mountain Road, at the 4.3-mile mark. Mountain Road climbs a short but steep 80-foot hill, before meeting Peck Road at a Y-intersection. Turn right onto Peck Road, up a longer, more gradual climb, through a dense and mostly undeveloped forest.

Cyclists looking to add distance may combine this route with the Torrington Loop (Ride 13), an 18-mile loop that overlaps ahead on Taylor Brook Road. Simply turn right instead of left and follow the Torrington Loop in reverse, resuming this route from Winsted Road on the return leg. This will cut out the ride down Burr Mountain Road. The total mileage will be roughly 27 miles and total elevation gain close to 2,000 feet.

Back on the original route, when Peck Road ends, turn left onto Taylor Brook Road, for a short, punchy climb up to 1,149 feet, the top elevation on this ride. After the peak, the road heads downhill, changing to Burr Mountain Road in a short stretch. For a quick scenic view of Burr Pond, take a quick detour into the boat launch parking lot ahead on the right.

Best Bike Rides Connecticut

A view from the flooded bridge of Highland Lake on a cloudy day.

After taking in the view, continue along the route with a fast, half-mile long, 300-foot descent down to Winsted Road and Burrville on an average grade of 9 percent.

Burr Mountain Road ends at the intersection with Winsted Road, in Burrville, a community of Torrington. Carefully cross Winsted Road onto Greenwoods Road, then turn left onto the Still River Greenway, a long-term trails project that currently functions as a 3-mile multi-use path paralleling the river and Winsted Road between Torrington and Winsted.

For a food stop, take a right instead, for a short detour down the trail to Noujaim's, a gourmet Lebanese market. The market serves a variety of Middle Eastern and Mediterranean dishes, both fresh-made and ready to go.

Continuing on the route, the Still River Greenway provides a scenic and car-free mile and a half ride back toward Winsted. The greenway is not fully completed so you must exit it near the 8.6-mile mark, turning right onto Torrington Road for the last 2.3 miles back to the East End Park and the finish of this ride.

Winsted does not have many options for coffee or post-ride meals, but two small spots near the ride start, Cackleberries and McGrane's on the Green, offer drip coffee and traditional diner fare for breakfast, lunch, and dinner.

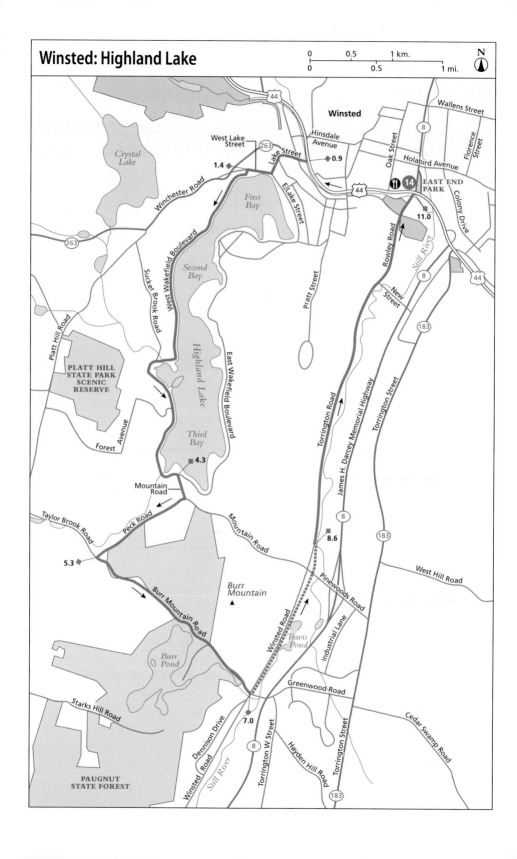

Winsted: Highland Lake

| 0 | 0.5 | 1 km. |
| 0 | | 0.5 | 1 mi. |

N

Winsted

44

Wallens Street

Crystal
Lake

West Lake
Street

263

Hinsdale
Avenue

Oak Street

Holabird Avenue

Florence Street

8

1.4

Lake Street

0.9

44

14 EAST END PARK

Colony Drive

Winchester Road

First
Bay

E Lake Street

11.0

263

West Wakefield Boulevard

Second
Bay

Rowley Road

Still River

8

Sucker Brook Road

Pratt Street

New Street

44

183

Highland Lake

East Wakefield Boulevard

Platt Hill Road

**PLATT HILL
STATE PARK
SCENIC
RESERVE**

Torrington Road

James H. Darcey Memorial Highway

Torrington Street

Forest Avenue

Third
Bay

4.3

Mountain
Road

8

183

Taylor Brook Road

Peck Road

Mountain Road

8.6

West Hill Road

5.3

Burr
Mountain

Pinewoods Road

Burr Mountain Road

Winsted Road

Industrial Lane

Burr
Pond

Travis
Pond

Starks Hill Road

Greenwood Road

Dennison Drive

7.0

Torrington W Street

Cedar Swamp Road

Still River

8

Hayden Hill Road

Torrington Street

183

**PAUGNUT
STATE FOREST**

MILES AND DIRECTIONS

0.0 Start on Main Street

0.9 Left onto Lake Street

1.3 Right onto West Lake Street

1.4 Left onto West Wakefield Boulevard

4.3 Right onto Mountain Road

4.5 Right onto Peck Road

5.3 Left onto Taylor Brook Road

5.6 Continue on Burr Mountain Road

6.9 Cross Winsted Road and left onto the Still River Greenway

8.6 Exit greenway and right onto Torrington Road

10.9 Left onto Main Street to finish

RIDE INFORMATION

Bike Shops
Bikers Edge 2: 427 Winsted Rd., Torrington; (860) 496-7770; bikersedge.com

Events and Attractions
Gilson Cafe and Cinema: This downtown theater screens new and old art-house films. American fare is served inside the theater.
Highland Lake: This lake and recreation area includes a popular beach and boat launch.
Burr Pond: This park, in nearby Torrington, has an interesting history as an industrial site: It was the first place where milk was condensed and evaporated for preservation. The park has bathrooms, a boat launch, and a small picnic area with beautiful views of the man-made pond.

Restaurants
Cackleberries: 242 Main St., Winsted; (860) 738-4113; cackleberriesrestaurant.com
McGrane's on the Green: 37 Park Place, Winsted; (860) 238-7828
Noujaim's Food and Catering: 2936 Winsted Rd., Torrington; (860) 618-5733; noujaims.com

Restrooms
1.5 Miles: Highland Lake Beach
6.7 Miles: Burr Pond Park

Litchfield Hills

Litchfield, the former county seat of Litchfield County, was once the economic and cultural center of the region and home to the first law school in America. Litchfield became a sleepy village in the mid-19th century but experienced a renaissance in the early 1900s, when a new commuter rail line brought tourists for the natural splendor, undeveloped lakes, and pristine forests. Visitors bought beautiful old homes in the town center as summer residences, and the town embraced the iconic white homes with black shutters of the Colonial Revival movement.

Start: Topsmead State Park

Length: 30.8 miles

Riding time: 2 hours

Best bike: Road bike

Terrain and trail surface: Asphalt, some dirt roads

Traffic and hazards: The first turn onto CT 118 can be hazardous. Watch for oncoming traffic. Some of the dirt roads may be daunting for inexperienced road cyclists, but they are incredibly scenic.

Things to see: Preserves, lakes and ponds, mountains, valleys, and farmland

Fees: None

Getting there: Take exit 42 from CT 8. Go west on CT 118 for 2.0 miles. Turn left onto Clark Road to the stop sign. Take a right at the stop sign then the first left onto Buell Road, to the entrance.

GPS: 41.744 / -73.15233

THE RIDE

This ride begins in Topsmead State Park in Litchfield and visits the small villages of Bantam and Morris and the neighboring town of Bethlehem, along rural, rustic roads, with a few stretches of hard-packed dirt, which are suitable for hardy road cyclists. If the weather has been particularly bad, or if the idea of a mile of dirt road doesn't appeal to you, follow the alternative roads offered below.

Ride out of the parking area on a tiny stretch of hard-packed dirt road and take a left onto Buell Road, which has views of beautiful meadows in the valley on the right and forest on the left.

Shortly ahead, turn left onto East Litchfield Road, another quiet street, which passes through forest and connects with 50-mph CT 118. Turn left to ride in the generous shoulder for a short stretch on 118.

Just ahead, pass Northfield Road and turn left onto Chestnut Hill Road. This quiet road offers views of Mount Tom, Mohawk Mountain, and the deep valleys around. The Haight-Brown Vineyard is on the left.

After another half-mile, before a pastoral farmhouse, turn right onto Camp Dutton Road, a mostly downhill connecting road that ends in 1 mile at South Plains Road (CT 63), a busier yet still scenic road.

Turn left onto CT 63 and ride in the narrow shoulder, passing Arethusa Farms on the right and then turning right onto Webster Road, through the farm property, before entering White's Woods on an easily navigable and very short hard-packed dirt road.

Turn left onto Whites Wood Road/Mattatuck Trail, which is well paved, quiet, and still very scenic. Turn right after the Morris town sign onto East Shore Road, through a wildlife preserve and along Bantam Lake on a rolling, curving road. After a long descent through evergreen forests and summer cottages, with the occasional lake view, the road descends into a fairy tale meadow. Turn right onto CT 109, West Street.

CT 109 is a slightly busier rolling road. Follow it for 1 mile up to a historic cemetery next to Jones Pond. Turn left just before the cemetery onto Todd Hill Road. In less than a half-mile, turn left onto Munger Lane, on an easy to miss turn, shortly after the town garage road. This is a beautiful road that quickly turns into a quiet, one-lane, dirt road. It is easy to ride with a road bike, although slightly wider tires are recommended.

Again, the unpaved section is very short before it returns to a well-paved road surface that heads downhill through dairy farms and pasture land, passing Hilltop Orchard, and then curving left past March Farm.

Meadow view from the road.

To avoid this dirt road, stay on Todd Hill Road to Woodcreek Road/Double Hill Road for a very slight detour that rejoins the route on Munger Lane by March Farm.

After March Farm, take a right to stay on Munger into the village of Bethlehem, making a left onto CT 132 and an immediate right along the Veteran's Memorial Park onto CT 61, South Main Street.

After passing the Sunny Ridge Supermarket, take a hard left onto Green Hill Road, a beautiful road with some fairly steep rolling hills. At a stop sign, turn left onto Nonnewaug Road. This very rural road runs through open spaces and small farms before curving right and running into a scenic stretch of CT 132, Kasson Road, past more farmland and a bucolic pond on the right.

In 1 mile turn left onto Hard Hill Road. Climb for a bit past some large homes before a beautiful descent through forest that opens into incredible views of farmland and meadows to the right.

The road ends in Morris and the route turns right onto CT 109. The road opens up again out of the center into a scenic rolling section for 3 miles. Continue to the Morris and Wigwam Reservoirs, with a very fast descent before a small bridge over the brook and great views of the water.

In another three-quarters of a mile, turn left onto Moosehorn Road, a quiet country road that is easy to miss. Moosehorn does have a short section of dirt. Keep to the left onto Wigwam Road, one of the most beautiful and peaceful roads on this route. Less than a half-mile is dirt, which could be slightly challenging but is worth the effort. This road passes many picturesque farmhouses and the Laurel Ridge Daffodil Fields. Bear left at the 26-mile mark onto Northfield Road, CT 254.

To detour around this section, skip the first left and continue on CT 109 for another 1.5 miles, then turn left onto Old Northfield Road to Northfield Road, CT 254, rejoining the mapped route. This adds 6 miles to the total.

Northfield Road is slightly busier than the quiet back roads you've been on, but it's still quiet and serene, affording many views of meadows, farmlands, forests, and valleys. After 3 miles, you reach East Street; turn right here, right again onto East Litchfield, and one last right onto Buell Lane to return to Topsmead State Forest.

MILES AND DIRECTIONS

0.0   Start on Chase Road in park, turning left onto Buell Road

0.7   Turn left onto East Litchfield Road

1.2   Turn left onto Route 118

1.8   Left onto Chestnut Hill Road

2.5   Right onto Camp Dutton Road

3.5   Left onto South Plains Road

4.1   Right onto Webster Road

5.0   Left onto Whites Wood Road

6.1   Right onto East Shore Road

8.6   Right onto West Street

9.7   Left onto Todd Hill Road

10.1   Left onto Munger Lane

13.6   Left onto West Road then right onto The Green

13.7   Continue on Main Street South

14.3   Left onto Green Hill Road

15.0   Left onto Nonnewaug Road

15.6   Cross East Street

16.2   Right onto Kasson Road

17.2   Left onto Hard Hill Road North

18.5   Cross Town Line Road and continue on Benton Road

20.0   Right onto CT 109

23.1   Left onto Moosehorn Road

26.0   Left onto CT 254

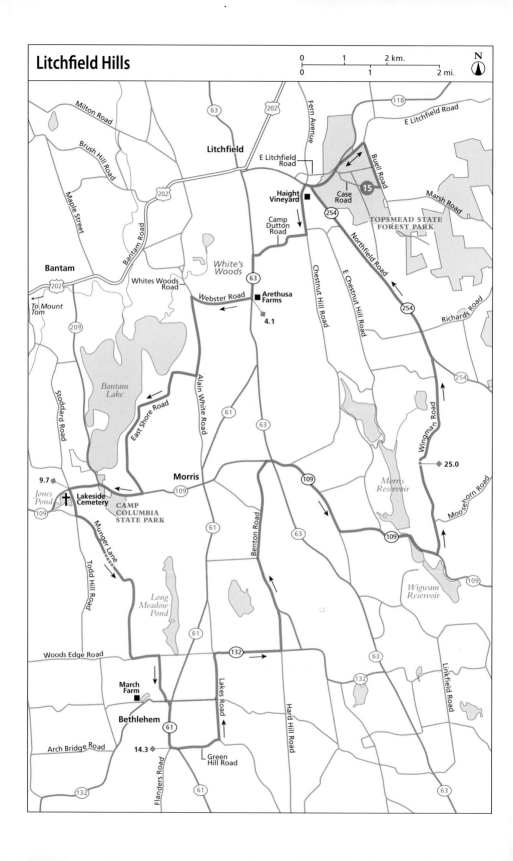

Litchfield Hills

0 1 2 km.
0 1 2 mi.

N

Litchfield

Milton Road

Brush Hill Road

Maple Street

Bantam Road

118

E Litchfield Road

202

63

202

E Litchfield Road

Fern Avenue

Buell Road

Case Road

Haight Vineyard ■

Camp Dutton Road

15

TOPSMEAD STATE FOREST PARK

Marsh Road

Bantam

202

209

Whites Woods Road

White's Woods

63

Webster Road

254

Chestnut Hill Road

E Chestnut Hill Road

Northfield Road

254

Richards Road

To Mount Tom

■ **Arethusa Farms**

◆ **4.1**

254

Bantam Lake

East Shore Road

Stoddard Road

Alain White Road

61

63

Wingman Road

Moosehorn Road

◆ **25.0**

9.7 ■

Jones Pond

109

✝ **Lakeside Cemetery**

Morris

109

61

Morris Reservoir

109

109

CAMP COLUMBIA STATE PARK

Munger Lane

Todd Hill Road

61

Benton Road

63

109

Long Meadow Pond

Wigwam Reservoir

61

Woods Edge Road

132

63

132

Linkfield Road

March Farm ■

Lakes Road

Hard Hill Road

Bethlehem

61

Arch Bridge Road

14.3 ◆

Flanders Road

Green Hill Road

132

61

63

29.0 Right onto East Street

29.5 Right onto East Litchfield Road

30.0 Right onto Buell Road

30.7 Right onto Chase Road

30.8 Finish ride

RIDE INFORMATION

Bike Shops
Bicycle Tour Company: 9 Bridge St., Kent; (860) 927-1742; bicycletour company.com
Bikers Edge 2: 427 Winsted Rd., Torrington; (860) 496-7770; bikersedge.com

Events and Attractions
Topsmead State Forest: The park is composed mostly of open field lands and was the summer estate of Miss Edith Morton Chase, a prominent business-woman and landowner, who left the property to the state upon her death in 1972. She provided a substantial endowment to keep the property undeveloped and open to the public. Free tours of her home are offered from June to October, and the grounds are open for walking, picnicking, and cross-country skiing year-round.

White Memorial Conservation Center: This 4,000-acre preserve consists of 40 miles of hiking trails and many ponds and waterways. The property abuts Bantam Lake and includes Caitlin Woods, a 30-acre old-growth forest. Some of the trees are estimated to be more than 200 years old. Camping is allowed in designated areas, and nonmotorized boating is allowed on the waterways and ponds.

Bantam Lake: This nearly 1,000-acre lake includes two beaches and boat launches.

Litchfield Historical Society: The society operates a full museum of local history and the Tapping Reeve House and Law School, a specialized exhibition space focused on the history of law and the legal profession in Litchfield. The History Museum will take an hour or two to fully explore and includes children-friendly hands-on exhibits. Most exhibits concern pre–Revolutionary War history. The society also operates a full research library, open year-round, in the Helga J. Ingraham Memorial Library.

Mount Tom State Park: This park includes a challenging hike to the 1,289-foot summit and an eponymous pond of clear, clean water for canoeing and swimming.

White Flower Farm: The garden center for the popular mail order plant and seed company is open every day for tours and sales.

South Farms: This family-run farm and market offers artisanal foods and a seasonal farmers' market with innovative selections.

Arethusa Farms: A working dairy farm, this was purchased by George Mal- kemus and Anthony Yurgaitis, co-executives of the famous Manolo Blahnik shoemaker, originally to safeguard the view from their beautiful home across the street. Now, however, they supply milk and cheese throughout the state, using a less common pasteurization technique reputed to make milk taste better.

March Farm: This family owned and operated farm offers berry and fruit pick- ing and farm activities for children and adults, including a farm store, corn mazes, hayrides, an animal yard, and other seasonal activities.

Bellamy-Ferriday House: This 18th-century home is one of twelve properties in the state managed by Connecticut Landmarks and is open for tours on a seasonal basis.

Laurel Ridge Daffodil Fields: Every spring, hundreds of thousands of daf- fodils bloom on the gently rolling hills and fields. The fields are on private property but are open to the public for walking and photography during daf- fodil season.

Laurel Ridge Farm: This family owned and operated grass-fed beef farm wel- comes visitors to learn more about their herd and their agricultural practices. In season, a farm stand in front of a picturesque windmill offers a pleasant break after a hilly ride.

Restaurants

The Village Restaurant: 25 West St., Litchfield; (860) 567-8307; village- litchfield.com

West Street Grill: 43 West St., Litchfield; (860) 567-3885; weststreetgrill.com

At the Corner: 3 West St., Litchfield; (860) 567-8882; athecorner.com

Meraki: 39 West St., Litchfield; (860) 361-9777

Bohemian Pizza: 342 Bantam Rd., Litchfield; (860) 567-3980; bohemian pizza.com

Little Town Deli: 22 East St., Bethlehem; (203) 266-6225

The Painted Pony: 74 Main St. S, Bethlehem; (203) 266-5771; paintedpony restaurantct.com

Restrooms

0.0 Miles: Topsmead State Park

Lakeville Lakes

Lakeville is a village in the town of Salisbury, in Litchfield County, named after Wononskopomuc Lake, the principal geographic feature. The town is on the border with New York and Massachusetts, in the northwest corner of the state. Salisbury is a quiet bucolic town with residents who work in Hartford and New York, and has a number of <u>celebrities and important figures</u>, including the actresses Meryl Streep and Laura Linney, who both currently live there. Georges Simenon, the Belgian author best known for the Maigret detective novels, lived in a home called "<u>Shadow Rock Estate</u>," which was fictionalized in one of his many mystery stories.

Start: Downtown Lakeville

Length: 27.4 miles

Riding time: 2 hours

Best bike: Road bike

Terrain and trail surface: Asphalt

Traffic and hazards: US 7 can be busy, but is fairly low-speed.

Things to see: The Housatonic River, mellow country roads, picturesque Falls Village, pastoral scenes

Fees: None

Getting there: Lakeville can be reached on US 44 from US 7. Turn onto CT 112W, and turn right onto US 44 into downtown Lakeville.

GPS: 41.96414 / -73.44047

THE RIDE

This 27.4-mile ride starts in downtown Lakeville, in the upscale commercial center, on CT 41, near Cannon Park. From here it follows scenic roads into nearby Falls Village, a tiny community in Canaan and one of the smallest towns in Connecticut. Falls Village is a cute, historic town that prides itself on looking and operating much like it did in 1851, when recently completed canals leaked, ending ambitions to industrialize around the waterfall that gave the town its name.

From the town center, head east on CT 41 and bear left at the fork onto Farnam Road, a quiet road with a few scattered homes through a well-forested and shaded area. The surroundings open up into meadow around the 2-mile mark, before the route turns right onto Salmon Kill Road, a rural country lane.

Some minor climbs are here but nothing too challenging for the next 1.25 miles, until the hard left turn onto Brinton Hill Road, a mile-long road that skirts Falls Mountain. The road climbs roughly 200 feet in 0.4 mile, with one steep switchback right in the middle, followed by the fastest, steepest descent on this route, ending at the T-junction, where the route turns left onto Dugway Road.

Dugway Road intersects the Appalachian Trail; expect to see a lot of hikers on this quiet, riverside road along the Farmington River. The route continues on Dugway Road for a half-mile before a right-hand turn over a scenic bridge onto Falls Mountain Road and then an immediate right onto Water Street.

This bridge is sometimes out due to weather or construction; in that case, take a somewhat lengthy detour southward on Dugway until a left turn onto Lime Rock Road. Bear left at the intersection with US 7 and stay left onto Warren Turnpike Road, which heads north and rejoins the mapped route at Falls Village.

Water Street is a steep climb up to the Falls Village downtown, the location of some charming homes and the Falls Village Inn, a historic property with lodging and a full restaurant spread out through several dining rooms. Take a right onto Railroad Street to visit this quaint village or take a left to follow the printed route northward toward North Canaan.

The route continues off of Railroad Street onto Point of Rocks Road just up ahead, a wide, slightly fast road, with a reasonable shoulder and abundant views of farmland and forests.

At the 6.8-mile mark, turn right onto Sand Road, a tranquil road through farmland and some old quarries. This 3.5-mile stretch, heading slightly uphill toward North Canaan, is one of the highlights of the route.

North Canaan isn't an ideal destination on a bicycle; the road is busy and there is a lot of automobile traffic and curbside parking, but it can provide a nice break at the 10-mile mark. To stay out of dense areas, turn off Sand Road early, at the 8.8-mile mark, by turning left onto Boinay Hill Road for a grueling, short and steep climb through a bucolic dairy farm. Boinay Hill Road ends on

An interesting boat house on one of the many lakes.

the mapped route just below US 44. Turn left onto 44 and follow the route to the Twin Lakes, cutting 4 miles.

Continuing on the mapped route, follow Sand Road until the end, where it meets US 7. Turn left here and follow US 7 through the heart of North Canaan to US 44, East Main Street.

After 0.4 mile, turn left to continue on US 44, Church Street. Church Street leads southwest, out of the dense area and up a short hill before the name changes to Salisbury Road and curves down to the Housatonic River. This scenic stretch of road provides a fast descent through a photogenic area.

Salisbury Road reaches a short bridge over the Housatonic, near Boinay Hill Road, which is the cut-off for anyone looking to shave a few miles off. The route then turns right onto Twin Lakes Road.

Farmland and fields on a peaceful road abut the next 0.8 mile. Stay left to follow Twin Lakes Road through dense woods, emerging with scenic lake views on your left in a small residential neighborhood.

The road curves right and heads away from the lake, close to the Massachusetts border, and meets Cooper Hill Road. Take the left again to stay on Twin Lakes Road, with a fairly steep climb, before the road ends in a junction with Taconic Road.

Turn right onto Taconic Road for a short but steep climb, turning left after a half-mile onto Hammertown Road.

16

Hammertown Road is quiet and remote, with beautiful valley and meadow views on either side, on a fast, steep descent. The road ends at CT 41, where the route turns left.

CT 41, Under Mountain Road, is busier but still quiet, and heavily shaded by forest canopy. In 1 mile the route passes along Fisher Pond on the left, then turns left onto Beaver Dam Road, another tranquil back road with pleasant views of the pond and surrounding marshes.

Beaver Dam Road features another challenging climb before it ends at Taconic Road. Turn right, heading south, for about 2.25 miles. Taconic Road ends where it meets US 44, Canaan Road, where you turn right for a 3-mile ride into and through downtown Salisbury on your way to the ride finish, where CT 41 meets 44 in downtown Lakeville.

MILES AND DIRECTIONS

0.0 Start in Lakeville's village district and turn onto Farnam Road

2.1 Right onto Salmon Kill Road

3.4 Left onto Brinton Hill Road

4.5 Left onto Dugway Road

5.0 Right onto Falls Mountain Road then right onto Water Street

5.4 Left onto CT 126

6.8 Continue on Sand Road

10.2 Left onto US 7 (High Street)

10.8 Left onto US 7 (East Main Street)/US 44

11.2 Left onto US 44 (Church Street)

12.1 Left onto US 44 (Salisbury Road)

13.8 Right onto Twin Lakes Road

14.6 Left onto Twin Lakes Road

18.5 Right onto Taconic Road

18.9 Left onto Hammertown Road

19.9 Left onto Under Mountain Road

20.9 Left onto Beaver Dam Road

21.9 Right onto Taconic Road

24.2 Right onto US 44 (Canaan Road)

27.3 Left onto Sharon Road

27.4 Finish in village district

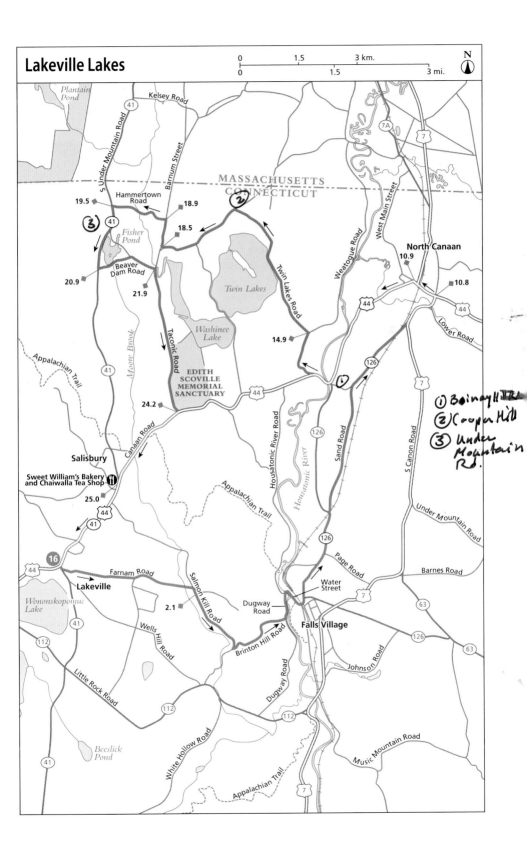

Lakeville Lakes

0   1.5   3 km.

0   1.5   3 mi.

N

Plantain Pond

Kelsey Road

7A

7

S Under Mountain Road

Barnum Street

Hammertown Road

19.5   18.9

3   41   18.5

Fisher Pond

MASSACHUSETTS
CONNECTICUT

Weatogue Road

West Main Street

North Canaan
10.9

10.8

Beaver Dam Road

20.9   21.9

Twin Lakes Road

Twin Lakes

Washinee Lake

44

Lower Road

44

Appalachian Trail

41

Moore Brook

Taconic Road

EDITH
SCOVILLE
MEMORIAL
SANCTUARY

14.9

126

1

126

7

① Boinay Hill TBA
② Cooper Hill
③ Under
   Mountain
   Rd.

24.2

44

Housatonic River Road

Housatonic River

Sand Road

S Canon Road

Under Mountain Road

Canaan Road

Salisbury

Sweet William's Bakery
and Chaiwalla Tea Shop   1

25.0

44
41

Appalachian Trail

126

Barnes Road

16
44

Farnam Road

Lakeville

Wononskopomuc
Lake

41

112

Salmon Kill Road

2.1

Wells Hill Road

Dugway Road

Page Road

Water Street

Falls Village

7

63

126

63

Little Rock Road

112

White Hollow Road

Brinton Hill Road

Dugway Road

112

Johnson Road

Beeslick Pond

41

Music Mountain Road

Appalachian Trail

7

Horses graze on a farm along Sand Road.

RIDE INFORMATION

Bike Shops

Bicycle Tour Company: 9 Bridge St., Kent; (860) 927-1742; bicycletour company.com
Bikers Edge 2: 427 Winsted Rd., Torrington; (860) 496-7770

Events and Attractions

This ride passes several major lakes, detailed below.
Wononscopomuc Lake: This is the deepest natural lake in Connecticut; once an industrial site for ore refining, it was never profitable and is now a protected lake used for fishing and swimming. The lake is stocked with trout, monitored for invasive plant species, and charges a parking fee for visitors. The first recorded name was simply Lakeville Lake, and no clear etymology of Wononscopomuc exists; some speculate it was a native word, and others that it was a garbled portmanteau. The lake is just off the route, being surrounded by higher-traffic roads that don't easily loop to other areas.

The Twin Lakes: These two very dissimilar lakes are, according to legend, named after the twin daughters of a Mahican tribal chief. Washinee, the southern lake, is an irregularly shaped lake, both longer and deeper than Washining, which is a shallow, round lake. Etymologists dispute the naming lore, citing irregularities in the structure of the words; the counter-theory is that they are more likely romanticized mash-up names invented by early European settlers.

Other attractions:

Bear Mountain: The highest peak in Connecticut is located in Salisbury. A short hike up to Lions Head will offer some coveted panoramic views of the surrounding forests and countryside, less than 3 miles from parking on Bunker Hill Road, just a few miles out of downtown Salisbury.

The Appalachian Trail: A section of the trail runs along the Housatonic River in Falls Village, through a particularly beautiful part of this route.

Restaurants

Black Rabbit: 2 Ethan Allen St., Lakeville; (860) 596-4227; blackrabbitbarand grille.com

Mizza's: 6 Ethan Allen St., Lakeville; (860) 435-6266; mizzas.com

On the Run: 4 Ethan Allen St., Lakeville; (860) 435-2007

Boathouse: 349 Main St., Lakeville; (860) 435-2111; theboathouseatlakeville.com

Chaiwalla: 1 Main St., Salisbury; (860) 435-9758

Sweet William's Bakery: 19 Main St., Salisbury; (860) 435-8889; sweet-williams.com

The White Hart Inn: 15 Under Mountain Rd., Salisbury; (860) 435-0030; whitehartinn.com

Burgers and Frites: 227 Main St., Lakeville; (860) 596-4112

West Cornwall Covered Bridge Ride

Cornwall is a charming little town in Litchfield County originally settled as a farming community, before a brief industrial phase shared with neighboring Kent, through the operation of two area furnaces. Many residents still derive employment from agriculture; others work in services, both for local residents and tourists.

Start: Covered bridge in West Cornwall

Length: 12.4 miles

Riding time: 1 hour

Best bike: Road bike

Terrain and trail surface: Asphalt

Traffic and hazards: With some exceptions, the route follows quiet back roads. CT 4 can be a bit fast, so use caution crossing.

Things to see: Covered bridge, beautiful back roads

Fees: None

Getting there: Take CT 4 to CT 188W/Litchfield Road, taking a slight right onto East Street, then a right onto North Street. Continue onto CT 63N/Goshen Road to a traffic circle. Take the third exit onto CT 4 to CT 128W, into West Cornwall.

GPS: 41.87151 / -73.36306

THE RIDE

This route is possibly the hilliest in the book, at 1,379 feet elevation gain over 12.4 miles. The route begins in the small community of West Cornwall, one of five neighborhoods that make up the town of Cornwall, four of which it visits. West Cornwall is a collection of quaint historic buildings, on a steep hill, beside a photogenic covered bridge.

Covered bridge in West Cornwall.

The narrow, one-lane bridge crosses the Housatonic River at a peaceful section, with an accessible grassy bank for picnics or rests, making for a very photogenic spot.

Start the ride with a right turn onto the Sharon-Goshen Turnpike, away from the bridge, and head up an imposingly steep section of road; most of the climbing on this route is found in the first mile and a half. The charming downtown ends just around the bend, and the road passes through a forested, scenic, rural section, with a tiny somewhat flat section just before the next turn, just past the half-mile mark.

Turn right onto Dibble Hill Road, a quiet little country road, for the briefest of respites in a fast downhill. As soon as the descent ends, the next section of the climb begins, in a steeper, more grueling section.

This part of the route is peaceful, with infrequent development, and very low traffic volumes. This makes for fairly safe surroundings as the road climbs at grades approaching and surpassing 20 percent over one of the steepest roads in the state.

These mountains are in the southernmost portion of the Green Mountains that Ethan Allen, Cornwall's most famous resident, named his late

18th-century militia after. Allen would use his militia both against the early colonial authorities and later in the Revolutionary War.

Dibble Hill Road continues on after reaching the peak, heading downhill, over a more gradual, less steep section of road, ending in a T-junction with Grange Hall Road.

Turn right onto Grange Hall Road, a still quiet, peaceful road sloping gently downhill. Just ahead on the right is the Cornwall Conservation Trust Ballyhack Preserve, a 55-acre property containing thick mountain laurel stands and an old-growth forest with 200-year-old white pine and hemlock trees. The preserve is largely a hiking property, without any exhibits or staff besides occasional rangers.

After the preserve and a quick descent, the road ends in a four-way intersection with CT 4. Cross this busy street onto Pine Street, passing a small town park on the left, into the Cornwall Village community.

After passing the Cornwall Historical Society barn, Pine Street continues through a tiny downtown of family homes and municipal buildings, ending at a T-junction with Jewell Street and a fantastic panoramic view of rolling fields and farmland straight ahead.

Bear right onto Jewell Street for a half-mile, turning left and then left again onto Furnace Brook Road (CT 4). This is a much busier street with a shoulder and some more open views on the left over the next 0.2 mile.

Take a gentle right onto Popple Swamp Road, a narrow, sometimes rough, asphalt road. This road passes more bucolic farms and quiet houses on a shaded, slightly uphill, stretch.

Shortly after Nash Pond, on the left, and a swampy area, the route heads downhill for a fast descent through farms and woods down to the Housatonic River. Turn left, following the curve of the road, and continue onto Brook Road, directly ahead now. Brook Road ends in less than a quarter-mile where it meets Furnace Brook Road.

Turn right onto Furnace Brook Road, by a scenic little green, passing a bank on the right, and entering the community of Cornwall Bridge. There aren't any coffee shops here, but there is a gas station just over the bridge ahead if a stop or food is needed. The road also passes the private Dark Entrance Road, which leads into a scenic forest and the property that once held a family farming community, now thought of as a ghost town.

Continuing on the route, cross the bridge, noting a scenic view of the Housatonic below and the picturesque church steeple to the right, and then bear right onto US 7.

This next section is a long, scenic road, passing along the Housatonic River. It can be busy, but the shoulder is comfortable, and area drivers are used to sharing with cyclists. This road continues for 4 mostly flat miles, past

View of the Housatonic.

campgrounds and bait and tackle shops, before finally arriving back at the covered bridge in West Cornwall. Carefully turn right, watching for other traffic, and cross the single-lane bridge back into the village.

West Cornwall has only two restaurants: RSVP and the Wandering Moose Cafe. RSVP is a celebrated upscale French restaurant serving a prix-fixe menu, where a kitted-out cyclist may not feel totally comfortable. The Wandering Moose Cafe is a slightly more laid-back establishment, with an outdoor patio, serving breakfast, lunch, and dinner. The restaurant operates out of a distinctive long red building on the corner, within sight of the covered bridge.

MILES AND DIRECTIONS

0.0 Start on Lower River Road and turn right onto Sharon-Goshen Turnpike

0.6 Right onto Dibble Hill Road

3.2 Right onto Grange Hall Road

3.9 Continue on Pine Street

West Cornwall Covered Bridge Ride

0   0.75   1.5 km.

0   0.75   1.5 mi.

N

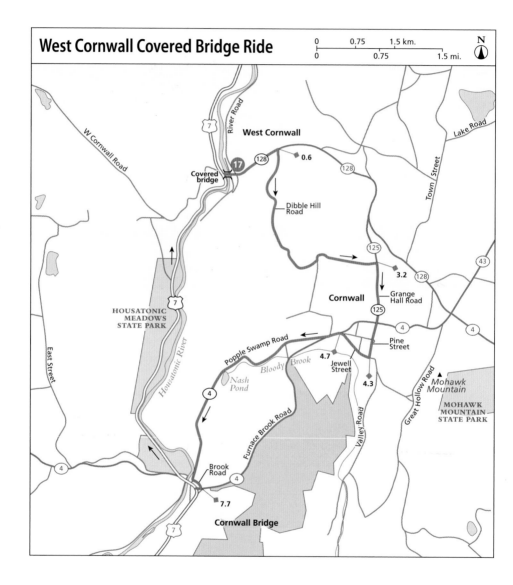

W Cornwall Road

River Road

7

West Cornwall

0.6

128

17

128

Covered bridge

128

Lake Road

Town Street

Dibble Hill Road

125

3.2

128

43

Cornwall

Grange Hall Road

HOUSATONIC MEADOWS STATE PARK

7

125

4

4

Pine Street

Popple Swamp Road

4.7

Jewell Street

East Street

Housatonic River

Bloody Brook

Nash Pond

4

4.3

Great Hollow Road

Mohawk Mountain

MOHAWK MOUNTAIN STATE PARK

Furnace Brook Road

Valley Road

4

Brook Road

4

7.7

7

Cornwall Bridge

4.3 Bear right on Jewell Street

4.8 Continue on Furnace Brook Road

4.9 Continue on Popple Swamp Road

7.7 Continue on Brook Road

7.9 Right onto Furnace Brook Road and continue on US 7/CT 4.

8.1 Continue on Cornwall Bridge Road

8.2 Continue on US 7

12.2 Continue on Cornwall Sharon Turnpike Connector

12.3 Right onto CT 128 and continue over West Cornwall Covered Bridge then right onto Lower River Road

12.4 Arrive at finish

RIDE INFORMATION

Bike Shops
Bicycle Tour Company: 9 Bridge St., Kent; (860) 927-1742; bicycletour company.com
Bikers Edge 2: 427 Winsted Rd., Torrington; (860) 496-7770

Events and Attractions
The Cornwall Historical Society: The society operates a seasonal exhibition space out of a renovated historic barn in Cornwall Village. When showing exhibits, the space is open on weekends.
Dark Entry Forest and Dudleytown: This is private land, but it attracts visitors every year, who face arrest for trespassing. They come for Dudleytown, a legendary ghost town. The mythic village was just a family farming community, but now in ruins, as the family left for better property elsewhere. The property gained a legendary status as a haunted ghost town and has since appeared in books, movies, and documentaries. The actual origin of the property as a family farm has been confused, replaced with fabricated tales of vengeful Englishmen and a curse that drove townspeople from a town that never existed.

Restaurants
RSVP: 7 Railroad St., West Cornwall; (860) 672-7787; rsvp-restaurant.com
Wandering Moose Cafe: 421 Sharon-Goshen Turnpike, West Cornwall; (860) 672-0178; thewanderingmoosecafe.com

18

Kent Hills

Kent is a rural community of some 3,000, located on the western border with New York, in scenic Litchfield County. The town has an incredibly quaint village district full of antiques, boutiques, and popular restaurants, but the chief attraction is the beautiful natural setting and miles of scenic roads. Kent is rich in undeveloped forests, with a number of preserves and conservation areas. Fittingly, it was a Kent resident, Birdsey Northrop, who brought Arbor Day to Connecticut, after the holiday originated in Nebraska in 1872. Northrop, a polymath who studied at Yale Divinity School, later spread the holiday to Japan in 1883, and the rest of America upon his return.

Start: Municipal parking lot in downtown Kent, behind post office

Length: 23.1 miles

Riding time: 2 hours

Best bike: Road bike

Terrain and trail surface: Asphalt

Traffic and hazards: South Kent Road can be a little fast, but most of these roads are low-volume, low-speed roads through quiet, minimally developed areas. The left turns onto US 7 from Brick School Road and Kent Falls can be a bit hairy; US 7 is a fast throughway for the region. The popular cycling road does have a wide shoulder, and drivers should expect to see cyclists.

Things to see: The Housatonic River, mellow country roads up Iron Mountain, downtown Kent, the Connecticut Antique Machinery museum and Kent Furnace Area, and the waterfalls at Kent Falls State Park

Fees: None

Getting there: Kent is not near any of the major interstates in Connecticut. The small town is on US 7, providing easy access from

Fairfield County. From the rest of the state, take CT 254N to Litchfield, then US 202W to CT 341W in Washington, finally turning right onto US 7N to downtown Kent.

Visitors from New York will take NY 22N to CT 37N and CT 39N to US 7N.

GPS: 41.72946 / -73.47345

THE RIDE

Kent is primarily known as a tourism destination and as home to several boarding schools. This route begins in downtown Kent, in a municipal lot near the post office and an IGA market. Ride from the parking lot onto North Main Street, and turn left, to head south toward the intersection with Maple Street. Navigate around the memorial in the road center and turn left onto Maple Street.

After a quarter-mile the route bears right onto South Kent Road, a fairly quiet but fast road that heads through river marshes and forest for 3.5 miles, passing two ponds, until it reaches South Kent. The next several miles will be along beautiful sections of road with stately homes, farms, and forests for scenery.

Turn left onto Camps Flat Road for a fairly steep road heading uphill past beautiful farmhouses, and in 0.6 mile, bear left onto Geer Mountain Road.

Geer Mountain Road is the start of the real climb up Iron Mountain; near the 6.2-mile mark, you see open farmland on your right, and scenic Irvings Pond, followed by a small dead-end road. Take the next right, at 6.3 miles, onto Flat Rock Road, making sure to take in the vistas along your right-hand side. This is considered one of the prettiest views in the area. The prime spot to survey the land around you is on a detour, about 500 feet after the next turn, onto South Road.

South Road is a short stretch of road that goes slightly up before dropping, over 0.8 mile; at the end, turn right onto Segar Mountain Road, a slightly busier street, with a comfortable shoulder.

After a slightly grueling short climb, the route passes between North Spectacle Pond and South Spectacle Pond, and then covers some rolling terrain through East Kent.

Near the 11-mile mark, the route turns left onto Brick School Road, heading downhill, through a quiet back road. After 0.9 mile, the route turns right to stay on Brick School Road, leading back uphill, with another elevation gain of over 300 feet in about 2.5 miles of road.

Turn right instead of left at Camps Flat Road for a short detour to Bulls Bridge.

Brick School Road is a long road with many scenic views, which starts out heading east, and then curves back west for a fast, turning descent, before ending at US 7.

Carefully cross the fast street and turn left, heading south on US 7; the Housatonic River will be visible on the right, and the road is mostly level here, with the occasional rolling hill. Kent State Falls Park will be on the left for a break and a possible hike up the waterfall.

After visiting the park, return to US 7, which remains relatively flat and steady for the rest of the 4.5 miles into downtown Kent and the finish of the ride. Along the way you pass a number of bed-and-breakfasts, including the scenic Spirit Horse Farm, and the Connecticut Antique Machinery Association and the Sloane-Stanley Museum, just shy of the 23-mile mark.

After finishing the ride, there are a number of food options, including two with outdoor patios, perfect for cyclists. The first on the left, J. P. Gifford Market, is an open-floor plan market with an eclectic menu of generous sandwiches and innovative Mexican and Asian-fusion cuisine. After J. P. Gifford is the House of Books, an independent bookstore with a wide-ranging inventory and a large selection of local trail guides and historic books, just before the Kent Coffee and Chocolate Company.

Cyclists seeking longer rides have two convenient options. The Macedonia Brook State Park ride, from Ride 19, overlaps with this route in downtown Kent. Simply follow the return leg of Macedonia after finishing this ride, ending where that ride arrives downtown. This would add 15.4 hilly miles, for 38.5 miles total, and a total of 3,656 feet of climbing.

The other option takes in the historic covered bridge of Cornwall from the previous ride, Ride 17. Turn right at the intersection with US 7 on the return leg, riding north to Cornwall Bridge, and then following the West Cornwall Covered Bridge Ride route. This loop would add 12.4 miles and 1,379 feet, for a total of 3,364 feet of elevation gain over 35.5 miles.

MILES AND DIRECTIONS

0.0   Proceed onto North Main Street

0.3   Left onto Maple Street

0.5   Right onto South Kent Road

4.0   Left onto Camps Flat Road

4.6   Left onto Geer Mountain Road

6.3   Continue on Flat Rock Road

7.0   Left onto South Road

7.8   Right onto Segar Mountain Road

10.9 Left onto Brick School Road

11.8 Right onto Brick School Road

16.5 Left onto US 7

23.1 Finish in downtown Kent

RIDE INFORMATION

Bike Shops
Bicycle Tour Company: 9 Bridge St., Kent; (860) 927-1742; bicycletour company.com
Bikers Edge 2: 427 Winsted Rd., Torrington; (860) 496-7770

Events and Attractions
Kent Falls State Park: This park is built around a series of waterfalls and pools that empty into the Housatonic River, from a peak elevation of 250 feet. This scenic attraction is best enjoyed with a somewhat strenuous hike up a steep

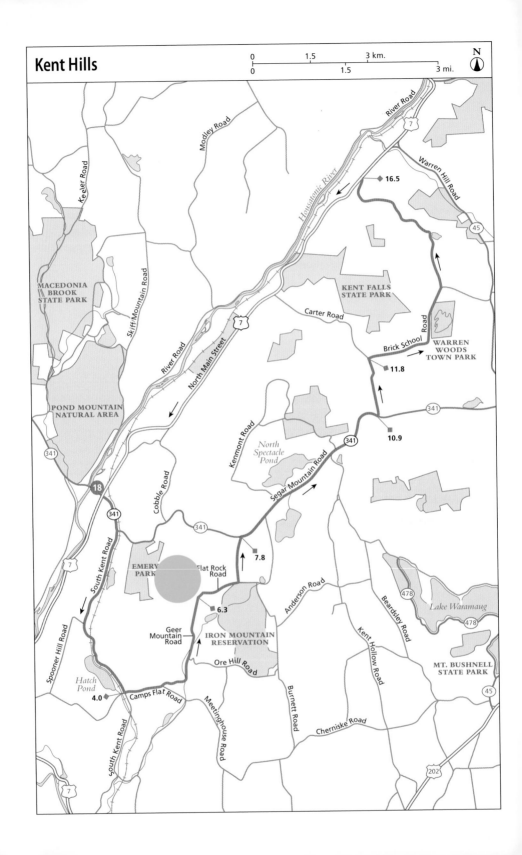

Kent Hills

0   1.5   3 km.

0   1.5   3 mi.

N

MACEDONIA
BROOK
STATE PARK

Keeler Road

Modley Road

Housatonic River

River Road

7

◆ 16.5

Warren Hill Road

45

Skiff Mountain Road

KENT FALLS
STATE PARK

Carter Road

River Road

North Main Street

7

POND MOUNTAIN
NATURAL AREA

341

Kennont Road

North
Spectacle
Pond

Brick School Road

WARREN
WOODS
TOWN PARK

■ 11.8

341

Cobble Road

18

341

7

South Kent Road

Spooner Hill Road

Segar Mountain Road

341

■ 10.9

EMERY
PARK

Flat Rock
Road

↑ 7.8

Geer
Mountain
Road

■ 6.3

IRON MOUNTAIN
RESERVATION

Ore Hill Road

Anderson Road

Beardsley Road

478

Lake Waramaug

478

Kent Hollow Road

MT. BUSHNELL
STATE PARK

45

Hatch
Pond

4.0 ◆   Camps Flat Road

Meetinghouse Road

Burnett Road

Cherniske Road

202

7

trail, with numerous vantage points and vistas. Water volume is greatest during the spring thaw, but this is also an ideal leaf-peeping spot in the fall.

Bull's Bridge: Bull's Bridge is one of two covered bridges in Connecticut still open to automobile traffic, on a scenic section of the Housatonic, with hiking trails for deeper exploration. This bridge can be part of a detour from the southernmost part of the route; turn right onto Bull's Bridge Road, instead of left onto Camps Flat Road, for a 3-mile trip to the bridge.

Eric Sloane-Stanley Museum House: Eric Sloane, author, painter, and Americana collector, is memorialized in the Sloane-Stanley Museum, adjacent to the Kent Iron Furnace, a historic pig iron furnace. A ticket from Sloane-Stanley will provide a half-off discount at three other state museums in Connecticut, including the Henry Whitfield House State Museum, covered in the Durham-Guilford Run (Ride 25), and the Prudence Crandall Museum, covered in Canterbury-Scotland Loop (Ride 37).

Connecticut Antique Machinery Association: CAMA is tucked behind the Sloane-Stanley Museum, in a collection of historic buildings containing an assortment of early machines from the industrial and agricultural eras of Connecticut. This sprawling museum offers tours and features a collection of artifacts from the early days of mining and industrial activity in the state.

Kent Historical Society: The Kent Historical Society occupies a building just off US 7 on Studio Road, where they offer tours and exhibits.

Restaurants

Kent Coffee and Chocolate Company: 8 N Main St., Kent; (860) 927-1445; kentcoffee.com

J. P. Gifford Market: 12 N Main St., Kent; (860) 592-0200; jpgifford.com

Kent Pizza Garden: 17 Railroad St., Kent; (860) 927-3733; kentpizzagarden.com

Restrooms

17.0 Miles: Kent Falls State Park

Macedonia Brook State Park

The area around Macedonia Brook State Park was once a farming settlement, where members of the Schaghticoke tribe were reputed to live in harmony with farmers originally from nearby Kent, even aiding them during the Revolutionary War. The tribe was made up of a coalition of groups, many formerly from Fairfield and the Connecticut shore, who had been displaced and pushed north following a harsh winter.

In 1796 the new tribe was given a reservation of 2,500 acres spanning the Housatonic River. Sadly, and despite the aid they gave during the Revolutionary War, most of their lands were sold by state-appointed agents of European-American descent from 1800 to 1911. Today, the remaining Schaghticoke people live on only 400 acres, solely on the western side of the Housatonic River.

Start: Hilltop Pond, north of Macedonia Brook State Park

Length: 15.4 miles

Riding time: 1.5 hours

Best bike: Road bike, cyclocross bike

Terrain and trail surface: Hard-packed dirt and asphalt

Traffic and hazards: The roads here tend to be low-volume with comfortable shoulders.

Things to see: The Housatonic River, Pond Mountain, Hilltop Pond, downtown Kent, views along Macedonia Brook State Park

Fees: There are no fees to park and picnic in Macedonia Brook State Park, or at Hilltop Pond. The park does charge a camping fee for overnight visitors. Fees are lower for Connecticut residents.

Getting there: US 7 runs directly through downtown Kent to the intersection with CT 341. Follow CT 341 (Macedonia Road) west, and turn right onto Macedonia Brook Road. Stay left at the intersection of

Macedonia Brook and Fuller Mountain Roads. Follow signs into the park and continue north to Hilltop Pond, where you should be able to park without difficulty on the roadside.

GPS: 41.79487 / -73.49083

THE RIDE

This is a hilly ride on peaceful back roads, through a 2,500-acre state park, with a stop in the downtown of nearby Kent. This route is the second hilliest in the book per mile, with a total elevation gain of 1,671 feet over 15.4 miles.

The route begins north of Macedonia Brook State Park, on a hard-packed dirt road beside Hilltop Pond, a picturesque pond full of reeds and lily pads, surrounded by wildflowers. Some might prefer a cyclocross bike for this ride, but a road bike with slightly wider tires is more than sufficient.

The first 3 miles are largely downhill, for some relaxed riding over a mix of hard-pack dirt and asphalt. Follow Weber Road south, into the park, and continue on the main path over an intersection and onto Macedonia Brook Road. This road travels through the main campground portion of the park, past numerous restrooms and water pumps, with a final stretch following the babbling brook down to the park entrance.

After the park entrance, take a hairpin turn left, onto Fuller Mountain Road, into a challenging, strenuous climb. The first mile in particular is the single-hardest part of the ride, with a 450-foot climb and grades approaching 12 percent. The scenery is breathtaking; deep, undeveloped forests border the road on both sides, and the area is full of wildlife, including numerous coyotes, which you may see near dawn or dusk.

After this first peak, enjoy a brief recovery on a quick downhill; two more climbs are still ahead. The second is more gradual, followed by a beautiful 100-foot descent through uninhabited woods. The third climb reaches the peak elevation of 1,113 feet with the single steepest section right in the middle. After a grade over 15 percent, the climb evens out, heading through gorgeous meadowland and peaking at the intersection with Skiff Mountain Road.

Turn right onto Skiff Mountain Road for a blistering descent; speeds up to and in excess of 50 mph are possible with the right gear combination and technical skill. Less technical riders will still enjoy this section; the asphalt road is mostly well maintained and bordered by heavy forests, keeping crosswinds at bay.

Hilltop Pond.

Follow the mild twists and turns to the base of the mountain, bearing right to stay on Skiff Mountain Road, for a flat mile-long ride along the Housatonic River on the left and a quiet neighborhood on the right.

At the end of Skiff Mountain Road, turn left onto Macedonia Road, then cross the scenic Housatonic on a generous shoulder. Entering downtown, you pass the picturesque cemetery of St. Andrew's Episcopal Church on the left, and then the Bicycle Tour Company, a small operation offering tour planning, rentals, repairs, and a limited inventory, all from a small outdoor kiosk.

After the church, turn left, circling the memorial in the middle of the intersection, onto North Main Street, for a short trip along Kent's charming and quaint downtown. Kent has a number of restaurants, but cyclists are encouraged to visit Kent Coffee and Chocolate Company and neighboring J. P. Gifford Market and Catering. Kent Coffee is a popular hangout for local cyclists offering a full espresso bar, fresh-made smoothies, baked goods made on premises, and a large selection of fancy chocolates and candies.

For more substantial lunch fare, J. P. Gifford serves an eclectic menu, ranging from generous deli sandwiches to innovative takes on Mexican cuisine and Asian-fusion dishes.

Field Trip: New York

A really beautiful 17-mile add-on is possible, through gorgeous farmlands in a deep valley just over the New York/Connecticut border, consisting of a loop through the towns of South Amenia, Wassaic, Amenia, and Leedsville.

From the start point, follow Weber Road until it ends in a T-junction, turning left onto Knibloe Hill Road. At the end of Knibloe Hill Road, turn left onto Amenia Union Road and head south, following the road as it curves west and north, around the mountains, into Amenia. The road frequently changes names, first becoming South Amenia Road, for a section with a lovely creek crossing and some beautifully desolate meadows. Next it is called Old NY Route 22 after a rightward curve and a narrowing where the road enters the hamlet of Wassaic. Continue following the road as it curves through the hamlet, passing a historic general store on the left, and next through a long section of farmland.

After crossing the Harlem Valley Rail Trail, the road ends in an intersection with busier South Street (NY 343). Turn right and ride the short distance into downtown Amenia, turning right at the post office onto East Main Street (also NY 343).

Follow East Main Street for 2.4 miles until an open field on the right, with a sign for a historic Episcopal church, and turn right, onto Leedsville Road. Leedsville Road winds past old farms and historic barns until the Connecticut border, just after the historic church from the earlier sign, where you turn right at the triangle, back onto Amenia Union Road.

Take a left ahead onto Knibloe Hill Road to Weber Road, and the original route start, at Hilltop Pond.

Nestled between the two is the House of Books; a small home converted to a bookstore, it carries a surprisingly deep and diverse range of books, including an excellent selection of local resources and guides. This is the best place to buy books on the local hiking trails and recreational opportunities.

After visiting scenic Kent, make a U-turn, and ride Main Street back to the intersection, marked by the memorial plinth, and take a right back onto Bridge Street onto Macedonia Road.

This section of the road, in a valley running through the Appalachian Mountain Range, is a hunting range for hawks and other birds of prey. The expansive open grounds of the Kent School and marshy areas ahead, on the

Macedonia Brook State Park

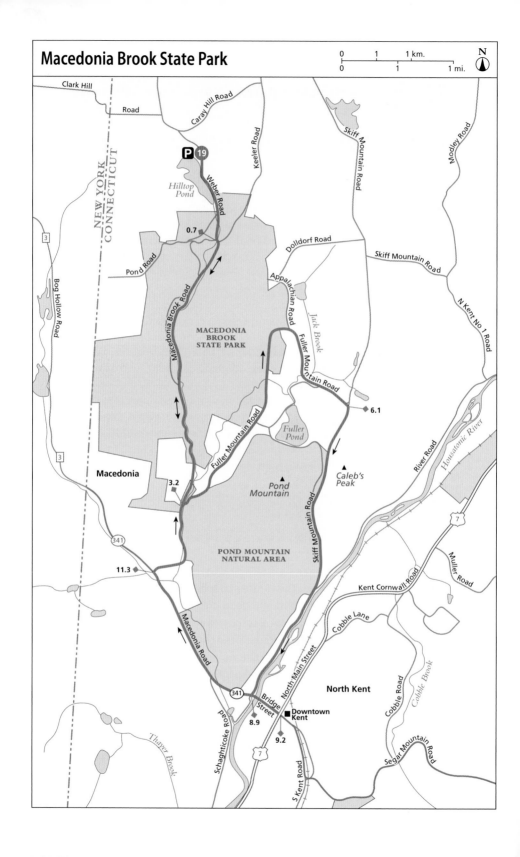

right, are prime areas to spot raptors. The Appalachian Trail runs through here, so be mindful of hikers making the crossing ahead.

At Brook Run Farm, an equestrian training center, take a gentle right onto Macedonia Brook Road, following park signs. This quiet road heads uphill for nearly a mile to the fork with Fuller Mountain Road, where you continue to the left into the park, and ride back through the campgrounds to finish the ride by Hilltop Pond, on a long, gradual climb of nearly 600 feet.

Macedonia Brook State Park makes an excellent camping destination; the prices are reasonable, and the park has a mix of closely situated sites and more remote spots. Each section has fire pits, grills, restrooms, and fresh water.

MILES AND DIRECTIONS

0.0 Start on Weber Road at Hilltop Pond

0.7 Proceed onto Macedonia Brook Road

3.2 Left onto Fuller Mountain Road

6.1 Right onto Skiff Mountain Road

8.9 Left onto Macedonia Road

9.2 Left onto North Main Street

9.5 Right onto Bridge Street

9.7 Continue on Macedonia Road

11.3 Right onto Macedonia Brook Road

14.6 Continue on Weber Road

15.4 Finish ride at Hilltop Pond

RIDE INFORMATION

Bike Shops
Bicycle Tour Company: 9 Bridge St., Kent; (860) 927-1742; bicycletour company.com
Bikers Edge 2: 427 Winsted Rd., Torrington; (860) 496-7770

Restaurants
Kent Coffee and Chocolate Company: 8 N Main St., Kent; (860) 927-1445; kentcoffee.com
J. P. Gifford Market: 12 N Main St., Kent; (860) 592-0200; jpgifford.com

Restrooms
1.0 Miles: Macedonia State Park

Lake Waramaug and Scenic Overlook

Lake Waramaug is a popular destination for boating, fishing, swimming, and picnicking. The 656-acre lake is exceptionally beautiful and easily accessed from local roads, making this one of the top cycling routes in the area. Development is moderate to sparse around the lake, and primarily centered on small residences with plenty of water views. Lake Waramaug is a great spot for leaf-peeping; the clear water is lined with trees and becomes incredibly colorful each autumn.

Start: Lake Waramaug parking lot

Length: 11.7 miles

Riding time: 1 hour

Best bike: Road bike, hybrid if skipping the scenic overview

Terrain and trail surface: Asphalt

Traffic and hazards: These roads are mostly quiet streets for local residents and lake visitors. Shoulders aren't wide, but visibility is good, and traffic speeds low.

Things to see: Lake Waramaug, scenic vineyards

Fees: None

Getting there: Take US 202 or CT 45 to CT 47. From CT 47, turn left onto North Shore Road and follow the signs around the lake to the park.

GPS: 41.70707 / -73.38303

THE RIDE

This ride starts at Lake Waramaug State Park on Lake Waramaug Road and heads northeast, following the shore. This route is more popular than the southerly route; the road tends to have a wider shoulder, and visibility is better in this direction. The opposite side of the road is more built up and has more interactions with road junctions as well.

View of the lake.

The first turn, onto North Shore Road, is just up ahead in about 0.1 mile. The view of the lake is largely open all along the right on this quiet, fairly flat road. Follow this scenic stretch for nearly 2.5 miles before turning left for the scenic overlook onto Lake Road/CT 45.

Lake Road is slightly faster and busier than the rest of the roads around the lake; for a shorter route, turn right instead, and continue following the lake for a flat 7-mile ride. The shorter 7-mile route is perfect for a hybrid bike.

Continuing on the mapped route, Lake Road is a fairly steep climb, with grades up to 10 percent near the beginning. Scenery on the left includes the back of the Vineyard at Strawberry Ridge. The road evens off, near the 4-mile mark, and the route turns right onto Woodville Road/CT 341.

The next mile is downhill, before a right-hand turn onto Rabbit Hill Road, a seriously steep section of climbing. The next mile includes more than 200 feet of climbing, with a sharp right-hand turn halfway through onto Tanner Hill Road.

Tanner Hill continues to climb, peaking near the 6-mile mark. Ahead is an incredible vista of Lake Waramaug. This is an especially scenic stop in the

Chief Waramaug

Chief Waramaug, also recorded as Wehanonaug, was one of the last native chiefs to reign in the region, with a tribe composed of the remnants of several tribal groups who had traveled north after being pushed out of their settlements by European settlers and colonists. Chief Waramaug formed a lasting peace with the settlers, and the two groups coexisted side-by-side in their respective villages.

Chief Waramaug lived in a much-admired long-house in the area which is now known as Lover's Leap State Park in New Milford. He was respected by his tribe of nearly 600 members, neighboring tribes, and even the local settlers, who left behind testaments to his genius, charm, and tact. He formed a friendship with the first minister of New Milford, the Reverend Daniel Boardman, which historians claim was based on mutual respect and affection. He ruled for 55 years before his death in 1735, which was attended by both traditional tribal shamans and his friend Reverend Boardman, who wrote a eulogy and participated in Chief Waramaug's burial under a monolith on a hill overlooking his long-house.

While the friendship formed between the tribes and the settlers persisted, the monument did not, and it was torn down in the 1880s by a family from Bridgeport, who incorporated stones from the monument in a pseudo-castle they built. Members of the Weantinock, one of the tribes that followed Chief Waramaug, migrated to the reservations set aside in southern Kent and continued a tradition of visiting the families in New Milford to sell handmade goods and exercise their fishing rights.

For more information about the regional tribes and native history, *Connecticut's Indigenous Peoples*, by Dr. Lucianne Lavin and available from Yale University Press, is a comprehensive and thorough work of original scholarship that was received with widespread praise. The work follows 13,000 years of history and is a very accessible academic work, available in cloth and paperback.

Out-of-print resources include *The Housatonic: Puritan River*, by Chard Powers Smith, which contains reproductions of source documents, mostly from the perspective of the settlers of the region. You can find archived copies in electronic formats online on a variety of websites, and the book is available in a number of libraries in northwest Connecticut.

Dr. Lavin's book is also available at the Institute for American Indian Studies, where she is the Director of Research and Collections. The institute features artifacts, a scale replica village, other museum exhibits, and a large collection of books and other resources on the various regional tribes and their history. The institute is open to the public, and holds talks and lectures. More information, and a complete schedule, is available on the website: www.iaismuseum.org/.

Road en route to overlook.

autumn, but the view remains year-round, even when the trees are full of healthy leaves.

After the break, settle in for a quick, fast descent down Tanner Hill Road; watch your speed, as the intersection with Lake Road is very abrupt. Turn left onto Lake Road/CT 45, which turns into East Shore Road just ahead, and then continues along the lake southward.

When the route reaches the Town of Washington public beach, around the 8-mile mark, turn right onto West Shore Road. This is a quiet stretch of irregularly maintained pavement—there are frequently some potholes and cracks in the road surface—but the view to the right is amazing and the traffic is fairly slow and low in volume. The road snakes around the southern part of the lake, with Mount Bushnell State Park and then the Lake Waramaug Country Club providing scenery on the left-hand side.

Turn right, back onto Lake Waramaug Road, after West Shore Road heads left and becomes Golf Links Road. Take the right and finish the ride just up ahead after this last stretch of quiet, flat road.

Lake Waramaug and Scenic Overlook

MILES AND DIRECTIONS

0.0 Start on Lake Waramaug Road

0.1 Right onto North Shore Road

2.4 Left onto Lake Road

4.0 Right onto Woodville Road

4.9 Right onto Rabbit Hill Road

5.5 Right onto Tanner Hill Road

6.7 Left on Lake Road

6.9 Continue on East Shore Road

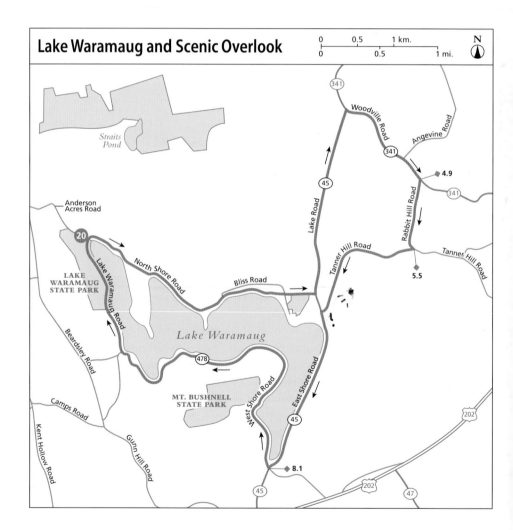

Lake Waramaug and Scenic Overlook

Best Bike Rides Connecticut

8.1   Right onto West Shore Road

10.9   Right onto Lake Waramaug Road

11.7   Finish at Lake Waramaug State Park

RIDE INFORMATION

Bike Shops
Bikers Edge 2: 427 Winsted Rd., Torrington; (860) 496-7770

Events and Attractions
Lake Waramaug State Park: This park offers a beach, restrooms, and camping facilities. The state built a new facility for concessions, but has had a hard time selling the contract, so food may or may not be available.

Hopkins Vineyard: One of the first vineyards in Connecticut offers tastings and meat and cheese plates. Open year-round.

Restaurants
Nine Main Bakery and Deli: 9 Main St., New Preston; (860) 868-1879; ninemain bakery.com

The Dutch Epicure: 491 Bantam Rd., Litchfield; (860) 567-5586; dutch epicure.com

Litchfield Catering and Deli: 722 Bantam Rd., Bantam; (860) 567-9878

Washington Food Market: 5 Bryan Hall Plaza, Washington Depot; (860) 868-7351; washingtonfoodmarket.com

The Hopkins Inn: 22 Hopkins Rd., Warren; (860) 868-7295; thehopkinsinn.com

Restrooms
0.0 Miles: Lake Waramaug State Park

Connecticut River Valley

The Connecticut River Valley is a collection of towns built along the longest river in New England. Many of these towns boomed as tourist destinations following the Industrial Revolution but fell out of favor as air travel became widespread.

The towns have retained their charm and character, and they are popular destinations for weekend visits and day trips. Historic accommodations include the Copper Beech Inn, a country inn in nearby Ivoryton, and the Griswold Inn, a historic tavern continuously operated since the 18th century. Alternative transit in the region includes the Chester-Hadlyme ferry, prominently featured in the River Valley Ferry Loop, and the Essex Steam Train.

These rides visit the beach town of Old Saybrook, previously mentioned Chester and Essex, the rural towns of East Haddam and Durham, and the impressive town green of historic Guilford. Mountain bikers will enjoy Millers Pond, a nearby location full of a variety of trails, all around a popular swimming hole.

The second longest ride in the area, the River Valley Ferry Loop, passes through Old Lyme, a town covered in more depth in the New London section, before taking a historic ferry ride over to the quaint waterfront villages of the Connecticut River.

None of these rides go all the way to Middletown, the biggest city in the area, but the area does have some attractive riding, especially west of the picturesque Wesleyan University campus. Check in with Pedal Power in downtown Middletown for guidance and group riding in the area.

The main highway, Route 9, offers a scenic drive through beautiful parts of the region, and mass transit users can easily reach Old Saybrook on the bike-friendly Shoreline East rail line.

Devil's Hopyard and Johnsonville Ghost Town

East Haddam is an ideal town for a bike ride. Geographically large with a small population and little automobile traffic, this rural town has evolved over the years into a quiet community with a small regional tourism industry. This ride highlights miles of hilly terrain, thousands of acres of forest, three waterfalls, and several day trip destinations.

Start: Devil's Hopyard lot at Foxtown Road

Length: 35.7 miles

Riding time: 2.5 to 3 hours

Best bike: Road bike

Terrain and trail surface: Asphalt

Traffic and hazards: Traffic can be fast on Hopyard Road and Mount Parnassus Road, and deer are abundant.

Things to see: Waterfalls, wildlife, abandoned mill town, and other historical points of interest

Fees: None

Getting there: From Route 9: take exit 7, then a left at the end of the exit ramp onto CT 82 east/154 north. Take a right at the first traffic light following CT 82 east and follow the signs.

GPS: 41.48417 / -72.3419

THE RIDE

First a fishing community, then a bustling mill town, East Haddam later went through a resort phase, attracting motorists from New York and the rest of Connecticut with scenic attractions. Major tourism dropped off as air travel became affordable, but East Haddam remains an excellent day trip destination.

Highlights include a natural park enshrouded in supernatural legends, the castle home of a famous 19th-20th century stage actor, a former industrial site turned ghost town, and a famous regional opera house beside an 899-foot swing bridge reputed to be the longest of its type in the world.

The first of the attractions, Devil's Hopyard State Park, is where this ride begins. The 1,000-acre property contains a 60-foot waterfall and extensive hiking trails. Signs posted around the property share possible origin stories behind the name and provide interesting local history and folklore. Check out the "potholes" by the waterfall; these circular holes were formed by glacier activity and are excellent examples of the geological phenomenon.

Starting on Foxtown Road, the route turns left onto Hopyard Road, along a glorious rolling road along the scenic Eight Mile River. At the 3.5-mile mark, take the hard left turn onto Norwich Salem Road (CT 82). Norwich Salem Road parallels Hopyard Road at first, curving away and climbing into the nearby town of Salem, and passing Mitchell Pond on the left. The route turns right onto Darling Road at local creamery Salem Valley Farms.

Bear right onto White Birch Road, descending quickly through deep forests and creeks, until crossing the second waterfall of the ride at Ed Bills Pond, a nationally designated Wild and Scenic River.

The road becomes Salem Road just before a short, punchy climb. Turn right at the end, onto Hamburg Road, beside a sprawling horse farm. At the T-junction with CT 82, Norwich-Salem Road, turn left toward Hadlyme Village.

The road remains scenic but becomes busier, with sightseers driving to or from the ferry launch. At Hadlyme Village Center, turn right to continue along CT 82 back toward East Haddam.

The road heads uphill over the next few miles, and continues climbing when it bears right onto Hungerford Road. This quiet wooded road quickly becomes Petticoat Lane, which climbs up through a quiet forest. Bear right to stay on Petticoat and turn right when you reach CT 82 again, passing Sanibel's and a small pond.

Turn left at the intersection, following CT 82, for a fast, curving descent into the scenic downtown of East Haddam. Make a U-turn, and bear left at the fork, following CT 149 down toward the Connecticut River and the village of Moodus, the small commercial center of East Haddam.

View of the waterfall at Devil's Hopyard State Park.

CT 149 travels past the Nathan Hale Schoolhouse and a beautiful Episcopal church, St. Stephen's, home to the oldest church bell in the New World. The bell was built for a Spanish monastery in AD 815, and abandoned in rubble after Napoleon destroyed the church during his invasion. It was later found by a Yankee sea captain, who used the bell as ballast for his journey home. A ship chandler bought the bell in New York, and had it transported to East Haddam, the hometown of his wife.

CT 149 continues past a number of grand historic homes, before bearing left with a scenic view of the Connecticut River. Turn left onto Johnsonville Road, through the "ghost town," until you reach Johnson Mill Pond. Turn left onto Neptune Avenue until it ends at CT 151.

Turn right onto 151, and head northeast through downtown Moodus, a more heavily developed commercial area. Just after downtown, start climbing again, and the road narrows; traffic can be slightly fast here, so be extra aware over this next mile. The route approaches a fork in the road just before the Moodus Reservoir Dam; take the right-hand path and then turn right onto Falls Bashan Road.

This is a peaceful residential street with suburban-style houses and low speed limits. Follow the road until it ends in a T-intersection with the East Haddam Colchester Turnpike, then turn right, and then make a quick left after a short hill onto Alger Road. Alger Road heads uphill through another quiet area, before you make a sharp left onto Smith Road, and an even more rural neighborhood. The pavement here isn't always well maintained, but the road is quiet and only lightly traveled.

Smith Road eventually passes an old cemetery, before you turn left and begin ascending Mount Parnassus Road, a long road with a maximum elevation of 561 feet, and three solid climbs, with fast descents between each. Automobile speeds can exceed 50 mph; be alert.

After a particularly fast descent, turn right onto Hopyard Road, which passes some scenic meadows and ponds before the left-hand turn onto Foxtown Road, ending the ride.

MILES AND DIRECTIONS

0.0 Start at the Devil's Hopyard Parking lot on Foxtown Road and left onto Hopyard Road

3.5 Left onto CT 82

7.1 Salem Valley Farms ice cream; take right onto Darling Road

7.3 Right onto White Birch Road

11.1 Right onto CT 156

11.2 Left onto CT 82

15.2 Right to stay on CT 82

16.1 Right onto Hungerford Road to Petticoat Lane

19.3 Right onto CT 82

20.0 Left to stay on CT 82

21.4 Right onto CT 149

22.1 Left to stay on CT 149

24.1 Left onto Johnsonville Road

24.7 Right onto Leesville Road then left onto Neptune Avenue

25.4 Right onto CT 151 to CT 149

27.3 Right onto Falls Bashan Road

28.2 Right onto East Haddam Colchester Turnpike then left onto Alger Road

29.1 Left onto Smith Road

30.9 Left onto Mount Parnassus Road

35.0 Right onto Hopyard Road

35.7 Left onto Foxtown Road to finish

Devil's Hopyard and Johnsonville Ghost Town

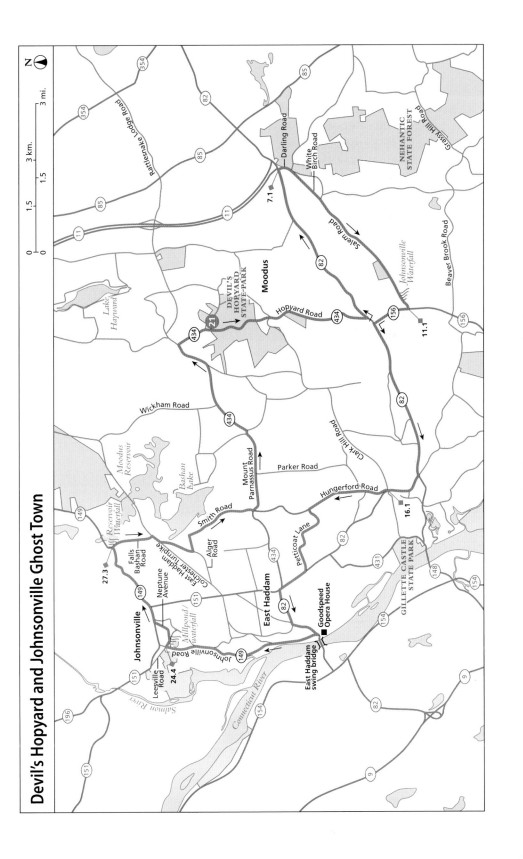

Johnsonville: Ghost Town in the Connecticut River Valley

Originally settled in the 1600s, Johnsonville was a bustling mill town before the decline of the twine industry, and was transformed into a replica of a Victorian village in the 1960s. The 64-acre property is now an abandoned ghost town, with a number of historic structures and industrial machines imported from other faded mill towns.

Johnsonville is located in the Moodus village of East Haddam, a small town settled in part of Machimoodus, a picturesque river valley of the Connecticut River.

During the 19th century, a series of twine mills were built, leading to the founding of Johnsonville, the "Twine Capital of America," where twine was produced for fishing nets. The first of these structures, the Neptune Mill, was built by Stanton S. Card in 1832. The Triton Mill, built in 1862 by Emory Johnson, came second. Johnson was an entrepreneur who left his family farm to build wagons and was later hired by Card.

Johnson married Eliza Card, daughter of Stanton, and joined the family business. He oversaw the development of the industrial village and tenement quality housing, and the name Johnsonville was both a critique and an homage.

The twine industry suffered through the Civil War and never fully rebounded. Johnsonville closed in the early 1900s. The mills were flammable, and only the Neptune survived until 1965, when Raymond Schmitt, aerospace industrialist, bought it and the surrounding property. Schmitt restored the property to create a model Victorian-era village and showcase for his collection of antique machinery.

The property was a special events venue but never became profitable, and the Neptune Mill was not restored after a fire caused by a lightning strike in the 1970s, although Schmitt maintained the property as a pet project up until his death in the 1990s.

The property was auctioned after his death and has changed hands many times. The grounds are technically closed to visitors, but the roads are public and afford views of a charming town that never properly existed.

You can enjoy your ride through this once bustling industrial town without fears of ghosts and goblins; while rumors of haunting circulate, they have no verifiable source or historicity and seem more likely to be modern inventions based on the property's lack of commercial success.

Waterfall at Ed Bills Pond.

RIDE INFORMATION

Bike Shops
Pedal Power Bicycle Shop: 359 Main St., Middletown; (860) 347-3776; pedal
powerct.com

Events and Attractions
Gillette Castle State Park: Is covered in greater detail in Ride 23, the River
Valley Ferry Loop. This historic replica castle is a state park, offering tours, hiking trails, and concessions.
The Goodspeed Opera House: Goodspeed hosts more than 400 musical theater performances each year, in a magnificent building overlooking the Connecticut River and the historic swing bridge.

Restaurants
Sanibel Farms: 328 Town St., East Haddam; (860) 873-9083
Hadlyme Country Market: 1 Ferry Rd., Lyme; (860) 526-3188

Restrooms
0.0 Miles: Devil's Hopyard

Old Saybrook Beach Loop

Old Saybrook is a classic shore town, full of islands, marshes, and quiet, low-volume roads. Bisected by I-95, Old Saybrook can feel like a bustling suburb; the highways exit onto a commercial strip of big box stores and parking lots. North and south of the small area between 95 and Route 1 are quiet, neighborhood-oriented areas. The south side contains a gorgeous beach community with a pedestrian-friendly town center and some spectacular views of Long Island Sound.

Visitors are drawn to Old Saybrook for the scenic waterways. Bordered by the Connecticut River and the Long Island Sound, Old Saybrook is a prime place to view shorebirds, raptors, and even river otters. Architecturally, the waterfront includes 17th- and 18th-century homes and two lighthouses, Saybrook Breakwater and Lynde Point.

Start: Kavanagh Park

Length: 8.2 miles

Riding time: 30 to 45 minutes

Best bike: Hybrid or road bike

Terrain and trail surface: Asphalt

Traffic and hazards: The causeway is narrow and can be rather hectic, either on the pedestrian sidewalk or the narrow roadway. Use caution and be respectful to other users. Downtown Old Saybrook has nose-in parking, and drivers may not see you when backing out of spots.

Things to see: Water views on the causeway, Willard Bay, Fort Saybrook Memorial Park, river otters, shorebirds

Fees: None

Getting there: I-95 provides easy access to Old Saybrook. From the east, take I-95S to exit 68 for US 1, and turn left onto Main Street. From the west, take I-95N to exit 67 for CT 154W to Main Street. From Main

Street, turn right onto Old Boston Post Road, then left onto Trask Road. The park will be on the left. The train station offers easy access for mass transit users. Exit the parking lot onto CT 154W to Main Street.

GPS: 41.2849 / -72.38533

THE RIDE

This 8.2-mile ride starts at Kavanagh Park and tours the beaches and bridges connecting the different sections of marshes, offering views of Indiantown Harbor during a crossing of the Back River, a ride along beautiful Willard Bay, and a long, scenic trip over the causeway, with views of lighthouses. After the water views, the route explores Old Saybrook's bustling main street for food and entertainment.

Start on Trask Road to Fairview, where the route turns right and then left onto CT 154 at the end of Fairview. This is a long, marshy stretch of road, which crosses over the Back River and past Indiantown Harbor, and provides excellent bird watching. Herons and other shorebirds are common.

After a bridge, the route passes Harvey's Beach around the 1.1-mile mark. This small town beach charges a parking fee and provides restrooms, water, and a seasonal concession stand.

After the beach, the route continues over a small bridge, with more water views on the left, following CT 154 as it twists and curves. Turn right at the fork after the Town Beach Store to continue on 154.

CT 154, also named Maple Avenue, continues through a quiet residential neighborhood with homes on either side until Willard Bay, where you have an unobstructed view of Long Island Sound. Overlooking the sound from an elevated vantage point, this section of road provides the most spectacular view of the ride. On clear days, you will be able to see Plum Island and parts of Long Island on the horizon.

The route continues along Willard Bay for nearly a mile before a slight left curve into the borough of Fenwick, where the late Katharine Hepburn lived in her retirement. This borough is the least populous municipality in the state of Connecticut, with only fifty-two residents.

The route exits Fenwick onto the Old Saybrook Causeway, with scenic views of South Cove. The causeway here is very narrow; slower cyclists may wish to take the pedestrian and bike path which adjoins the main road. The causeway road lanes are quite narrow and will not comfortably allow space for cars to pass you when the road is busy, but the bike and pedestrian path can be very congested with fishing, walking, and other activities. You may

Lighthouses

Saybrook Breakwater Lighthouse, or Outer Saybrook, and Lynde Point Light, or Inner Saybrook, are both along this route. Outer Saybrook is a sparkplug-operated lighthouse built in the 1880s and featured on the Connecticut "Preserve the Sound" license plate. This lighthouse was staffed until 1959. The older of the two, Inner Saybrook, was first built in 1803 and actively staffed until 1970.

While the lighthouses are romantic to view, the work apparently isn't; historically, local newspapers have run op-eds by lighthouse keepers, and their spouses, complaining about the tedium and long hours. Outer Saybrook is now a privately owned property, but both lighthouses are still operational, albeit automated. Outer Saybrook can only be reached by boat, and Inner Saybrook is on a private road and still minimally staffed by the Coast Guard in order to deter vandalism. Neither lighthouse can be visited by the public, but there are several places to view them from the Fenwick area and the South Cove.

have to dismount and walk your bike in order to share the pathway with users who are fishing or walking. Use your best judgment whichever option you choose, but make sure to look to the right and back to see Old Saybrook's historic lighthouses.

Once you've crossed South Cove, you make a hard left to stay on 154, passing Fort Saybrook Memorial Park on the right, an attraction dating to the European settlement of Connecticut. Before the English, the Dutch settled the area in 1624 as an early trading post, named Kievits Hoek or Plover's Corner, which was later abandoned in favor of consolidating in New Amsterdam. In 1631, English viscounts Saye and Sele and Baron Brook built the first fortified settlement in New England, named Fort Saybrook from a portmanteau of Saye and Brook.

Fort Saybrook failed by 1648, a casualty of the Pequot War. The original location of the fort is uncertain, but the history of the town is memorialized in the 17-acre park, open from dusk to dawn. Elevated boardwalks lead visitors by historical plaques and views of scenic marsh.

Take the first right onto Cromwell Place. After a short stretch, turn left onto North Cove Road for a quiet, scenic stretch where the Connecticut River enters the North Cove. Turn right back onto CT 154 at the end of North Cove, following the road as it becomes Main Street, heading directly into downtown Old Saybrook.

South Cove in Old Saybrook.

Maple Avenue is part of an important training circuit for local sports cyclists. The 5-mile loop takes Maple to CT 154, over the causeway you just passed, skips the detour, and then turns left again onto Maple to repeat.

The mapped route bypasses Maple, into downtown Old Saybrook, passing first the Old Saybrook Historical Society and then The Katharine Hepburn Cultural Center just a few hundred feet later.

Pay careful attention here, as the parking spaces are all pull-in; watch for drivers backing out of spots, who may not see you if you're too close to the parked cars.

There are a few ideal stop options for cyclists in kit. The Paperback Cafe is a cozy and casual spot with a surprisingly broad menu; they have a full espresso bar and extensive gluten-free options. Cafe Toscana is a newer establishment, operating out of a small storefront with an exterior modeled after rustic Italian cafes. Cafe Toscana also offers a full espresso bar, with a smaller menu, and outdoor seating. Finally, Tissa's Le Souk Du Maroc, also on Main Street, is a creative little Moroccan market with only a few tables. The food is diverse, offering traditional fare alongside beach treats like ice cream, and Moroccan-inspired sandwiches and wraps. For chain options, there is a Starbucks, located just after Cafe Toscana.

Follow Main Street to the intersection with Route 1, a high-volume road and an active commercial zone for big box stores with large parking lots. Carefully make a U-turn and back onto Main Street, to ride out of downtown and back toward the ride start. Be aware again of traffic, and turn right onto Old

Photos of riders along Willard Bay by John Ho.

Boston Post Road, then left after a half-mile onto Trask Road, which continues to the town park.

MILES AND DIRECTIONS

0.0   Ride start at Kavanagh Park on Trask Road. Turn right immediately onto Fairview Avenue.

0.3   Turn left onto CT 154 (Great Hammock Road)

2.0   Bear right to stay on CT 154 (Maple Avenue)

4.0   Lighthouses are visible behind you on the right

4.7   Turn right onto Cromwell Place

5.0   Turn left onto North Cove Road

5.7   Turn right onto CT 154 (Main Street)

7.0   Visit Old Saybrook's village district for food or refreshment, then turn around

7.5   Turn right onto Old Boston Post Road

8.0   Turn left onto Trask Road

8.2   Ride finishes back at town park

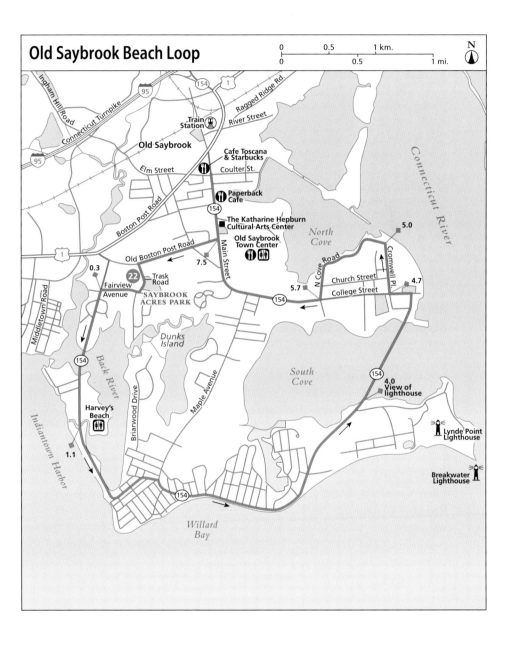

Old Saybrook Beach Loop

0   0.5   1 km.

0   0.5   1 mi.

N

Ingham Hill Road

Connecticut Turnpike

95

154

1

Ragged Ridge Rd.

River Street

Train Station

Old Saybrook

Elm Street

95

Cafe Toscana & Starbucks

Coulter St.

Paperback Cafe

154

The Katharine Hepburn Cultural Arts Center

Old Saybrook Town Center

North Cove

5.0

Connecticut River

Boston Post Road

Old Boston Post Road

7.5

N Cove Road

Cromwell Pl.

1

Main Street

Church Street

4.7

0.3

22

Trask Road

Fairview Avenue

SAYBROOK ACRES PARK

5.7

College Street

Middletown Road

Dunks Island

154

South Cove

154

4.0 View of lighthouse

154

Back River

Maple Avenue

Briarwood Drive

Harvey's Beach

Lynde Point Lighthouse

1.1

Indiantown Harbor

Breakwater Lighthouse

154

Willard Bay

The Kate

The Kate was built in 1908 as Old Saybrook Town Hall and became a venue for music, stage, and film until the mid-1950s, when the performing arts rooms were renovated into offices and conference spaces. Hepburn moved back to Old Saybrook for her retirement in 1997, where she lived until her death in 2003.

That year, the town government moved into a new building, and the residents decided to preserve the old building by returning it to its original use as a theater. In 2005, planners received permission to use Hepburn's name, and The Kate was born.

The venue hosts eighteen performances per month; the performances range from live comedy, stage plays, and musical performances to classic films and HD streams from the Bolshoi Ballet and Met operas.

You can view their schedule, purchase tickets, or learn more about the theater on their website: http://katharinehepburntheater.org/.

RIDE INFORMATION

Bike Shops
Action Sports of Old Saybrook: 1385 Boston Post Rd., Old Saybrook; (860) 388-1291; actionsportsct.com

Local Events and Attractions
Old Saybrook Memorial Fort: Just off the causeway on the right, this 17-acre park is an outdoor history exhibit in a beautiful natural setting.
The Kate: A major performing arts venue named in honor of the legendary actress and town resident.

Restaurants
Penny Lane Pub: 150 Main St., Old Saybrook; (860) 388-9646; pennylanepub.net
Red Hen Restaurant: 286 Main St., Old Saybrook; (860) 388-8818; redhen restaurant.com
Paperback Cafe: 210 Main St. #9, Old Saybrook; (860) 388-9718; paperback cafect.com
Cafe Toscana: 25 Main St., Old Saybrook; (860) 388-1270

Restrooms
Miles 0.0: Kavanagh Park
Miles 1.1: Harvey's Beach
Miles 7.0: Various eateries, grocery store at start of Main Street

River Valley Ferry Loop

This route follows in the footsteps of the early European colonists; Old Saybrook was the base camp for European settlers to explore Connecticut. The English settlers of Old Saybrook fanned out into the surrounding region and eventually sought permission to found their own parishes in order to worship at churches closer to their homesteads. Essex, Deep River, Chester, Lyme, Old Lyme, and Westbrook all originated as religious parishes for the colonial inhabitants of the original settlement at Old Saybrook. Today, these towns all host rich cultural attractions, from stage theaters to a preserved colonial inn where sea shanties are still sung the way they were in the 18th century.

Start: Main Street, Old Saybrook

Length: 30.1 miles

Riding time: 2.5 hours

Best bike: Road bike

Terrain and trail surface: Asphalt

Traffic and hazards: The causeway is narrow and can be rather hectic, either on the pedestrian sidewalk or the narrow roadway. Use caution and be respectful to other users. Downtown Old Saybrook has nose-in parking, and drivers may not see you when backing out of spots.

Things to see: Connecticut River, beautiful back roads, historic downtowns

Fees: Small ferry walk-on fee for pedestrians and cyclists

Getting there: I-95 provides easy access to Old Saybrook. From the east, take I-95S to exit 68 for US 1, and turn left onto Main Street. From the west, take I-95N to exit 67 for CT 154W to Main Street. The train station offers easy access for mass transit users. Exit the parking lot onto CT 154W to Main Street.

GPS: 41.29243 / -72.37634

THE RIDE

The ride takes advantage of the Chester-Hadlyme Ferry, one of the oldest continuously operated ferry services in the United States. The ferry is seasonal, from April 1 to November 30. If closed, an alternate crossing is available, adding roughly 10 miles to the trip, documented in the directions below.

From the start, ride up Main, and turn right onto the Boston Post Road, Route 1, for one of the busiest and least scenic stretches of the ride, starting with a fairly large bridge, without a real shoulder, along four lanes of traffic. After the bridge, turn right to stay on Boston Post Road, and then turn right again onto Ferry Road, which curves around and under the Raymond E. Baldwin Bridge, a long bridge that crosses the Connecticut River into Old Lyme.

When Ferry Road ends, take a left onto Essex Road, following signs for the pedestrian and bicycle bridge access. Right around the 3-mile mark, turn onto the paved off-road path that leads over the Baldwin Bridge.

The bridge ride is about 1 mile long, and has great views of the Connecticut River below through the barrier fencing. Note the exhibit on the history of the bridge on the Old Lyme side. At the end of the path, take a left off the trail onto CT 156, Neck Road.

This is a slightly busy road that runs north-south along the Connecticut River, affording views of marinas and large homes set back from the road. In roughly 2 miles, turn right onto Bill Hill Road for a quick detour past a coffee shop and farmers' market.

After climbing up Bill Hill Road, turn right, back onto CT 156, and take the immediate left onto Ely's Ferry Road.

Ely's Ferry Road is a quiet rural street through conservancy lands; the road ends with preserves. Take a right after a half-mile onto Cove Road, another quiet side road, that leads past Camp Claire before rejoining CT 156.

Take a left onto CT 156, riding through Hamburg village. In less than a half-mile, carefully turn left onto Old Hamburg Road; use caution because oncoming traffic speeds can be quite fast and the road curves here, limiting visibility.

At Joshuatown Road, turn left, onto one of the single most beautiful stretches of road in the region. This road is roughly 5 miles long, and features three incredible hills, over a total gain of close to 700 feet of climb and descent. Scenery consists of deep forests, beautiful homes, and undeveloped natural woods, and automobile traffic is rare.

At the end of Joshuatown Road, turn left onto Ferry Road, and board the Hadlyme-Chester Ferry. The ferry operators tend to be gregarious and helpful; they can talk about nearby Gillette Castle (a short trip up River Road, which you passed as you approached the ferry) or other local attractions.

Joshuatown Road.

If the ferry isn't running, turn around, and turn left onto Geer Hill Road to River Road, then left onto CT 82. Turn left from CT 82 onto Ray Hill Road, down a fast descent, and turn left onto another spur of 82 through downtown East Haddam, over the historic swing bridge. Turn left after a shopping plaza to continue on CT 82 to CT 154, meeting the mapped route where it continues onto Water Street.

Assuming the ferry is running, disembark and ride up Ferry Street, crossing the tracks still in use for the Essex Steam Train. Cross Middlesex Avenue and continue on Water Street, a pretty street leading into downtown Chester.

Take a left onto Main Street, and after visiting Chester, turn right off Main and up Maple Street, a quiet suburban road that winds up and out toward Deep River. Turn left onto Straits Road at the end of Maple.

Straits Road becomes Union Street ahead, after a four-way stop, and continues through the outskirts of Deep River. Deep River is a charming town; to detour through it, turn left onto Bridge Street, then right onto Main Street, and then another right onto Elm Street back to the route.

Continuing on the mapped route, cross the intersection with Bridge Street, onto Union Street, and take a right in just under a mile onto CT 80, Elm Street. This road curves around the Pratt Read Reservoir with some scenic water views before becoming West Elm Street. In 1 mile, the route turns left onto Warsaw Street, a narrower road that becomes Main Street and passes through the small villages of Ivoryton and Centerbrook, through quaint downtowns.

Keep right at the 25-mile point, and the road becomes CT 154, passing under a highway overpass and by the Essex Steam Train, before traffic speeds pick up slightly and the road becomes a faster commuter route. These last 4–5 miles can be slightly busy, but there is a small shoulder, and bicyclists are fairly common here. The road should feel safe and comfortable for solo riders or group riders in single file.

The route here is mostly downhill into downtown Old Saybrook, through a somewhat busy suburban area with car lots. Be careful near the 29-mile mark, where a large, high-speed on-ramp for Route 9 bears right; you want to make sure you're highly visible and attentive to the traffic around you as you cross over the ramp to continue on CT 154.

Shortly after the on-ramp, cross the large bridge that leads to the train station, then turn left onto Main Street with the light, ending the ride.

MILES AND DIRECTIONS

0.0 Start on Main Street

0.3 Right onto Boston Post Road

0.7 Right onto Boston Post Road

1.9 Right onto Ferry Road

2.7 Left onto Essex Road

4.0 Left onto CT 156 (Neck Road)

6.2 Right onto Bill Hill Road

7.7 Right onto CT 156 (Hamburg Road)

7.8 Left onto Ely's Ferry Road

8.6 Right onto Cove Road

9.8 Continue on Hamburg Road

10.2 Continue on Old Hamburg Road

10.5 Left onto Joshuatown Road

15.2 Left onto Ferry Road

16.2 Board the Hadlyme-Chester Ferry

River Valley Ferry Loop

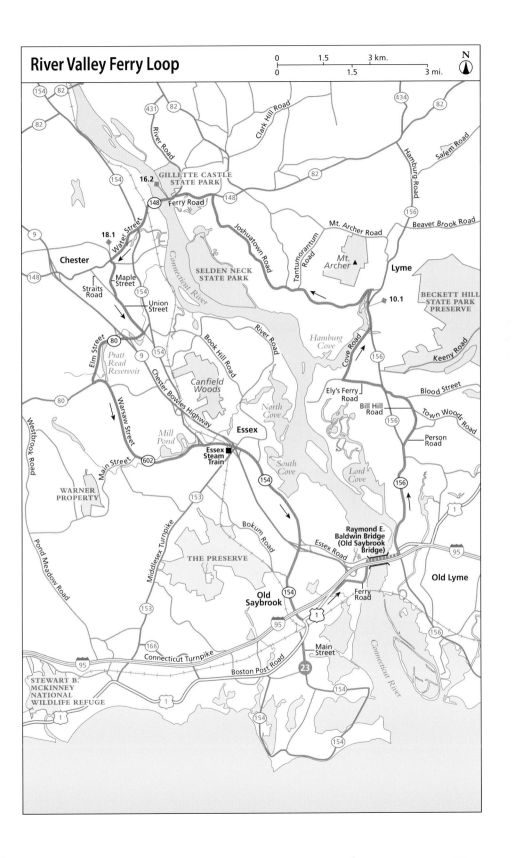

N

0		1.5		3 km.
0		1.5		3 mi.

GILLETTE CASTLE STATE PARK

16.2

Ferry Road

18.1

Chester

Water Street

Maple Street

Straits Road

Union Street

Pratt Read Reservoir

SELDEN NECK STATE PARK

Connecticut River

River Road

Book Hill Road

Clark Hill Road

Joshuatown Road

Tantumorantum Road

Mt. Archer Road

Beaver Brook Road

Hamburg Road

Salem Road

Mt. Archer

Lyme

10.1

BECKETT HILL STATE PARK PRESERVE

Keeny Road

Hamburg Cove

Cove Road

Elm Street

Warsaw Street

Chester Bowles Highway

Canfield Woods

North Cove

Mill Pond

Essex

Essex Steam Train

Main Street

WARNER PROPERTY

Westbrook Road

Pond Meadow Road

Middlesex Turnpike

Bokum Road

THE PRESERVE

Ely's Ferry Road

Bill Hill Road

Blood Street

Town Woods Road

Person Road

South Cove

Lord Cove

Raymond E. Baldwin Bridge (Old Saybrook Bridge)

Essex Road

Old Lyme

Ferry Road

Old Saybrook

Connecticut Turnpike

Boston Post Road

Main Street

STEWART B. MCKINNEY NATIONAL WILDLIFE REFUGE

Connecticut River

16.5 Proceed onto Ferry Road

17.1 Cross Middlesex Avenue, continue on Water Street to downtown Chester

18.3 Left onto Main Street then right onto Maple Street

19.1 Left onto Straits Road

19.2 Continue on Union Street

20.0 Right onto CT 80 (Elm Street)

20.7 Continue on CT 80 (West Elm Street)

21.7 Left onto Warsaw Street

22.9 Continue onto North Main Street

25.6 Right onto CT 154 (Middlesex Turnpike, Main Street)

29.7 Continue on Boston Post Road

30.1 Continue on Main Street to finish

Gillette Castle and William Hooker Gillette

This replica castle was built by William Hooker Gillette, a stage actor, originally from Hartford, Connecticut, and a descendant of the Reverend Thomas Hooker, who founded Hartford. His father was a member of the US Senate who supported the abolition of slavery, women's suffrage, and the temperance movement.

Gillette grew up surrounded by literary figures, including Mark Twain and Harriet Beecher Stowe, and he eventually became famous in his own right for portraying Sherlock Holmes on the stage. Gillette wrote the adaptations he starred in and was responsible for the most enduring image of Holmes in a deerstalker cap with a distinctive, curved pipe.

After achieving fame, Gillette built this mansion, styling it with the facade of a European castle, on 184 acres in East Haddam. As a stage manager, Gillette invented a number of props and stage pieces, and his home contains a number of these innovations. Tables and decor were designed to slide and move, providing multi-use spaces.

Gillette died unmarried, without heirs, and the property eventually came into the possession of the State of Connecticut. You can learn more about this unique property and plan a visit or tour on the state website at ct.gov/deep/gillettecastle.

RIDE INFORMATION

Bike Shops
Pedal Power: 4 Essex Plaza, Essex; (860) 347-3776; pedalpowerct.com
Action Sports of Old Saybrook: 1385 Boston Post Rd., Old Saybrook; (860) 388-1291; actionsportsct.com

Events and Attractions
Gillette Castle State Park: Hiking trails, seasonal events, and guided tours of the fascinating historical home, on 184 acres overlooking the river.
Essex Steam Train: This historical steam-powered train runs regular trips on tracks by the Connecticut River.

Restaurants
Paperback Cafe: 210 Main St. #9, Old Saybrook; (860) 388-9718; paperbackcafect.com
Cafe Toscana: 25 Main St., Old Saybrook; (860) 388-1270
Ashlawn Farm Coffee: 78 Bill Hill Rd., Old Lyme; (860) 434-3636; farmcoffee.com
Simon's Marketplace: 17 Main St., Chester; (860) 526-8984; simonsmarketplacechester.com
River Tavern: 23 Main St., Chester; (860) 526-9417; rivertavernrestaurant.com
Griswold Inn: 36 Main St., Essex; (860) 767-1776; griswoldinn.com
Black Seal: 15 Main St., Essex; (860) 767-0233; theblackseal.net

Restrooms
6.9 Miles: The Farmers' Market/Ashlawn Farm Coffee
16.2 Miles: Ferry launch

Millers Pond State Park

This ride takes place in Millers Pond State Park, a nearly 300-acre property surrounding a picturesque pond, created in 1704 by a Durham resident seeking a water source for his gristmill. The trails here are ideal for beginners. The most challenging hazards can be avoided easily on bypasses that are immediately visible. This route covers two routes: a roughly 2-mile beginner loop and a longer, more varied loop, which covers just under 10 miles.

Start: Millers Pond State Park parking lot off Foothills Road

Length: Varies: between 2 and 10 miles

Riding time: Varies: between 30 minutes and 2.5 hours

Best bike: Mountain bike

Terrain and trail surface: Singletrack, gravel, dirt, and doubletrack

Traffic and hazards: There is no traffic. Use caution around hikers, who have the right of way. Some areas are popular with dog walkers and joggers, so be aware of other users. Make sure to bring water, snacks, and a cell phone in case of problems. The southern portion of this route is very challenging and should not be attempted by solo riders. The rest of the park has bailout sections by each hazard, making for a great course for beginner riders looking to improve. All routes must be ridden clockwise, except for the practice loop.

Things to see: Millers Pond is the centerpiece of this ride. The park is a beautiful forested, undeveloped preserve.

Fees: None. Millers Pond State Park is open year-round with no parking fees.

Getting there: Take exit 11 on Route 9 to CT 155W. Turn left onto Millbrook Road, then bear left onto Foothills Road. The parking area will be on the right.

GPS: 41.48028 / -72.62959

Millers Pond view from trail.

THE RIDE

The pond was created in 1704, but the park was established more recently, in 1955. The property was acquired at the turn of the 20th century by Thomas MacDonough Russell, a one-time mayor of Middletown, and the grandson of the local naval hero who defeated the British on Lake Champlain, leading to the Treaty of Ghent and the end of the War of 1812.

The state purchased the initial property with money left in a trust by George Dudley Seymour, a preservationist and close friend to President Taft, whose generous donations were used to establish eight state parks and one state forest.

This ride can be broken into three segments: the Practice Loop, the northwest section of the red-blazed trail, and the southern section of the red-blazed trail. The practice loop is an under 2-mile beginner section that is ridden counter-clockwise. The red-blazed trail is a mix of the very technical southern section and the much less challenging, cyclocross-oriented, northwest section.

The Practice Loop is the easiest to follow. Simply head north from the parking lot and follow the trail for just under a half-mile. Bear right where the trail meets the red-white trail, staying on the Practice Loop, for another 0.4 mile, heading north and then west. Turn left and continue to the white trail, by the pond, where you turn left and ride along the water back to the parking lot.

To just ride the northwest section of the red-blazed trail, also start on the Practice Loop. Follow it to the pond, as above, but turn right onto the white-blazed trail. Take the next right to the red-blazed trail, and then turn right to follow the red blazes in a long, 3.5-mile loop into the woods and past some narrow creeks.

This is a very easy route, suitable for a cyclocross bike even, but it has jumps and drops available if you're seeking to increase the challenge. When you reach the Practice Loop from earlier, turn right onto it and then left onto the white-blazed trail by the pond back to the parking lot.

To start with the more challenging southern section, or ride the entire red-blazed trail in full, head south from the parking lot, onto a small dirt and gravel road. The red-blazed trail entrance is just ahead. This first section contains a beautiful free-ride loop, with a plethora of challenges and hazards. Most have bypasses and bailouts if they prove too daunting. There are a number of log bridges and ramps, and many intersections with other trails.

This route passes the yellow-blazed trail, to the left, and then intersects with the blue-blazed trail. Continue riding south, over another intersection, and then head to the right, and follow the trail as it curves left and to the south.

The trail winds back to the right, heading north for a short bit, before curving back to the south just before an intersection with the B Line.

Continue south, noting the red and white trail on the right; this is a return option if the going is rougher than expected.

Continuing on, the red-blazed trail intersects a road ahead, and then a singletrack, before reaching the southernmost portion and curving to the right. The path heads north, back over a singletrack, into a longer, fairly straight section that crosses the blue-blazed trail. To finish the southern section, turn right onto the blue-blazed trail to the white-blazed trail, and ride that back to the parking lot, keeping the pond to your right. This loop is roughly 5 miles long, and would take about 1.5 hours.

To continue the full red-blazed loop, cross the blue-blazed trail, and follow the route as it curves left and west, into the fairly easy section detailed above. This full loop is roughly 10 miles long and should take about 2.5 hours.

MILES AND DIRECITONS

0.0 Start on red-blazed trail south from parking area
0.1 Right to stay on red-blazed trail
0.2 Cross the blue-blazed trail and continue on red
1.1 Turn right to stay on red-blazed trail
2.3 Cross an unblazed hiking trail and continue on red trail
2.4 Cross the blue-white hiking trail, continue left on the red trail

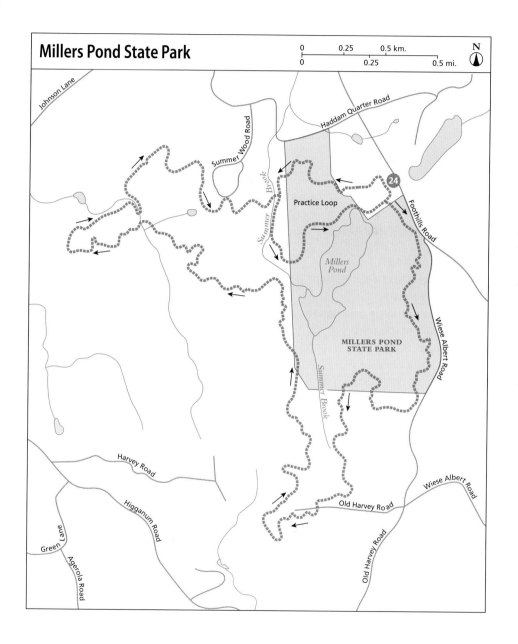

Millers Pond State Park

0   0.25   0.5 km.

0   0.25   0.5 mi.

N

Johnson Lane

Haddam Quarter Road

Summer Wood Road

Summer Brook

Practice Loop

24

Foothills Road

Millers Pond

Wiese Albert Road

MILLERS POND
STATE PARK

Summer Brook

Harvey Road

Higganum Road

Old Harvey Road

Wiese Albert Road

Green Lane

Agerola Road

Old Harvey Road

2.5 Cross the blue-white hiking trail, continue on red trail

3.9 Cross the blue-blazed hiking trail (Mattabasset Trail) and continue on the red trail Rockland

7.4 Turn right onto the gravel road

7.6 Turn left onto the white-blazed trail

8.0 Finish the ride at the parking area

Optional

8.2 Take the practice section (red-blazed trail north) and follow it to the northwest, back to the gravel road from before

9.0 Turn left onto the gravel road

9.2 Turn left onto the white-blazed trail

9.6 Finish the ride at the parking area

RIDE INFORMATION

Bike Shops
Pedal Power Bicycle Shop: 359 Main St., Middletown; (860) 347-3776; pedal powerct.com
Cheshire Cycle and Repair: 3550 Whitney Ave., Hamden; (203) 891-5320; cheshirecycle.com
North Haven Bike: 510 Washington Ave., North Haven; (203) 239-7789; northhavenbike.com

Local Events and Attractions
Durham Fair: The largest agricultural fair in Connecticut is held annually on the last weekend in September. The fair hosts competitions, live games, shopping, and food and local produce (durhamfair.com).

Restaurants
Perk on Main: 6 Main St., Durham; (860) 349-5335; perkonmain.com
Time Out Taverne: 100 New Haven Rd., Durham; (860) 349-1721; timeout taverne.com

Restrooms
7.0 Miles: Bathrooms at Stony Creek Beach

Durham-Guilford Run

Durham is a former agricultural town in Middlesex County, north of the shoreline. The small town hosts the largest agricultural fair in Connecticut and is largely a residential community, with the majority of residents working in nearby job centers. This ride follows a popular local route into nearby Guilford, spins around the historic green, and then returns on an alternative route.

Out of the two towns, Guilford is the primary tourist attraction; this picturesque shoreline town has an attractive, walkable green surrounded by boutiques, restaurants, and coffee shops.

Start: Parking lot on Main Street in Durham by Perk on Main coffee shop

Length: 28 miles

Riding time: 2 hours

Best bike: Road bike

Terrain and trail surface: Asphalt

Traffic and hazards: CT 79 can be rather hectic with traffic, so use caution exiting and entering Durham. CT 77 is a fairly fast road with a narrow shoulder, but bicycles are common here, and most drivers should be respectful.

Fees: The parking lot is free to use.

Getting there: The parking is on CT 79, which can be easily accessed via exit 61 on I-95. From I-91, take exit 15 to CT 68E, and turn right onto CT 15, Main Street, in Durham. Look for the coffee shop and parking lot on the left. Mass-transit users may wish to ride this route in reverse. The Shoreline East train station in Guilford is near the green, and is a very bike-friendly train line.

GPS: 41.46625 / -72.67898

First pass by Quonnipaug Lake.

THE RIDE

The majority of this ride takes place along one long stretch of road (nearly 13 miles in total), visits the Guilford Green, and then returns on parallel roads that rejoin the main road near the end. CT 77 is a staple of many shoreline bike clubs' weekend rides and can be included in a much longer route or ridden in the alternate direction, from Guilford to Durham. The longer, roughly 65-mile, route is included in the sidebar.

Starting at the parking lot, turn right onto Main Street, and stay right at the triangle, onto CT 17 (New Haven Road).

In 0.1 mile, carefully bear left onto CT 77 (Guilford Road), and out of the busy downtown section of Durham. The road has a wide shoulder here, and heads mostly straight and with few interruptions or stops over the next 12 miles; scenery includes the Quonnipaug Lake and forested yards along the residential route.

You cross some busy intersections as you approach downtown Guilford; when the road narrows and becomes Church Street, just shy of the 13-mile mark, you will be close to Perk on Church, which will be on your right in a unique quonset hut building. This was once Cafe Grounded, a popular Sunday brunch spot for the longer metric-century route detailed later.

Take the next right onto Broad Street, and then the first left onto Whit-field Street; use caution here, as cars park in diagonal spots, mostly nose-in, and visibility is poor. You should ride as far to the left as possible.

Metric Century Route

You can also ride this as part of a much larger metric-century, roughly 65 miles, starting in New Haven.

Start on the Back of the Giant Route and bear right on Hartford Turnpike, instead of left onto Ridge Road; the Turnpike has a generous shoulder and is fairly rolling with interesting terrain for a long stretch up to Wallingford, where you take a hairpin turn right onto Toelles Road, under a highway overpass, and onto US 5, where you turn left, and follow the busy street for a short section until a right on Northfield Road.

Northfield Road is a short quiet residential street that ends at Pond Hill Road, where you turn left, and head uphill before the road ends at Harrison Road; a quick right and a left onto Kondracki Lane heads through another residential neighborhood and through the intersection with CT 150, onto South Airline Road. This road reaches East Center Street, near the I-91 ramps, where you turn right for a scenic ride down to a pond, and a choice between taking a right up Whirlwind Hill Road (a very steep set of three climbs) or straight onto Scard Road, which climbs more gradually around the hill on a curving path, with a right-hand turn onto North Branford Road to the summit.

At the summit, you take a left if you rode the more gradual climb, or head straight from the steeper option, onto Whirlwind Hill Road for a fast descent through quiet meadows and a dairy farm.

Whirlwind Hill Road becomes Howd Road, which ends at CT 17, where you turn left and ride up to the Time Out Taverne. Turn right here onto Birch Mill Road, and then right again on CT 77, Guilford Road, to follow the route mapped here.

After following CT 77 into Guilford, ride around half the green to CT 146. CT 146 is a beautiful road through marshes and wetlands, which has a cross-over with the Branford–Stony Creek Route; follow CT 146 through Branford, bearing left onto Indian Neck Road from that route, and then turn left when it ends, onto Maple Street.

Follow Maple Street through a residential neighborhood until it ends at CT 142 (Short Beach Road); turn left for a very scenic ride through a beach-front village.

After Granite Bay, you cross a small bridge, and the road curves to the right up a very steep hill; shortly after this you cautiously turn left onto CT 337 (Silver Sands Road), across busy CT 142.

CT 337 curves around, coming to a small intersection with a housing development directly ahead; turn left here to stay on CT 337 until the next stop sign, where you turn right to remain on the road.

The town line for New Haven is just ahead, on your right; in a short distance, you reach the intersection of Lighthouse Road and Townsend Avenue from the Lighthouse Point Route. You can now follow that route's return leg to get back to downtown New Haven. Orange Street is the most recommended road to get back to the East Rock neighborhood where this route began.

25

When the green ends, after passing The Marketplace and Cilantro, you turn left onto CT 146 (Boston Street), and then take the next left onto Park Street, to head back up the green toward Broad Street.

Make a right turn onto Broad Street, and then a left onto State Street, in 0.1 mile. This is the return road, a less traveled and quieter set of roads. After roughly 4 miles on State Street, you turn left onto South Hoop Pole Road for a mile and a half before crossing CT 80.

In 1.75 miles, take a right onto Lake Drive, which follows the opposing shore of Quonnipaug Lake back to CT 77. Take a right when you reach CT 77, and follow it back to CT 17 (New Haven Road), which returns to Perk on Main for the finish.

MILES AND DIRECTIONS

0.0 Start the ride on Main Street in Durham and turn right onto CT 17 (New Haven Road)

0.1 Left onto CT 77 (Guilford Road)

2.4 Continue on Durham Road

12.9 Continue on Church Street

13.8 Right onto Broad Street, and then take first left onto Whitfield Street.

14.0 Left onto CT 146 (Boston Street)

14.1 Left onto Park Street

14.2 Right onto Broad Street

14.3 Left onto State Street

18.3 Left onto South Hoop Pole Road

19.9 Cross CT 80 onto Hoop Pole Road

21.4 Right onto Lake Drive

23.1 Right onto CT 77 (Durham Road)

25.5 Continue on CT 77 (Guilford Road)

27.8 Continue on CT 17 (New Haven Road)

28.0 Left onto Main Street and finish

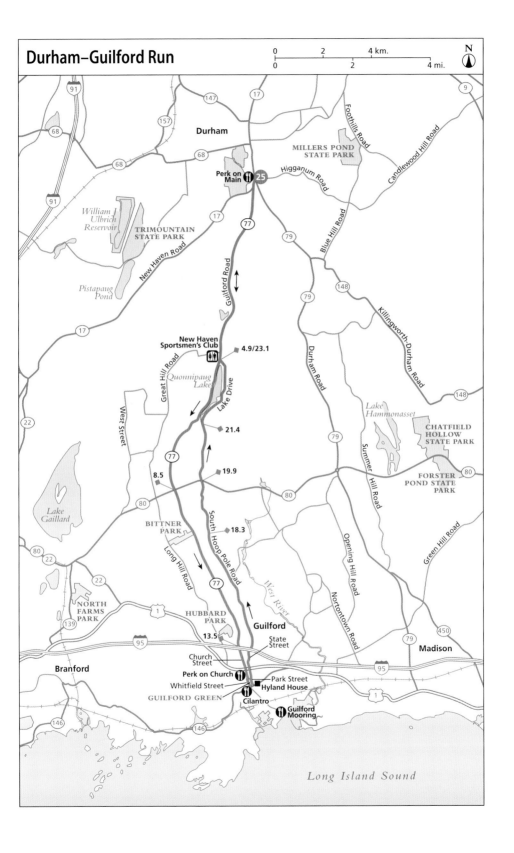

Durham–Guilford Run

0 2 4 km.
0 2 4 mi.

N

91

147

17

9

68

157

Durham

MILLERS POND
STATE PARK

Foothills Road

Candlewood Hill Road

68

68

Perk on
Main 25

Higganum Road

William J
Ulbrich
Reservoir

TRIMOUNTAIN
STATE PARK

91

17

77

79

Blue Hill Road

Guilford Road

New Haven Road

Pistapaug
Pond

148

17

79

New Haven
Sportsmen's Club

4.9/23.1

Great Hill Road

Quonnipaug
Lake

Lake Drive

Durham Road

Lake
Hammonasset

Killingworth-Durham Road

148

22

West Street

CHATFIELD
HOLLOW
STATE PARK

21.4

79

77

South Hoop Pole Road

19.9

80

FORSTER
POND STATE
PARK

80

8.5

Summer Hill Road

80

Lake
Gaillard

BITTNER
PARK

Long Hill Road

18.3

80

West River

Green Hill Road

80

22

22

NORTH
FARMS
PARK

139

HUBBARD
PARK

77

13.5

Guilford

Opening Hill Road

Nortontown Road

79

450

1

95

State
Street

Madison

Church
Street

95

Branford

Perk on Church

Park Street

Whitfield Street

Hyland House

1

GUILFORD GREEN

Cilantro

Guilford
Mooring

146

146

Long Island Sound

Durham History

The area where Durham was established was named Coginchaug by the Mattabesset, a branch of the Algonquian tribe, who are believed to have used the rivers as shipping lanes for trade. The Coginchaug River retains the Algonquian name, believed to mean "great swamp" or "long swamp," an apt description for the marshy wetlands around the waterway. When English settlers from nearby Guilford acquired the land through a deed, the surrounding towns had been long settled, and there were few Mattabesset left. The deed was signed by Tarramuggus, the Mattabesset chief, or sachem, and several other representatives of the tribe.

The history of Durham is surprisingly prosaic as rendered in an 1866 treatise titled *History of Durham, Connecticut: From the First Grant of Land in 1662 to 1866*. The author, William Chauncey Fowler, was an American scholar and Yale graduate who lived in the Durham area. The book is long out of copyright but still available from Cornell University Library in paperback, and portrays the settlement of Durham as a peaceful exercise of unity, in sharp contrast to the neighboring towns, which Fowler notes were founded by people in conflict with their former neighbors or government.

RIDE INFORMATION

Bike Shops

Pedal Power Bicycle Shop: 359 Main St., Middletown; (860) 347-3776; pedalpowerct.com

Cheshire Cycle and Repair: 3550 Whitney Ave., Hamden; (203) 891-5320; cheshirecycle.com

North Haven Bike: 510 Washington Ave., North Haven; (203) 239-7789; northhavenbike.com

Zane's Cycles: 330 E Main St., Branford; (203) 488-3244; zanes.com

Action Sports: 324 W Main St., Branford; (203) 481-5511; actionsportsct.com

Local Events and Attractions

Durham Fair: The largest agricultural fair in Connecticut is held annually on the last weekend in September. The fair features competitions, live games, shopping, and food and local produce (durhamfair.com).

Road view into Guilford.

Trip Planning: Guilford offers a comprehensive list of historic sites, lodging, and recreation on one of the better Connecticut tourism websites, visitguilford ct.com.

Henry Whitfield State Museum: This three-story stone building is the oldest house still standing in Connecticut, dating to 1639. Full-price museum tickets can be re-used at three other state museums for half-price admission. Two of these, the Sloane-Stanley (Ride 18: Kent Hills) and the Prudence Crandall (Ride 37: Canterbury-Scotland Loop), are covered in other routes.

Hyland House: This not-for-profit preservation site charges a very small admission fee to tour a two-story colonial sandbox home, built in 1713.

Restaurants

Perk on Main: 6 Main St., Durham; (860) 349-5335; perkonmain.com

Perk on Church: 20 Church St., Guilford; (203) 689-5060; perkonmain.com/ perk-on-church

Cilantro Specialty Foods: 85 Whitfield St., Guilford; (203) 458-2555; cilantro coffee.com

The Place: 901 Boston Post Rd., Guilford; (203) 453-9276; theplaceguilford.com

Time Out Taverne: 100 New Haven Rd., Durham; (860) 349-1721; timeout taverne.com

Shoreline and New Haven County

New Haven County is best known for its principal city New Haven, the home of Yale University and some of the most famous pizza restaurants in the world, but the region is also home to beautiful shoreline towns and bucolic, wooded communities.

New Haven is a hotbed of culture, with famous museums, restaurants, and musical venues. Each summer, the International Arts and Ideas Festival brings a wide range of mostly free performances, lectures, and other events. The surrounding towns are also rich in offerings, particularly on the water. Nearby Branford is home to a number of craft breweries and Stony Creek, a quaint waterfront community.

Distance cyclists can create a longer route incorporating New Haven's Sleeping Giant outbound route, the Durham-Guilford run from the previous chapter, the shore in Branford, and a return along the Lighthouse Point route. This 65-mile ride is a regular club ride for area cyclists and offers a "best of" collection of the county, showcasing new urbanist cityscapes, hills, rural roads, and the shoreline.

Mountain bike riders of all skill levels will love the Rockland Preserve, one of the best-marked trail systems in the state, created and maintained by local enthusiasts who add miles of trails each year.

Visitors from New York may look into using Amtrak; New Haven has a number of bike lanes and a fast-growing bicycle community, and it is a great city to tour by bike. Locals who want to get more involved are encouraged to look into Elm City Cycling, an advocacy nonprofit central to these efforts.

Back of the Giant

Hamden, nestled between the city of New Haven and the bucolic, rural communities of Bethany and Woodbridge, combines the best elements of city dwelling with a small-town feel and rural countryside views. The town has many popular cycling routes, along slower streets with wide shoulders. This ride covers one of the principal routes, starting in the walkable East Rock neighborhood in New Haven, and circling behind Sleeping Giant State Park through a lovely orchard.

Start: Orange Street at the intersection of Linden Street, New Haven

Length: 22.4 miles

Riding time: 1.5 to 2 hours

Best bike: Road bike

Terrain and trail surface: Asphalt

Traffic and hazards: Use caution on CT 10 in Hamden, and watch for potholes on some of the back roads after the orchard behind Sleeping Giant. Watch the "door zone" on Orange Street, staying to the outer edge of the bike lane. Mt. Carmel can be busy around the Quinnipiac campus, and watch out around the busy flea market on a short segment of Hartford Avenue on the weekends.

Things to see: Orchards, forest, quiet back roads, East Rock Park

Fees: Free parking is ample in this neighborhood. Just pay attention to signage and don't park in bus lanes or resident-only spots.

Getting there: New Haven is easily accessible by bike or car, a short distance from the Metro-North train station and numerous bus stops. Local bus lines stop across the street; Connecticut buses have bike racks for multi-modal transit.

GPS: 41.3214 / -72.91226

Cyclists taking a snack break after climbing up the orchard road hill.

THE RIDE

This ride starts at the intersection of Linden Avenue and Orange Street, by a popular local deli and Italian market.

Start the ride in the separated bike lane along the parking lane on Orange Street. Orange Street is a fairly slow neighborhood street with steady traffic.

After a short distance, you pass College Woods, the park at the base of East Rock, on your left. East Rock is the mountainous ridge, directly ahead of you, that overlooks the neighborhood and lends it its name. When you reach the end of Orange Street, and the start of East Rock, turn left onto Farnam Drive, which runs around and partially up the ridge. Total elevation gain is only about 100 feet, although the park road does continue up to the 367-foot summit if you're craving additional climbing or distance.

At the top of the climb up Farnam Drive, you pass the inner park road, and descend to Davis Street. Turn right and then take the next left onto Ridge Road, a faster but safe road popular for cycling, which heads slightly uphill.

After three-quarters of a mile, cross Hartford Turnpike at the traffic light to stay on a more rolling Ridge Road. This is a suburban neighborhood with schools and parks, and two signalized intersections; the first with Skiff Street at the 3.5-mile mark, and the second with Dixwell Avenue, at 4.6 miles.

Ridge Road overlaps with CT 22 at the 5.2-mile mark, and then you turn left to stay on Ridge Road in less than a half-mile. Be extremely careful on this turn; it's on a sharply descending right-hand curve, and other traffic may be moving very fast. Oncoming cars do not have a stop sign, and cars behind you may not see you around the corner. Typical traffic flow here is low, but it can be busy during weekday afternoons.

The rest of Ridge Road is very rural and quiet, with heavily forested homes and park land on either side of the road. You climb quite a bit here, before turning left to stay on Ridge Road at the 6.7-mile mark, where the road flattens out and becomes more level.

Turn left again at Blue Hill Road to stay on Ridge Road, which curves and then has a fast, steep descent. Use caution, as the road levels out and then ends very quickly where it meets with Mt. Carmel Avenue at the base of Sleeping Giant State Park.

Mt. Carmel Avenue leads to Quinnipiac University, a college with a large number of commuters; this road can get fairly busy between weekend recreational travel to the state park and student commuters. Speeds tend to be slower, however, because the road is narrow, rolling, curvy, and scenic; it's a fun and somewhat challenging biking route.

Mt. Carmel Avenue ends in a T-intersection with the Hartford Turnpike up ahead, a wider road with a generous shoulder. After the flea market, climb a short hill, and carefully turn left at the 10.2-mile mark onto Mansion Road. This is the serious climb of the ride; a consistently steep ascent of over 250 feet will bring you to the top, in the middle of a picturesque apple orchard.

Mansion Road has one more small climb up ahead, and then curves downhill to Tuttle Avenue, a gorgeous back road through Sleeping Giant. You pass streams and fields on this sometimes poorly maintained road before it crosses the northernmost part of the Mill River and meets CT 10/Whitney Avenue.

Whitney Avenue is a busy thoroughfare that connects the different towns in the region; you cautiously take a left-hand turn onto it, and then ride in the wide shoulder, passing Wentworth's Ice Cream on the left.

Shortly after Wentworth's, you pass Cheshire Cycles on the right, and then take a left-hand turn at a traffic signal back onto Mt. Carmel Avenue, heading toward the Quinnipiac University main campus.

Take the first right onto New Road, which runs along the Mill River and past a large pond, through a neighborhood of single-family homes and student housing. At the 16.1-mile mark you take a left onto Ives Road (CT 22) and

East Rock, New Haven: Sidewalk Society and Cafe Culture

The neighborhood of East Rock is known for having a sidewalk society and cafe culture; coffee shops and markets offer outdoor seating to the local residents, who are primarily professional families and Yale University graduate students.

Two stand-outs include Romeo and Cesare's Gourmet and East Rock Coffee, in the space formerly occupied by Lulu's European Coffee House.

Romeo Simeone, originally from Caserta, Italy, and daughter Francesca oversee every aspect of the market. The father and daughter team know the tastes and preferences of the neighbors and friends who make up their customer base. During quiet moments they can be found out front, under the vine-covered pergola, having an espresso with local patrons or taking on challengers in a game of foosball. Nearly everything is cooked in-house, including the meatballs that Julia Child, a repeat visitor, raved about.

The market was opened in 1988, following earlier import shops located in the Fair Haven neighborhood. He opened a restaurant and coffee shop on Orange Street, closer to downtown, called Cafe Romeo, which is frequently confused with the market, known colloquially as Romeo's.

Some locals still call East Rock Coffee by the previous business's name, Lulu's, out of habit or loyalty to a neighborhood institution. Lulu's was as beloved as its dynamic proprietor, Louise "Lulu" de Carrone, who gave the spot her name and good cheer. Lu banned laptops after noticing an increasing trend of people working and studying in silence at her little shop; counter-intuitively, this brought her more customers and high reviews. Customers still reminisce about the tight bonds they formed with neighbors.

Lu came into the cafe business as an outsider; she saw a "for rent" sign the same day she was dismissed from her position as a receptionist in 1991. Her focus on human interaction and comfort established a cafe culture where literary talents, world-class medical experts, carpenters, and short-term graduate students mingled together for lively conversations and fellowship. Lu retired in early 2015, but her spirit is present in East Rock Coffee, which still encourages face-to-face interactions and prohibits the use of laptops.

then bear right over a small bridge to continue onto Broadway, another quiet neighborhood street following the Mill River.

You pass a town line sign on your right and Broadway becomes Davis Road, before ending where it meets back with Ridge Road. Take a right onto a familiar street, and follow the road back over Dixwell, Skiff, and the Hartford Turnpike before taking a right onto Davis Street and then the first left onto Farnam Drive.

This is a good moment to decide if you'd like to extend the ride; you can either continue down Farnam and onto Orange to the end, or turn left onto the East Rock Park Road to the summit. If you do decide to do the summit, you add 2.5 miles, nearly 300 feet of climbing, and an incredible view over East Rock and the City of New Haven to your ride. The climbing is mostly steady, except one particularly challenging switchback.

MILES AND DIRECTIONS

- **0.0** Start on Orange Street
- **0.4** Left onto Farnum Drive
- **1.5** Right onto Davis Street, then a left onto Ridge Road.
- **2.2** Cross Hartford Turnpike
- **3.5** Cross Skiff Street
- **4.6** Cross Dixwell Avenue
- **5.6** Left to stay on Ridge Road
- **6.7** Left to stay on Ridge Road
- **7.3** Left to stay on Ridge Road
- **7.7** Right onto Mt. Carmel Avenue
- **8.8** Left to stay on Mt. Carmel Avenue
- **9.4** Left onto Hartford Turnpike
- **10.2** Left onto Mansion Road
- **12.3** Left onto Tuttle Hill Avenue
- **14.1** Left onto Whitney Avenue
- **14.6** Left onto Mt. Carmel Avenue
- **14.9** Right onto New Road
- **16.1** Left onto Ives Street
- **16.2** Continue on Broadway
- **16.9** Continue on Davis Road
- **17.1** Right onto Ridge Road
- **20.8** Right onto Davis Street
- **20.9** Left onto Farnum Drive
- **22.0** Left onto Orange Street
- **22.4** Finish ride on Orange Street

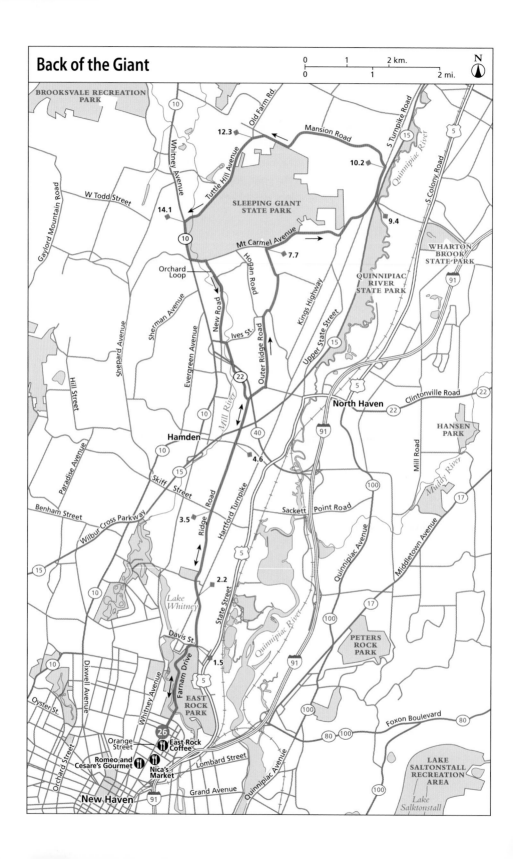

Back of the Giant

| 0 | 1 | 2 km. |
| 0 | 1 | 2 mi. |

N

BROOKSVALE RECREATION PARK

10

12.3

Old Farm Rd.

Mansion Road

S Turnpike Road

15

5

Whitney Avenue

Tuttle Hill Avenue

10.2

Quinnipiac River

S Colony Road

W Todd Street

14.1

SLEEPING GIANT STATE PARK

9.4

Gaylord Mountain Road

10

Mt Carmel Avenue

WHARTON BROOK STATE PARK

91

Orchard Loop

Hogan Road

7.7

QUINNIPIAC RIVER STATE PARK

New Road

Sherman Avenue

Evergreen Avenue

Ives St.

Outer Ridge Road

Kings Highway

Upper State Street

15

Shepard Avenue

Mill River

22

Hill Street

10

40

91

North Haven

22

Clintonville Road

22

Hamden

10

HANSEN PARK

Paradise Avenue

15

Skiff Street

Ridge Road

Hartford Turnpike

4.6

100

Mill Road

Muddy River

17

Benham Street

Wilbur Cross Parkway

3.5

Sackett Point Road

Quinnipiac Avenue

Middletown Avenue

15

10

5

2.2

5

100

17

PETERS ROCK PARK

Lake Whitney

Quinnipiac River

100

91

Davis St.

Farnam Drive

1.5

State Street

Foxon Boulevard

80

Dixwell Avenue

Whitney Avenue

EAST ROCK PARK

10

80

100

LAKE SALTONSTALL RECREATION AREA

Oyster St.

Orchard Street

26

East Rock Coffee

Orange Street

Romeo and Cesare's Gourmet

Nica's Market

Lombard Street

Quinnipiac Avenue

100

New Haven

91

Grand Avenue

Lake Saltonstall

RIDE INFORMATION

Bike Shops
Cheshire Cycle and Repair: 3550 Whitney Ave., Hamden; (203) 891-5320; cheshirecycle.com
Devil's Gear Bike Shop: 137 Orange St., New Haven; (203) 773-9288; the devilsgear.com
College Street Cycles: 252 College St., New Haven; (203) 865-2724; college streetcycles.com

Local Events and Attractions
Sunday Lulu's Ride: Every Sunday at 10 am, local riders meet in front of Lulu's Coffee Shop for a group ride that goes as far as Guilford. Check with the Devil's Gear for latest information on this ride.
New Haven Century: Every year, Elm City Cycling, a local advocacy group, hosts a ride from 20 to 100 miles. Check the Resources section to find out more about the group and the event.
Rock to Rock: On Earth Day each year, Rock to Rock hosts a number of rides to benefit local environmental groups.

Restaurants
East Rock Coffee: 49 Cottage St., New Haven; (203) 785-9218; eastrock coffee.com
Archie Moore's: 188½ Willow St., New Haven; (203) 773-9870; archie moores.com
Romeo and Cesare's Gourmet: 771 Orange St., New Haven; (203) 776-1614; romeoandcesare.com

Restrooms
0.3 Miles: In College Woods Park, on the left
14.9 Miles: Ahead and to the left, in Sleeping Giant State Park

27

Branford Lakes and Stony Creek

Branford is a shoreline town a few miles east of New Haven, perhaps best known for being home to the Thimble Islands, an archipelago of more than one hundred small islands in Long Island Sound. Many of the islands have beautiful summer cottages owned by seasonal residents, accessible only by boat. This ride follows the water into Stony Creek, a cute waterfront community, and then loops back through the tranquil Branford Supply Ponds.

Start: Branford Town Green

Length: 15.3 miles

Riding time: 1 hour

Best bike: Road bike

Terrain and trail surface: Asphalt

Traffic and hazards: Watch the "door zone" around the Branford Green. Most of these roads are low-volume scenic roads used by neighborhood residents and sightseers.

Things to see: Thimble Islands, Stony Creek village, Branford Supply Pond

Fees: Branford offers free and hourly parking. Pay attention to local signs.

Getting there: Branford is easily accessible by car or mass transit. By train, exit the Shoreline East station left onto Kirkham Street. Turn right at the end of the road, onto Main Street, to the green. By car: From I-95N, take exit 54 for Cedar Street toward Branford. Turn right onto Cedar Street, then left onto Main Street. From I-95S, take a left onto Cedar Street from exit 54, and then a left onto Main Street.

GPS: 41.28105 / -72.81198

View of a Thimble Island.

THE RIDE

Start on the Branford Town Green, on Main Street, heading toward a left turn onto Kirkham Street.

Kirkham is a half-mile stretch of road, with a train track crossing, heading toward the shore. It intersects and continues onto Maple Street; make a sharp left-hand turn here, and follow Maple over a small causeway where it becomes Indian Neck Avenue in a quarter-mile.

Indian Neck Avenue ends in a half-mile, with the Indian Neck School on your right, where you turn right onto Scenic Route 146, known here as South Montowese Street. The rest of the ride will mostly follow Route 146, which changes names several times, with a few detours down side roads for additional views or stops.

South Montowese continues into the Indian Neck neighborhood, named for the waterway, and the name changes to Sybil Avenue. You can take a short detour here onto Linden Avenue, on the right, for some spectacular views of the water. Local regulations forbid building houses on the coastal side of Linden Avenue, leaving a scenic view from the road and from the tastefully designed water-facing homes in the neighborhood.

> ## The Thimble Islands
>
> The Thimble Islands are actually the tops of mountains and hills, moved by glaciers, which melted into Long Island Sound and left behind this stable island chain. They are known scientifically as "terminal moraines"; terminal refers to the end of the glacier's advancement, and moraine is the geological term for any accumulation of rock and solids deposited by glaciers. Other islands in New England were created by the same process, including Cape Cod, Martha's Vineyard, Nantucket, and Long Island.

Sybil Avenue continues forward, to the water, before the road turns left, continuing along Limewood Beach, with a view of populated Green Island. The name of CT 146 changes again here to Limewood Avenue, which the route follows for a half-mile before turning right, onto 9th Avenue, and then immediately left onto Seaview Avenue, at the 2.8-mile mark, to provide better views of Hotchkiss Cove.

Seaview Avenue continues along the cove for a quarter of a mile, ending with a left-hand turn onto 1st Avenue, which heads back to CT 146, where you turn right, in another quarter of a mile.

CT 146 is Elizabeth Street here, for the next third of a mile, until the neighborhood of Pine Orchard, where the route is again renamed as Pine Orchard Road. This is a somewhat exclusive neighborhood with beautiful homes on carefully manicured estates; you turn left to stay on CT 146, now named Blackstone Avenue, at the 3.8-mile mark, heading uphill.

The road passes Youngs Pond on the left and winds through the Pine Orchard Golf Course, an expansive rolling course with a natural feel aided by copses of marshland vegetation. After 0.6 mile, the route reaches a little intersection with a triangle of greenery in the middle; stay left and follow CT 146, now named Totoket Road, northward.

This short stretch of road continues through a suburban neighborhood to another spread-out intersection, in 0.6 mile, where the route turns right, climbing up some steeper grades. Stay right to continue on a hilly stretch of CT 146, named Stony Creek Road here, which travels through marshes and forests with some housing for the next mile and a half.

At the 6.4-mile mark, you reach a little intersection with commercial buildings on the right and a large cemetery across the street on the left. Turn right, off of CT 146, and onto Thimble Islands Road, for a quick descent into the seaside village.

Marsh views near the route at Branford Point.

Most of the views can be enjoyed by riding down to the marina where cruises are offered, and then making a U-turn to ride back out of the village, climbing the road back up to CT 146. Cross here onto Leetes Island Road, which heads uphill and into a denser, more populated commercial district near the highway exit and entrance ramps.

The road passes over I-95 and is renamed School Ground Road, which continues through a heavy commercial zone with large parking lots for a half-mile, before ending at North Branford Road. Turn left here into a light industrial area similar to the previous road, and then a right in 0.4 mile onto Thompson Road.

Thompson Road heads back into scenic forested areas after 0.1 mile, when it becomes Flax Mill Road, which continues until it ends in a T-junction with Northford Road in roughly a half-mile. Turn left onto Northford Road, a quiet and lightly populated residential street, for the next mile, before the road is renamed as Mill Plain Road.

Near the 12.9-mile mark, just before a highway underpass, the route turns right onto Short Rocks Road. This turn can be easy to miss and isn't well marked; if you reach the highway, you've just overshot.

This is a quiet rural lane that leads to and through the Branford Supply Ponds. The road turns left, becoming Chestnut Street and crossing a narrow section of the pond on a rustic bridge. Chestnut Street heads away from the park for 0.6 mile, passing a small suburban housing development, and continuing under I-95, before intersecting with Route 1.

Very carefully turn left on this busy street, North Main Street, and ride 0.3 mile to the right-hand turn onto East Main Street, which passes the majority of downtown restaurants and stores before a left-hand turn onto Main Street at a signalized intersection, and the end of the ride on the Branford Town Green ahead.

MILES AND DIRECTIONS

0.0 Start at Branford Green on Main Street

0.3 Left onto Kirkham Street

0.7 Left onto Maple Street

0.9 Continue on Indian Neck Avenue

1.5 Right onto South Montowese Street

2.1 Continue on Sybil Avenue

2.3 Continue on Limewood Avenue

2.8 Right onto 9th Avenue, then immediate left onto Seaview Avenue.

3.1 Left onto 1st Avenue

3.3 Right onto Elizabeth Street

3.6 Continue on Pine Orchard Road

3.8 Left onto Blackstone Avenue

4.4 Continue on Totoket Road

5.0 Right onto Stony Creek Road

6.4 Left onto Thimble Islands Road

7.9 Continue on Leetes Island Road

9.7 Continue on School Ground Road

10.2 Left onto North Branford Road

10.6 Right onto Thompson Road

10.7 Continue on Flax Mill Road

11.3 Left onto Northford Road

12.2 Continue on Mill Plain Road

12.9 Right onto Short Rocks Road

13.5 Continue on Chestnut Street

14.1 Left onto North Main Street

14.4 Right onto East Main Street

15.0 Continue on Main Street

15.3 Finish ride on the Branford Green

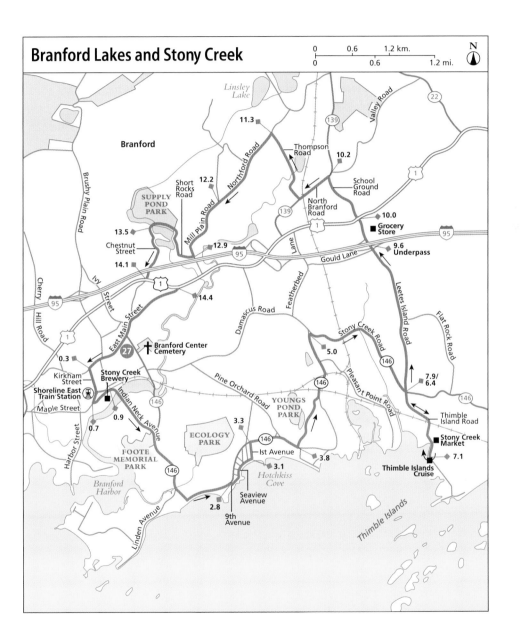

Branford Lakes and Stony Creek

0   0.6   1.2 km.

0   0.6   1.2 mi.

N

Linsley Lake

Branford

Valley Road

22

139

11.3

Thompson Road

10.2

Short Rocks Road

12.2

Northford Road

School Ground Road

1

SUPPLY POND PARK

North Branford Road

139

10.0

Grocery Store

95

13.5

Chestnut Street

12.9

9.6 Underpass

95

Gould Lane

Brushy Plain Road

14.1

1

Ivy Street

Mill Plain Road

Featherbed Lane

Leetes Island Road

Flat Rock Road

Cherry Hill Road

95

1

14.4

Damascus Road

Stony Creek Road

146

7.9/ 6.4

East Main Street

Branford Center Cemetery

5.0

146

0.3

27

Kirkham Street

Stony Creek Brewery

Pine Orchard Road

146

Pleasant Point Road

146

Thimble Island Road

Shoreline East Train Station

Maple Street

Harbor Street

Indian Neck Avenue

146

YOUNGS POND PARK

Stony Creek Market

7.1

0.7

0.9

3.3

ECOLOGY PARK

146

Thimble Islands Cruise

FOOTE MEMORIAL PARK

1st Avenue

3.8

146

Branford Harbor

3.1

Hotchkiss Cove

Linden Avenue

2.8

Seaview Avenue

9th Avenue

Thimble Islands

RIDE INFORMATION

Bike Shops
Zane's Cycles: 330 E Main St., Branford; (203) 488-3244; zanes.com
Action Sports: 324 W Main St., Branford; (203) 481-5511; actionsportsct.com

Local Events and Attractions
Stony Creek Brewery: Located near downtown Branford, this hip brewery offers scenic water views with a wide assortment of beers.
DuVig Brewing Company: This brewery offers easy-drinking beers in a relaxed tap room on the east side of Branford.
Thimble Islands Brewery: This brewery, located north of Stony Creek on the east side, serves ale and stout-style beers in a large, modern tap room.
Thimble Islands Cruise: Take a scenic tour of the islands, departing from Stony Creek.
Stony Creek Puppet House: Historic Sicilian puppets continue a 50-year-old tradition for locals and visitors alike.

Restaurants
Whole G Cafe: 1008 Main St., Branford; (203) 208-0930; gcafebakery.com
G-Zen: 2 E Main St., Branford; (203) 208-0443; g-zen.com
Som Siam: 1209 Main St., Branford; (203) 208-4204; somsiam.com
Le Petit Café: 225 Montowese St., Branford; (203) 483-9791; lepetitcafe.net
Common Grounds: 1096 Main St., Branford; (203) 488-2326
Stony Creek Market: 178 Thimble Island Rd., Branford; (203) 488-0145

Restrooms
7.0 Miles: Bathrooms at Stony Creek Beach

New Haven to Lighthouse Point

Although best known for Yale University, New Haven was once an important harbor city during the Industrial Revolution. Eli Whitney, a former Yale student, developed the cotton gin and manufactured firearms in a local factory; the harbor, railroad, and short-lived canal made the city a shipping center for weapons, known as "The Arsenal of America" during the Civil War.

Start: Northwest corner of the New Haven Green

Length: 13.6 miles

Riding time: 1 hour

Best bike: Road bike or hybrid

Terrain and trail surface: Asphalt, park roads, concrete boardwalk

Traffic and hazards: Downtown New Haven can be busy and hectic. Watch the "door zone" on Chapel Street. The bridge on Route 1 can be fast, and the railroad tracks at the end are dangerous. Use caution crossing them and dismount if needed.

Things to see: Several parks, harbor views, the Quinnipiac River, and many historic sites

Fees: Varies. There are a number of parking garages and lots nearby, as well as street parking with some restrictions. Pay careful attention to posted rules and signs.

Getting there: Downtown New Haven can be reached by mass transit or car. From Union Station, convenient signs lead to the green and downtown New Haven. Connecticut buses also have bike racks and regular service on a number of lines.

By car: From I-95N, take exit 47 for CT 34 West toward New Haven/Downtown, and then follow the Oak Street Connector toward North

Frontage/MLK Boulevard, and finally make a right onto Church Street. From I-95S, take exit 34, and then follow the steps above.

From I-91S take exit 3, for Trumbull Street, and then turn left onto Orange Street. Orange Street reaches Chapel, where you turn right, and the green is one block up.

GPS: 41.30707 / -72.92516

THE RIDE

New Haven doesn't enjoy the same scenic reputation as neighboring shore-line towns, but the city has a number of park properties along the water and a historic district developed during the height of oyster fishing. This route visits several hidden gems, with the centerpiece being Lighthouse Point Park. Other highlights include a ride along the Quinnipiac River, historic forts, and town parks and greens.

This route begins on the northwest corner of the upper New Haven Green, on Chapel Street, by the Pierre Lallement plaque.

Turn left onto Chapel Street for roughly a half-mile, taking a right onto Olive Street at a signalized intersection. The route skips Wooster Square at the start, but passes through it on the return leg.

The route turns left one block ahead, onto Wooster Street, passing by famous pizzerias, on a busy, pedestrian-filled street. The road ends in about a quarter-mile, where you turn right onto Franklin Street, a small side street, then left onto Chestnut Street.

From Chestnut, turn left again onto Route 1, Water Street. Follow the bridge over the harbor, and bear right onto Waterfront Street, taking extra caution with the curved railroad tracks.

After 0.3 mile through factories and warehouses, turn left onto Alabama Street, and then right onto Connecticut Avenue, which ends at the back entrance to East Shore Park, at the 2.8-mile mark.

Usually the gates are open just enough for bicycle entry, but if not, you need to dismount and lift your bike over the short automobile barriers. Once inside, keep right and follow the park road, for a leisurely 0.75-mile ride to the main park entrance at Woodward Avenue.

Turn right onto Woodward Avenue and follow the road out along the water. You see signs for Fort Hale and Black Rock Fort on your right. Just past the fort entrance, the road curves up and to the left with a short but steep climb, and then ends at Townsend Avenue, a major thoroughfare.

View of Black Rock Fort.

Turn right onto Townsend Avenue and ride along the generous shoulder through a quick descent, with a beautiful view of the Sound on your right, over a small park. The route goes through a residential neighborhood with small waterfront homes, and then turns right onto Morris Cove Road.

This quiet connecting street skips the larger intersection ahead. Follow it for 0.1 mile before a hard left turn, and then a right just ahead onto Lighthouse Road.

The road climbs slightly uphill here for a half-mile, before reaching the park. Take a left around the island in the middle of the road, and then a right onto the park road, and follow that straight past the attendant booths. The road ends at the beach, with a paved walkway suitable for biking; take a right to follow this along the beach, past the food kiosks, to the carousel building, where you turn right to follow the park road out to where you entered.

When you've finished at the park, you exit back on Lighthouse Road to coast down to the signalized intersection with Townsend.

Turn left onto Townsend and follow that back to a left-hand turn onto Woodward Avenue, using St. Bernadette's church on your right as a landmark. This time, skip the park; proceed through two roundabouts, reaching the intersection with Main Street Annex and Route 1, and cross these roads on the highway overpass bridge.

Woodward Avenue curves to the right, where Townsend Avenue and Fairmont Avenue meet; cross the street onto Quinnipiac Avenue, a one-way road that runs downhill toward the river.

New Haven Green and Pierre Lallement

New Haven Green was the historic town center of New Haven. The 16-acre park is privately owned by a self-electing five-person group, the Committee of the Proprietors of Common and Undivided Lands at New Haven, who have been responsible for management and ownership of the land since 1683.

The Proprietors are charged with preserving the historic character and public access of the green, and to this end, have barred commerce, but allow musical performances, movie showings, theater productions, and other cultural and artistic events, open to all, and free of charge.

The green is where many public rides begin, and it has a historic claim in the development of the bicycle. Frenchman Pierre Lallement was inspired by the "dandy horse," an early wheeled device propelled by walking, to build the first true bicycle, with a transmission built out of cranks, pedals, and a front hub. He tried to market his idea to industrialists in Paris and ended up in America, where he sought a manufacturer to mass-produce the bicycle.

Some historians maintain that Lallement's ideas were stolen by Parisian industrialists and used by Ernest Michaux, who may have employed Lallement; others believe that Lallement himself copied ideas from Michaux. Lallement failed to find interest for his device in America and returned to Europe, where he learned that Michaux's invention had sparked a craze for bicycles across the continent. Lallement later would die in obscurity.

Despite the unclear history, Lallement does hold the first and only American patent for the bicycle, and a plaque on the northwest edge of the upper green commemorates his legacy.

The road turns sharply right and becomes a two-lane road, running along historic homes and landmarks. This road used to be particularly dangerous, but a traffic-calming process in New Haven in the mid-aughts brought down speeds and made the road safer; the small rotary you pass through is one of the many steps taken.

When the route reaches a signalized intersection with East Grand Avenue, it turns left over the historic bridge, and then left onto Chapel Street. The road passes the Quinnipiac River Park and curves right and uphill.

Ahead, turn left at the light, onto Ferry Street, and then right onto River Street, a low-volume road that bypasses the heavier traffic on narrow Chapel Street. This area is home to Fairhaven Furniture, a local handmade furniture company, and a number of depressingly unkempt industrial buildings that seem ready for a conversion to loft spaces and artist studios. The road ends at Criscuolo Park, where you turn right and then left back onto Chapel Street, which crosses the Mill River, and continues back up toward the New Haven Green.

After a former industrial zone, you ride under a highway overpass and into Wooster Square Park. The route continues up Chapel, through the intersection with Olive Street, finishing back up on the New Haven Green.

MILES AND DIRECTIONS

0.0   Left onto Chapel Street from the New Haven Green

0.4   Right onto Olive Street and then left onto Wooster Street

0.7   Right onto Franklin Street

0.8   Left onto Chestnut Street

0.9   Left onto Route 1 (Water Street)

1.4   Cross the Tomlinson Bridge

1.7   Right onto Waterfront Street

2.0   Left onto Alabama Street

2.2   Right onto Connecticut Avenue

2.8   Enter the park and turn right to follow the park road

3.5   Right onto Woodward Avenue

4.1   Right onto Townsend Avenue

4.8   Right onto Morris Cove Road

4.9   Left onto Bristol Place

5.0   Right onto Lighthouse Road

5.4   Left onto Park Avenue and stay left to follow the park road

5.8   Turn right at the beach to follow the park road

6.1   Turn right to follow park road around through the rest of the park

6.4   Turn left onto Park Avenue back to Lighthouse Road

7.2   Left onto Townsend Avenue

8.0   Left onto Woodward Avenue

9.6   Cross over Main Street Annex and Route 1

9.9   Cross Townsend Avenue onto Quinnipiac Avenue

11.1   Left onto East Grand Avenue

11.2   Left onto Front Street to Chapel Street

11.7   Left onto Ferry Street

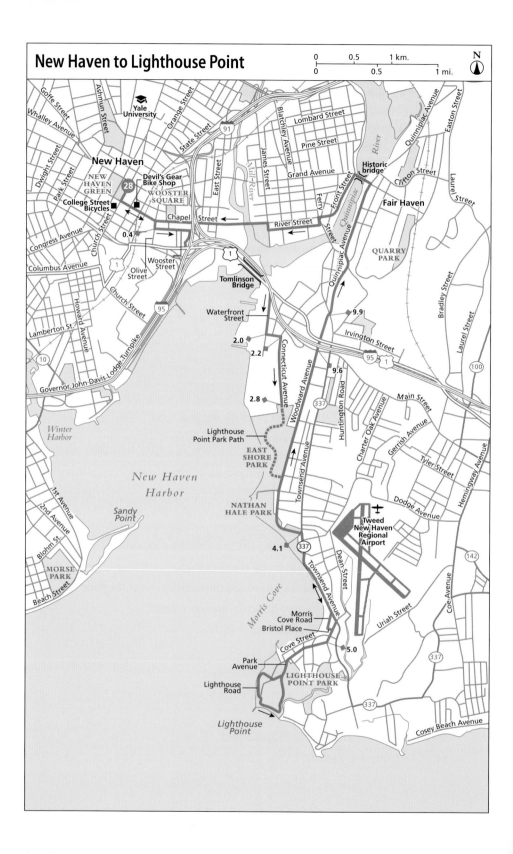

New Haven to Lighthouse Point

N

0   0.5   1 km.

0   0.5   1 mi.

Goffe Street
Whalley Avenue
Ashmun Street
Orange Street
Yale University
Lombard Street
Blatchley Avenue
Pine Street
Quinnipiac Avenue
Easton Street

Dwight Street
Park Street
State Street
East Street
James Street
Grand Avenue
Front Street
Historic bridge
Clifton Street
Laurel Street

New Haven
NEW HAVEN GREEN
Devil's Gear Bike Shop
WOOSTER SQUARE
Ferry Street
Quinnipiac
Fair Haven

College Street Bicycles
28
Church Street
Chapel   Street
River Street
QUARRY PARK

Congress Avenue
0.4
Quinnipiac Avenue
Bradley Street

Columbus Avenue
Olive Street
Wooster Street
9.9
Laurel Street

Church Street
Tomlinson Bridge
Irvington Street

Howard Avenue
95
Waterfront Street
95   1
100

Lamberton St.
2.0
2.2
Connecticut Avenue
9.6
Charter Oak Avenue
Main Street

10
Governor John Davis Lodge Turnpike
2.8
Woodward Avenue
337
Huntington Road
Gerrish Avenue
Tyler Street
Hemingway Avenue

Winter Harbor
Lighthouse Point Park Path
EAST SHORE PARK
Townsend Avenue

New Haven Harbor
Sandy Point
NATHAN HALE PARK
Dodge Avenue

1st Avenue
2nd Avenue
4.1
337
Tweed New Haven Regional Airport
142

Blohm St.
Dean Street
Uriah Street
Coe Avenue

MORSE PARK
Beach Street
Morris Cove
Townsend Avenue

Morris Cove Road
Bristol Place
5.0
337

Cove Street
Park Avenue
LIGHTHOUSE POINT PARK

Lighthouse Road
337
Cosey Beach Avenue

Lighthouse Point

11.8 Right onto River Street

12.2 Right onto James Street

12.3 Left onto Chapel Street

13.6 Ride arrives at finish on the New Haven Green

RIDE INFORMATION

Bike Shops
Devil's Gear Bike Shop: 137 Orange St., New Haven; (203) 773-9288; the devilsgear.com
College Street Cycles: 252 College St., New Haven; (203) 865-2724; college streetcycles.com

Events and Attractions
Lighthouse Point: Lighthouse Point Park is a beachfront park with a historic carousel and a lighthouse, both occasionally open to visitors. The carousel, open through the summer, is one of only a few remaining from the 1920s.
Cherry Blossom Festival: In season, you can ride around Wooster Square to see the cherry blossoms on Hughes Place, which have been tended by neighbors since they were planted in 1973. The trees usually bloom in late April and last for a few weeks. The neighborhood association holds an annual celebration, which may or may not occur at peak bloom, depending on luck and conditions.
Fort Hale and Black Rock Fort: These forts were used in the Civil War and Revolutionary War respectively. The two forts are part of the same free attraction, which has a small visitors station for donations, tours, and merchandise sales. Knowledgeable tour guides will explain the history of the region, from early settlements to the 1950s and urban renewal, all while strolling through an open-air exhibit, with up-close viewing of red-winged blackbirds and several species of swallows.

Restaurants
Sally's Apizza: 237 Wooster St., New Haven; (203) 624-5271; sallysapizza.com
Frank Pepe Pizzeria: 157 Wooster St., New Haven; (203) 865-5762; pepes pizzeria.com
Frank Pepe's The Spot: 163 Wooster St., New Haven; (203) 865-7602; pepes pizzeria.com
Fuel Coffee Shop: 208 Wooster St., New Haven

Restrooms
0.0 Miles: Port-a-johns on the Green
6.2 Miles: Restrooms at Lighthouse Point Park

New Haven Hills

Westville is a thriving and distinct neighborhood of New Haven, located on the northwest border with the suburban communities of Woodbridge and Orange. The village consists of mixed-use development, impressively maintained old homes, several parks, and a quaint, historic downtown. All of these factors give Westville a unique sense of place, distinct from the rest of New Haven.

Highlights include Edgewood Park, a 120+-acre park designed by Frederick Law Olmsted Jr., son of the more famous Olmsted Sr. who planned Central Park in NYC. The park includes waterways, bridges, and a rose garden, and hosts a weekend farmers' market for the neighborhood. The other major park, West Rock Ridge State Park, is partially located within the neighborhood, extending northwest to form the boundary between Hamden and Woodbridge. The park is named for the visually striking ridge, towering 627 feet over the city below.

Start: Corner of Edgewood Park

Length: 27.1 miles

Riding time: 2 hours

Best bike: Road bike

Terrain and trail surface: Asphalt

Traffic and hazards: The start can be hairy, in a built-up urban environment. The return leg on Whalley Avenue/ CT 63 is fast, but the most dangerous spot is closer to New Haven, in a car-centric commercial strip with heavy traffic.

Things to see: Brookvale Recreation Park, West Rock Ridge, the Farmington Canal Linear Trail, Edgewood Park, quaint downtown Westville

Fees: None

Getting there: Take exit 59 from CT 15 (Wilbur Cross Parkway) for CT 63/ New Haven/Woodbridge. Turn right onto CT 69 S/Whalley Avenue and follow Whalley Avenue to the park.

GPS: 41.32555 / -72.95805

THE RIDE

This ride starts at the corner of Edgewood Park, by the intersection of West Rock and Whalley Avenues. The route follows beautiful long roads past tranquil preserves into water company land, before entering a small valley followed by a 400-foot climb and a long, fast descent back into Westville. The climb, up Bethany Mountain Road, is referred to by area cyclists as Holiday Hill, named after the longtime resort at the top.

Carefully exit the park, onto Whalley Avenue, bearing right on the fork to stay on Whalley. This major intersection in a thriving commercial district is the most hectic spot on the ride; pay attention to traffic and follow traffic signs and signals.

After a short stretch, curbside parking ends, leaving a comfortable shoulder to ride in on this frequently backed up road. Continue up the hill past a library on the left, and turn right at the next major intersection, onto Emerson Road.

This one block street affords excellent views of the West Rock Ridge high above. At the end, turn left onto Valley Street, a quiet neighborhood street bordered by sidewalks and multi-family homes.

In under a mile, Valley Street ends in a T-junction with Pond Lily Avenue. Turn left, and ride past a motel chain on the right and highway ramps, until the road ends at the Litchfield Turnpike.

Turn right to head north through a sometimes busy section with a narrow shoulder. The road becomes safer just ahead where it narrows to one lane with a comfortable shoulder.

After riding past some single-family homes and through an intersection, development spreads out, with natural scenery making a reappearance in a more suburban neighborhood. Finally, near the 3-mile mark, the houses disappear entirely, and the route passes town open space and some scenic farmlands, followed by views of Lake Dawson on the right.

After passing the lake, the road gets steeper, and you bear right onto Downs Road after a short stretch of climbing.

View of Lake Watrous from the causeway on Downs Road.

Downs Road is one of the most scenic roads in the county, passing a waterfall on the right and then crossing Lake Watrous on a causeway with excellent views. The route continues along this narrow, low-volume road, up a short, steep hill, until reaching a stop sign and a cheerful red barn on the left.

Turn right onto Carmel Road, just past the 7-mile mark, along patched, sometimes cracked asphalt. Carmel Road ends in a T-junction with Brooks Road; turn left onto Brooks, for another quiet, sometimes curvy, wooded road.

Brooks becomes West Woods Road in 0.3 mile, continuing along much the same. In a half-mile, at a stop sign, West Woods Road turns right; continue straight onto Gaylord Mountain Road, up a curving, sometimes steep climb past low stone walls and scenic woods.

At a stop sign around the 9.1-mile mark, turn right onto West Todd Street, a quiet neighborhood road. Follow the road to the intersection with Still Hill Road, at the 10-mile mark, before the West Woods School.

Still Hill Road continues for a mostly flat half-mile, until turning sharply right, and heading downhill into a forested valley. The sometimes choppy road parallels the Farmington Canal Linear Trail until ending in a T-junction at Brooksvale Avenue.

Turn left onto Brooksvale, another sometimes choppy, low-volume back road, riding past modest homes separated by greenways and stone walls. Note Brooksvale Recreation Park, on the left, a historic farm operated as a town park by Hamden. Visitors can experience a variety of animals up close, including miniature horses, pygmy goats, sheep, chickens, and bunnies. The park offers educational programs in addition to a petting zoo and hiking.

At the end of Brooksvale Avenue, turn left onto Mount Sanford Road, to continue on another stretch of flat road through a rural neighborhood, for a little over a half-mile. Carefully turn left when the road ends onto South Brooksvale Road; this road can be a little busy and oncoming traffic does not stop.

At the sign for CT 42, turn left onto Bethany Mountain Road (CT 42), for the hardest and longest climb of the ride, as the road twists and curves on a mile-long 400-foot ascension. Continue following the main road to the top, then cross the signalized intersection with CT 69, staying on CT 42.

CT 42 continues for roughly a mile, reaching the next intersection with Cheshire Road (CT 63) at the 17-mile mark. Turn left with the light for a short, steep climb, before a nearly 9-mile section primarily heading downhill.

This is a busy thoroughfare but mostly feels safe, with a comfortable shoulder and expansive forests to either side, passing through the rural communities of Bethany and Woodbridge. Be mindful of cars behind you, particularly as you approach wide right turns, and remain alert for road hazards, as the length and grade of the descent will make for a fast ride.

As the road approaches Westville, near the 26-mile mark, the streetscape becomes increasingly built up, with big box stores, car dealerships, and popular food chains on either side. Use caution in this area, as it's the longest stretch of busy, car-centric development.

Not all of the businesses here are chains, however; local favorite New England Brewing Company operates a tasting room in their facility, on the left, just before traveling under the CT 15 (Wilbur Cross Parkway) highway overpass.

After the highway overpass and the big box stores, turn right onto Dayton Street, at an intersection next to a large gas station. This tiny neighborhood ends in one block, with Fountain Street, where the route turns left, reaching Whitney Avenue and Edgewood Park in a half-mile to end the ride.

There are a number of food options in Westville, from taverns and pubs to small coffee shops. Manjares is a local favorite, started by a proprietor who learned the craft at local institution Lulu's, across town in the East Rock neighborhood. Manjares has a patio, drip coffee and espresso, and baked goods.

A newer arrival, the Coffee Pedaler, is a satellite outlet from the popular East Rock shop of the same name. The name is a holdover from the first incarnation of the business, a bike-driven cart that the owner used to sell specialty coffee at live events.

MILES AND DIRECTIONS

0.0	Start at Edgewood Park on Whalley Avenue
0.4	Right onto Emerson Street
0.5	Left onto Valley Street
1.4	Left onto Pond Lily Avenue
1.6	Right onto Whalley Avenue/Litchfield Turnpike
4.8	Right onto Downs Road
7.2	Right onto Carmel Road
7.5	Left onto Brooks Road
7.9	Continue on West Woods Road
8.4	Continue on Gaylord Mountain Road
9.2	Right onto West Todd Street
9.9	Left onto Still Hill Road
11.2	Left onto Brooksvale Avenue
12.5	Left onto Mount Sanford Road
13.0	Left onto South Brooksvale Road
13.7	Left onto Bethany Mountain Road
14.8	Continue on Mountain Road
15.2	Continue on Cheshire Road
17.1	Left onto Amity Road
26.5	Right onto Dayton Street
26.6	Left onto Fountain Street
27.1	Continue on Whalley Avenue to finish

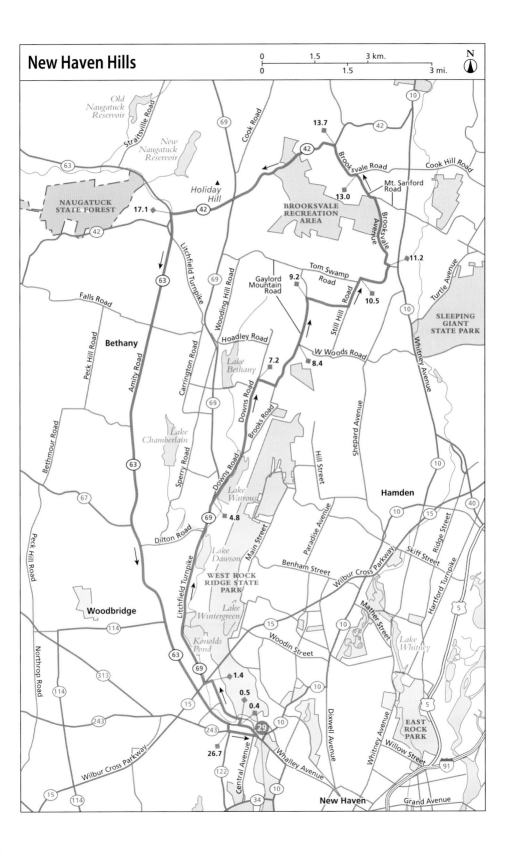

New Haven Hills

0   1.5   3 km.
0   1.5   3 mi.

N

Old Naugatuck Reservoir

New Naugatuck Reservoir

Straitsville Road

Cook Road

69

13.7

42

Brooksvale Road

Cook Hill Road

63

Holiday Hill

42

17.1

NAUGATUCK STATE FOREST

42

42

BROOKSVALE RECREATION AREA

Mt. Sanford Road

13.0

Brooksvale Avenue

11.2

Turtle Avenue

63

Litchfield Turnpike

Wooding Hill Road

69

Gaylord Mountain Road

Tom Swamp Road

9.2

Still Hill Road

10.5

10

SLEEPING GIANT STATE PARK

Falls Road

Peck Hill Road

Amity Road

Bethany

Carrington Road

Hoadley Road

Lake Bethany

7.2

8.4

W Woods Road

Shepard Avenue

Whitney Avenue

Bethmour Road

Lake Chamberlain

Sperry Road

69

Downs Road

Brooks Road

Hill Street

Hamden

67

63

Lake Watrous

Paradise Avenue

10

15

40

Dilton Road

69

4.8

Main Street

Benham Street

Wilbur Cross Parkway

Skiff Street

Ridge Street

Hartford Turnpike

5

Woodbridge

Litchfield Turnpike

Lake Dawson

WEST ROCK RIDGE STATE PARK

Lake Wintergreen

15

Woodin Street

10

Mather Street

Lake Whitney

114

Konolds Pond

1.4

0.5

0.4

10

Northrop Road

313

63

69

29

10

EAST ROCK PARK

5

114

15

243

26.7

122

243

Central Avenue

Whalley Avenue

Dixwell Avenue

Whitney Avenue

Willow Street

91

Wilbur Cross Parkway

15

114

34

10

New Haven

Grand Avenue

RIDE INFORMATION

Bike Shops
Devil's Gear Bike Shop: 137 Orange St., New Haven; (203) 773-9288; thedevils gear.com

College Street Cycles: 252 College St., New Haven; (203) 865-2724; college streetcycles.com

Local Events and Attractions
Edgewood Farmers' Market: CitySeed, a local nonprofit, hosts a Sunday market from May to December.

Restaurants
Manjares Bistro: 838 Whalley Ave. #3, New Haven; (203) 389-4489; manjares finepastries.com

The Coffee Pedaler: 911 Whalley Ave., New Haven

Stone Hearth: 838 Whalley Ave., New Haven; (203) 691-1456; stoneheart hnh.com

Deja Brew: 763 Edgewood Ave., New Haven; (203) 389-1518; dejabrewcafe.net

Restrooms
0.0 Miles: Edgewood Park

30

Rockland Preserve State Park

One of the best mountain bike projects in New England can be found in the Rockland Preserve in Madison, Connecticut. This 649-acre property, bordered to the west by Durham and to the south by Guilford, was established around Coan Pond, the centerpiece of the preserve. The marshy pond has dark, rich soil and a diversity of wildlife, including families of beavers. In addition to wildlife, rare wildflowers and vegetation are abundant: lady's slipper orchids, asters, several berry species, laurel, and massive oak trees all grow here.

Start: CT 79 parking lot in Durham

Length: 7.1 miles

Riding time: 1.5 hours

Best bike: Mountain bike

Terrain and trail surface: Singletrack, gravel, dirt, and doubletrack

Traffic and hazards: There is no traffic. Bring a cell phone, water, and snacks, in case of emergency or if you spend longer than planned. It is important to follow the direction trails go in, and stay out when wet. Don't braid the trails by riding around obstacles; if something is beyond your skill level, dismount and carry the bike. Avoid brushing leaves off the trail in fall. Current conditions and advisories are detailed on a Facebook page established by the trailmakers at https://facebook.com/MadisonTrailmakers/.

Things to see: Coan Park is the visual centerpiece, but also look for wildlife, wildflowers, and other attractive natural sights.

Fees: None

THE RIDE

These routes follow miles of tracks through Rockland Preserve, which only recently gained legitimate mountain bike trails. Town leaders felt the property was under-utilized and entertained plans to develop it into a golf course. The plans fell through when they discovered just how difficult construction would prove. The town continued trying to find uses for nearly 450 acres of land, until 2011, when teacher Jason Englehardt proposed constructing singletrack mountain bike trails.

Englehardt led a student cycling club that had been looking for places to ride. His proposal would solve three problems at once: increasing use, preserving the ecology, and giving his students a perfect mountain biking venue. It took a year for approval and another year for Englehardt and a small group of volunteers to build the red trail, a small lollipop to the west of Coan Pond.

Trail creation sped up dramatically when Jon Petersen, a well-known Connecticut cyclist, joined the work. Petersen plans trails all over the state and has a big network of friends and fellow-enthusiasts who volunteer with him. The two work as a team now, with Englehardt handling official business and approvals, and Petersen planning and implementing routes. The preserve now has dozens of trails, beautifully marked, and offers absolute beginner to double black diamond expert routes.

This ride covers one route, the Rockland Preserve Tour, with some of the connectors and sections called out separately. Starting in the parking lot, follow the green sign for the East loop on the left.

The route dips to the left and loops back up, turning right onto the Glades Trail, which heads uphill, before turning right briefly onto the orange trail and then right again, then take the immediate left, onto the Waterfall Connector. This short connector trail heads over a bridge to the summit station, providing an information kiosk and a good place to take a break.

Bear right to the Summit Area trails, skipping the quick right turn onto Mary's Ghost, and continue to the start of Thunderdome, a 2-mile ascent to the summit over a variety of challenges including log bridges, drops, and pits and rock formations to jump over. This long, curvy section of trail eventually

The entire trail is well-marked with these large signs.

ends, back onto the regular Preserve Tour loop, in a section with berms and jumps. Follow the route south, curving left and back north, to the Darkside.

Darkside is just over a mile and a half of intermediate challenges and features, breaking up a long gradual climb, headed west and away from the rest of the route. Darkside ends in a winding section called Bambi, which loops around back to the east, and meets the orange trail. This is a fast downhill section, mostly straight, which intersects near the Glades from earlier. Break left with blue arrows, crossing trail you rode earlier, and onto the Zipline, another fast section of downhill riding.

The Zipline crosses a stream before a section called Moebius Rip, a quick section of snaking turns, followed by one more real descent and a swampy area with a bridge.

After the bridge, take a quick left, and the ride ends a short distance ahead, back in the parking lot.

MILES AND DIRECTIONS

0.0 Start on the East Loop from the route 79 parking area and turn left onto Stinger

0.5 Cross the orange Rockland Trail

0.6 Cross the orange Rockland Trail again and continue onto Glades, then turn right onto Orange

Start of the trail around Rocklands Preserve.

0.8 Turn right onto and then right at the intersection onto doubletrack

0.9 Continue left on Waterfall Connector, following signs for the summit

1.2 Bear right and then past the Mary's Ghost trail (Optional: expert level short trail detour that exits ahead at Thunderdome)

1.6 Exit onto the Thunderdome trail

3.8 Turn right onto the Darkside trail

5.2 Exit Darkside onto orange-blazed Rockland trail

5.4 Cross Glades onto East Loop ("Zipline")

5.8 Hard right to follow East Loop around

6.1 Cross Rockland Trail onto Moebius Rip

6.7 Exit Moebius Rip on a straight section of the East Loop

7.1 Finish at route 79 parking area

RIDE INFORMATION

Bike Shops
Pedal Power Bicycle Shop: 359 Main St., Middletown; (860) 347-3776; pedal powerct.com

Cheshire Cycle and Repair: 3550 Whitney Ave., Hamden; (203) 891-5320; cheshirecycle.com

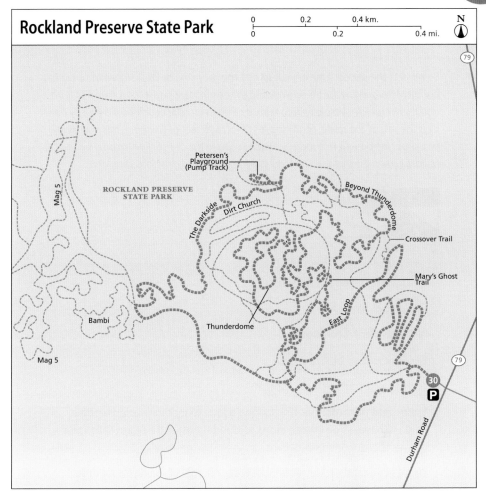

Rockland Preserve State Park

0   0.2   0.4 km.
0   0.2   0.4 mi.

N

North Haven Bike: 510 Washington Ave., North Haven; (203) 239-7789; northhavenbike.com

Restaurants
Perk On Main: 6 Main St., Durham; (860) 349-5335; perkonmain.com
Lino's Market: 472 Main St., Durham; (860) 349-1717; linosmarket.com
Cozy Corner Restaurant and Pizza: 5 New Haven Rd., Durham; (860) 349-2161; cozycornerdurham.com

Summer is the perfect time of year to ride the shoreline of West Haven into neighboring Milford. Enjoy the boardwalk and the ocean view, pause for coffee in Milford, and then return to West Haven to relax by the ocean. The beachfront is mostly flat, as is the rest of the route. Featuring less than 500 feet of climbing, this ride would be a great introduction to road cycling. Excepting the one tricky turn on the road to Milford's town green, the route follows cycle paths and generous shoulders.

Start: West Haven boardwalk

Length: 21.8 miles

Riding time: 1.5 to 2 hours

Best bike: Road bike or hybrid

Terrain and trail surface: Asphalt

Traffic and hazards: This ride follows a low- to medium-volume public road, with two large intersections, a roundabout, and a boardwalk open only to bicycles and pedestrians.

Things to see: West Haven beaches, the boardwalk, Savin Rock Point, Milford's charming downtown

Fees: There should be parking at Beach and 3rd Avenue; if not, continue down Beach Street to Captain Thomas Boulevard. Non-residents can only park in the beach lot out of season.

Getting there: West Haven is very accessible from I-95, the Amtrak train station, or Connecticut buses. From the train station on CT 162, turn left onto Main Street, and after 1 mile, turn right onto 1st Avenue to Beach Street. From I-95S, take exit 42. Turn right onto Saw Mill Road, then left onto Main Street, and follow the directions above. From I-95N, take exit 43, and turn right onto Campbell Avenue, then left onto Richards Avenue. Turn right onto 1st Avenue to Beach Street.

GPS: 41.26462 / -72.93178

THE RIDE

This ride follows the boardwalk of West Haven before exiting on a low-volume road with a generous shoulder. After a roundabout, winding neighborhood streets lead onto Milford's scenic town green. The return trip consists of one-way shoreline streets, a park road, and the most beautiful stretches of road from the first half of the ride.

At the apex of the ride is Cafe Atlantique, on the Milford Green. The coffee shop is warm and cozy with an open kitchen area and an outdoor patio area in a tiny municipal park. The menu offers espresso drinks, crepes, baked goods, sandwiches, and traditional breakfast fare.

Riders seeking a longer trip may wish to add on the Milford Beaches and Downtown Loop, which intersects with this ride on River Street; after turning left onto River Street, simply follow the Milford route. This will add a little more than 6 miles, mostly flat, to your total ride.

The boardwalk starts as asphalt, rough in places, before a wood section, separated from the street by housing and restaurants. Public restrooms are located along the beach, and there are several seasonal restaurants serving shellfish and seafood.

You will be sharing the boardwalk with dog walkers, joggers, and other recreational users; make sure to adjust your speed, stay in the demarcated bicycle lane, and use audio cues to alert other users before passing.

The trail follows the beach for nearly 2 miles, before exiting on a two-lane road that quickly becomes Ocean Avenue, a low-volume road with a wide shoulder. After 3.5 miles of beach riding, you have reached the roundabout between Milford and West Haven, a perfect turning point if you're interested in a shorter, under-10-mile, loop. There are a few options for ice cream and food here as well.

The rest of the ride into Milford (7 miles) is a mix of narrower, higher-volume roads and back streets through neighborhoods. Milford is a sprawling town with a well-developed commercial strip and scenic natural attractions. This ride avoids the busy traffic of Route 1 in favor of shore and parks.

You start seeing nests of vibrant green monk parakeets, a South American parrot residents have reported seeing since the 1960s. Popular theories for their origin include mislaid shipping crates and released pets. The parrots nest on utility poles, and benefit from the heat of transformers during cold Connecticut winters.

After the roundabout, you ride for a mile before bearing left at the fork onto Kings Highway from New Haven Avenue. Use caution; the oncoming traffic does not have a stop sign, and automobile speeds are quicker here than at any other point on the route.

Savin Rock and Colonel George Kelsey

George Kelsey, civil war veteran and entrepreneur, moved to Savin Rock from Middletown, Connecticut, in the 1850s and patented belt buckles. He would later leverage his inventions to reorganize the American Buckle Company before purchasing a horse-drawn trolley business.

After his early success in business and transportation, Kelsey built a 1,500-foot pier at Savin Rock and started ferry service to New Haven. He built a 150-room luxury hotel for visitors, and encouraged other development around the hotel, leading to zoos, parks, and amusements.

Inspired by the 1893 World's Fair in Chicago, he replicated the famous "White City" exhibit, which drew regional tourists for three-quarters of a century. The hotels, amusement parks, and attractions suffered frequent fires, and a hurricane in 1938 destroyed the pier.

White City and the Savin Rock attractions survived until 1967 despite the natural disasters. The only business that remains from that era is Jimmies, a large family-owned seafood restaurant opened in 1925 by Jimmie Gagliardi as a modest hot dog stand.

Kings Highway is a residential road with a fast, curvy descent to the next right turn onto Mark Street, which continues onto Abigail Street for a short jog before exiting onto CT 736. CT 736 has a wide shoulder and low traffic volumes. Sadly, the beach view is mostly cut off by houses and neighborhoods that aren't accessible on the outbound trip.

Eventually, CT 736 narrows and enters a more built-up suburban neighborhood. At the 8-mile point you turn right on Odell Avenue and climb until you reach the end, where you turn left onto Welchs Point Road. Be careful turning; traffic from the left has no stop sign.

Welchs Point Road rises before a fast descent which turns into Gulf Road, and travels along some beautiful stretches of beach. There are restroom facilities and water, and marshland to your right, where you spot an osprey platform on your right, in Gulf Pond, around the 9-mile mark.

Gulf Street narrows again after the beach, and goes through a residential area, before you come to a high-volume intersection with New Haven Avenue.

Watch the lights, and when safe, turn left for the approach into the historic Milford Green. At the Green, the road becomes one-way; turn right to follow it, and you come around to a quaint New England town green, with shopping, food, and coffee shops.

After turning right to stay with the one-way, you turn left onto River Street. You can turn right to explore the rest of the green, or turn left and go back onto New Haven Avenue to finish the ride.

Cross back over the bridge, and take the first right past the Milford Library on Shipyard Lane. Stay to your right, following signage for Wilcox Park, a local hiking spot, and you come out on Harborside Drive after a pleasant ride through this scenic area.

The rest of the return trip is similar to the first half of the ride, but when possible, diverts onto quiet, one-way streets that follow the shoreline back to West Haven. Harborside Drive turns into Bedford Drive and terminates in a right back onto Gulf Street, or CT 736. After riding back over Gulf Pond, you turn right onto Deerfield Avenue to Field Street to Bayshore, a beach-front neighborhood, which exits back onto CT 736.

In a half-mile you reach the second neighborhood. Turn right onto Platt Street and follow the road until you get to Point Beach Drive, turning left when the road ends, and following the neighborhood streets back up to CT 736. All of these neighborhoods have beautiful views of Milford's beach, and have one-way streets with minimal traffic.

A short distance ahead, a right turn on Yale Avenue leads into a forested neighborhood, before turning right onto Ridgewood; Ridgewood loops around the neighborhood and ends at Morningside Drive, which turns left and follows the ocean for one of the most beautiful stretches of shoreline riding in the area before exiting back onto CT 736.

An almost immediate right turn onto South Street to Hillside Avenue is your fourth neighborhood, and it's another scenic road along the ocean, before returning to CT 736.

After a few miles, you take a quick side-trip down Abigail Street onto Mark Street to Kings Highway, and then right onto Beach Avenue, your last neighborhood road. Beach Avenue is a beautiful one-way street that follows the ocean for another mile, before returning to New Haven Avenue, just before the roundabout between Milford and West Haven, and leading back to the public beach where you began.

West Haven Shoreline

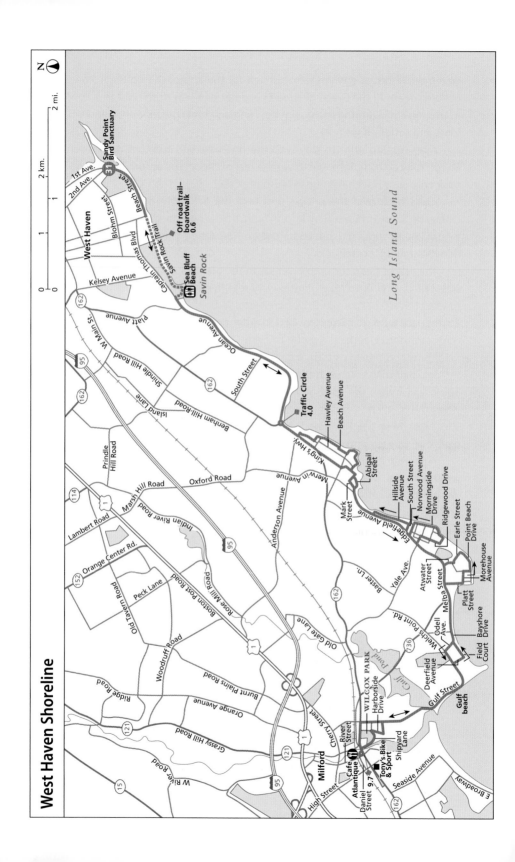

N

2 mi.
2 km.

Sandy Point Bird Sanctuary

1st Ave.
2nd Ave.

West Haven

Blohm Street
Beach Street

Off road trail—boardwalk 0.6

Savin Rock Trail

Captain Thomas Blvd

Kelsey Avenue

Sea Bluff Beach

Savin Rock

Platt Avenue

Ocean Avenue

W Main St.

Shingle Hill Road

South Street

Island Lane

Benham Hill Road

Traffic Circle 4.0

Hawley Avenue

Beach Avenue

Prindle Hill Road

Oxford Road

Anderson Avenue

Merwin Avenue

King's Hwy

Abigail Street

Hillside Avenue

South Street

Norwood Avenue

Morningside Drive

Marsh Hill Road

Lambert Road

Indian River Road

Mark Street

Edgefield Avenue

Ridgewood Drive

Earle Street

Point Beach Drive

Orange Center Rd.

Peck Lane

Rose Mill Road

Boston Post Road

Old Gate Lane

Baxter Ln.

Yale Ave.

Atwater Street

Melba Street

Morehouse Avenue

Old Tavern Road

Platt Street

Odell Ave.

Welch's Point Rd.

Field Court

Bayshore Drive

Woodruff Road

Burnt Plains Road

Deerfield Avenue

Gulf Street

Gulf beach

Ridge Road

Orange Avenue

WILCOX PARK

Gulf Pond

Grassy Hill Road

Cherry Street

River Street

Harborside Drive

Shipyard Lane

Seaside Avenue

Milford

Cafe Atlantique

Daniel Street 9.7

Tony's Bike & Sport

High Street

W River Road

E Broadway

Long Island Sound

0.0   Start on Beach Street

0.6   Carefully go onto the off-road boardwalk trail

1.9   Left onto Ocean Avenue

4.0   Enter traffic circle and take the second exit onto CT 162, New Haven Avenue

4.6   Left onto Kings Highway

5.1   Right onto Mark Street

5.3   Continue on Abigail Street to Merwin Avenue to Edgefield Avenue

7.5   Right onto Odell Avenue

7.7   Left onto Welchs Point Road

9.4   Left onto CT 162, New Haven Avenue

9.7   Right onto Daniel Street

9.8   Left onto River Street

9.9   Left onto New Haven Avenue then right onto Shipyard Lane

10.2   Right onto Harborside Drive

10.4   Left onto Bedford Avenue

10.5   Right onto Gulf Street

11.8   Right onto Deerfield Avenue

12.0   Left onto Field Court

12.1   Left onto Oakland Avenue then right onto Bayshore Drive

12.9   Right onto Platt Street

13.1   Continue on Morehouse Avenue

13.2   Right onto Elaine Road

13.3   Left onto Point Beach Drive

13.6   Left onto Earle Street

13.7   Right onto Atwater Street

13.8   Right onto Melba Street

14.2   Right onto Yale Avenue

14.3   Continue on Ridgewood Drive

14.6   Left onto Little Pond Road then left onto Morningside Drive

15.0   Continue on Norwood Avenue

15.2   Right onto Edgefield Avenue then right onto South Street

15.3 Left onto Hillside Avenue

15.7 Continue on Merwin Avenue

16.1 Right onto Abigail Street

16.3 Right onto Mark Street then left onto Kings Highway

16.4 Right onto Beach Avenue

16.7 Left onto Chapel Street

16.8 Right onto Beach Avenue

16.9 Right onto Clinton Street then left onto Beach Avenue

17.2 Left onto Bonsilene Street then right onto Hawley Avenue

17.5 Right onto CT 162, New Haven Avenue

17.7 Enter traffic circle, take the first exit for Ocean Avenue

19.9 Right onto off-road trail

21.0 Exit off-road trail carefully back onto Beach Street, with traffic

21.8 Finish on Beach Street

RIDE INFORMATION

Bike Shops
Chapman's Orange Bicycle: 284 Boston Post Rd., Orange; (203) 795-5701
Tony's Bike and Sports: 108 Broad St., Milford; (203) 878-5380; tonysbikes.com

Local Events and Attractions
Savin Rock Boardwalk: This long boardwalk features public parks and monuments, and is a popular place to walk, bike, or play bocce.
West Haven Beaches: These beaches provide miles of public shore access.

Restaurants
Cafe Atlantique: 33 River St., Milford; (203) 882-1602; cafeatlantiquedtm.com
Jimmies of Savin Rock: 5 Rock St., West Haven; (203) 934-3212

Restrooms
0.0 Miles: West Haven Beach
2.0 Miles: Sea Bluff Beach
8.5 Miles: Gulf Beach

Milford Beaches and Downtown Loop

Although technically a city of over 50,000, much of Milford feels like a quintes-sential New England coastal town. The remarkable town green is surrounded by locally owned taverns, coffee shops, and boutiques, and the municipal buildings are situated in front of a long, lovely pond used for weddings and picnics. Other highlights include a historic shipyard district on the harbor, an Audubon center, and quiet, sandy beaches.

Start: Downtown Milford, by the Metro-North station

Length: 6.4 miles

Riding time: 30 minutes

Best bike: Road bike or hybrid

Terrain and trail surface: Asphalt

Traffic and hazards: Most of these roads are pleasant, low-speed roads, but use caution crossing by the hospital on Seaside Avenue, and turning left from New Haven Avenue, after the bridge, onto Prospect Street.

Things to see: Silver Sands State Park, Charles Island, marshes, the Milford Harbor, historic buildings, charming bridges, and the upper and lower lagoon

Fees: Parking in the Milford train station is free on weekends, and there is ample on-street parking near the ride start. Make sure to check signs for time limits and other restrictions, even on the weekend in the station.

Getting there: Milford is conveniently located just off I-95 and has a Metro-North train station in downtown. By car, take exit 38 from I-95 to a left turn onto Route 1, Boston Post Road, and then turn right onto CT 121, to the intersection with New Haven Avenue, CT 162. Turn right onto CT 162 and take the first right over the bridge, onto Daniel Street, directly to the train station, crossing River Street into the parking lot.

GPS: 41.22295 / -73.05698

THE RIDE

This mostly flat ride of 6.4 miles follows small local streets down to Silver Sands State Park, cuts through the parking lot, and then follows the coastline back into downtown Milford for a tour of the river, ponds, and green spaces of the historic town.

From the train station, take a right onto River Street to start the route, cycling up a short hill toward the green. Turn right before the intersection, onto one-way South Broad Street, for a half-mile stretch along the scenic green. Continue on up the two-way road ahead where the green ends, onto a two-way road, turning left onto Osborn Street after two blocks.

Osborn Street crosses busy Bridgeport Avenue (CT 162) ahead, onto Seaside Avenue, past the Milford Hospital to the right. Seaside is a mellow road bordered by street trees, bushes, and modest single family homes.

In 0.4 mile, the route turns right, off of Seaside and onto Meadowside Road, another quiet neighborhood street. Note the possible view, depending on foliage and season, of Walker Pond on the right, followed by a slightly built-up intersection with the Robert Treat Parkway. Cross and continue on Meadowside into an even quieter section, turning left at the 1.8-mile mark, onto Silver Sands Park Way. This is a low-speed road leading into Silver Sands State Park, a beautiful collection of interior tidal wetlands and sand dunes, with a number of bird habitats and an attractive boardwalk for low-impact marsh exploration.

The road ends in 0.6 mile, where the mapped route continues left on Silver Sands Park Road, but nature-seekers can continue on the car-free gravel road past the gate ahead to Myrtle Beach, returning on the boardwalk to the silver beach area, just up the road on the mapped route.

Follow Silver Sands Park Road for nearly a quarter-mile until the road ends at the beach, turning left onto East Broadway. From here, or from the boardwalk to the right linking to Myrtle Beach, visitors can see Charles Island in the distance.

This 14-acre island has hosted indigenous people, a soon-to-be executed Captain Kidd, tourist attractions, and even a religious retreat operated by the Dominican order, in the 1930s. The island is now a state preserve, home to nesting seabirds, and is accessible with some risk by foot during low tide, when a sand bar is exposed for more than 2 hours. Local legend and folklore claims the island is haunted, and others believe that some of Captain Kidd's treasure is still buried here, although no evidence has ever been found. His principal treasure was recovered from Long Island, where he buried it before sailing to his arrest in Boston.

Downtown Milford.

East Broadway continues, back toward Milford, with a number of scenic beach views between cottages and seasonal homes on the right. A young Bill Clinton lived in one of these homes while attending Yale University in nearby New Haven. At the intersection with Seaside Avenue, at the 3.5-mile mark, turn right, and then left onto Trumbull Avenue for a third of a mile, with a beautiful scenic vista of the Sound along the right.

Turn left onto Rogers Avenue, following the water for the next half-mile, and turn left at the three-way intersection. Ahead is the Milford Yacht Marina, on a dead-end road built up with many houses; the route follows Rogers Avenue, on the left, past some commercial properties and then over the marshes on a low bridge affording views to either side.

After a half-mile, turn right onto Pond Street, a narrow, quiet little neighborhood road connecting to Green Street ahead. At the sharp bend, look ahead and to the right to see moored boats in the harbor, behind a lovely Victorian home.

When Pond Street ends, turn right onto Green Street, and then take the first right onto High Street, then a left onto Helwig. This is an area with a rich maritime tradition; note signs for historically important boatwrights and shipbuilders.

The Milford Historical Society owns three houses here, seasonally open for touring. Look for the Eells-Stow House, a renovated brown clapboard home believed to date back to 1700. The Clark-Stockade House, dating to the late 18th century, was moved from a location near the hospital; look for the saltbox-style home with a light-brown shingled exterior and symmetrically arranged windows. The other saltbox, the Bryan-Downs House, was also moved, after having been dismantled and stored. This home is believed to be a few years younger than the Stockade House; look for the same window symmetry with long, red boards.

Follow Helwig past condominiums and marinas, heading back into downtown Milford, and note the scenic bridge over the harbor to the right where the road becomes Factory Lane.

On the left, the route passes Archie Moore's Bar and Restaurant, a popular local tavern-style place with another location in New Haven. Archie Moore's is mostly known for their chicken wings and a healthy list of local craft beers on tap.

When Factory Lane reaches the green, turn right, onto New Haven Avenue (CT 162), and ride over the picturesque bridge leading to and from the downtown.

Carefully turn left onto Prospect Street, the first turn, past a view of the upper lagoon to the left, and through an overpass bridge ahead. Stay on Prospect Street, which becomes North Street ahead at the 5.5-mile mark, and passes a particularly beautiful section of the lower lagoon on the left.

Turn left onto Bridge Street, with more scenic views on the left of an area where couples hold weddings, and then left again onto West River Street, a quiet little neighborhood road that forks as it approaches a traditional white Congregational church. Stay right to follow the road to the intersection with West Main Street, and cross the road, continuing along West River Street past the Mayor's Office, the Superior Court, the Post Office, and several historic churches, all along the picturesque lagoon. West River Street becomes River Street, and the ride ends back at the start, in front of the train station and Cafe Atlantique on the left.

Food options in Milford are plentiful. Cafe Atlantique, at the start of the ride, is a local cyclist favorite. The shop serves crepes, baked goods, sandwiches, and other classic coffeehouse fare, along with an espresso bar and drip coffee. Other options include the aforementioned Archie Moore's, popular micro-brewery chain Southport Brewery and Restaurant, and a mix of local establishments and chain offerings.

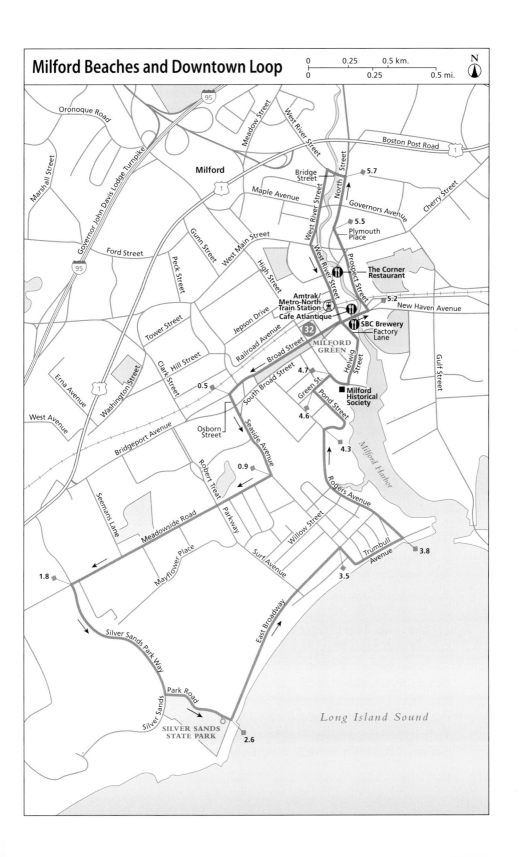

Milford Beaches and Downtown Loop

| 0 | 0.25 | 0.5 km. |
| 0 | 0.25 | 0.5 mi. |

N

Oronoque Road

95

Meadow Street

West River Street

Boston Post Road

1

Milford

Bridge Street

North Street

5.7

Maple Avenue

Governors Avenue

Cherry Street

West River Street

5.5

Plymouth Place

Ford Street

Gunn Street

West Main Street

High Street

Prospect Street

The Corner Restaurant

Governor John Davis Lodge Turnpike

Peck Street

West River Street

Amtrak/ Metro-North Train Station

5:2

New Haven Avenue

95

Tower Street

Jepson Drive

Cafe Atlantique

SBC Brewery

Factory Lane

Erna Avenue

1

Hill Street

Clark Street

Railroad Avenue

32

MILFORD GREEN

Helwig Street

Gulf Street

Washington Street

Broad Street

0.5

South Broad Street

4.7

Green St.

Pond Street

Milford Historical Society

West Avenue

Bridgeport Avenue

Osborn Street

Seaside Avenue

4.6

4.3

Milford Harbor

Seemans Lane

Robert Treat Parkway

0.9

Rogers Avenue

Meadowside Road

Willow Street

Mayflower Place

Surf Avenue

Trumbull Avenue

3.8

1.8

East Broadway

3.5

Silver Sands Park Way

Park Road

Silver Sands

SILVER SANDS STATE PARK

2.6

Long Island Sound

MILES AND DIRECTIONS

0.0 Start on River Street and turn right onto South Broad Street

0.5 Left onto Osborn Street

0.6 Continue on Seaside Avenue

0.9 Right onto Meadowside Road

1.8 Left onto Silver Sands Park Way

2.4 Left onto Silver Sands Park Road

2.6 Left onto East Broadway

3.5 Right onto Seaside Avenue

3.8 Left onto Rogers Avenue

4.3 Right onto Pond Street

4.6 Right onto Green Street

4.7 Right onto High Street

4.8 Left onto Helwig Street

5.0 Continue on Factory Lane then turn right onto New Haven Avenue

5.2 Left onto Prospect Street

5.5 Continue on North Street

5.7 Left onto Bridge Street

5.8 Left onto West River Street

6.1 Right onto West River Street

6.4 Finish ride on River Street

RIDE INFORMATION

Bike Shops
Tony's Bike and Sports: 108 Broad St., Milford; (203) 878-5380; tonysbikes.com

Local Events and Attractions
Silver Sands State Park: This park consists of nearly 300 acres of beach, dunes, salt marsh, and forest.

Connecticut Audubon Society Coastal Center at Milford Point: This Audubon center is located on a barrier beach, with indoor exhibits and outdoor bird habitats, visible from hiking trails.

Milford Historical Society: The Historical Society operates several properties for tours and exhibits: milfordhistoricalsociety.org.

Marsh views of nesting birds just west of the route, near the Audubon Center.

Restaurants
Cafe Atlantique: 33 River St., Milford; (203) 882-1602; cafeatlantiquedtm.com
Archie Moore's Bar and Restaurant: 15 Factory Ln., Milford; (203) 876-5088; archiemoores.com

Restrooms
2.5 Miles: Silver Sands State Park

New London County

The Pequot tribes once flourished throughout this region, using the Connecticut River and shore to conduct a widespread trade network. This area was heavily contested during the Pequot Wars in the early 17th century and later became a powerful trading post and naval center for early European settlers.

Most of the major towns are located on or near the water. The history of the region has perhaps been best preserved in Stonington and Mystic, two communities on the water that boast lighthouses, tall ships, and quaint downtowns made up of historic buildings nestled side-by-side.

This section focuses on Old Lyme, a historic arts community and seafaring village at the confluence of the Connecticut River and the Long Island Sound, and the village of Mystic and nearby Stonington, toured in one 30-mile loop.

Other areas of interest include Groton, home to a naval submarine base, and New London, location of the Coast Guard Academy. Locals flock to Rocky Neck State Park, on I-95 between Old Lyme and New London, for fishing, sunbathing, and a quiet getaway on a stretch of beautiful, rocky shore.

Weekend visitors may want to check out the Bee and Thistle and Old Lyme Inn, both located within walking distance of the many art museums and galleries near the town green.

To avoid busy I-95 on a weekend, check out the Shoreline East, a bike-friendly train line with service to Old Saybrook, New London, and many other shoreline towns, including New Haven.

33

Mystic-Stonington Loop

The harbor village of Mystic is one of the most popular tourist destinations in New England. Once an important trading post, Mystic has retained the character and charm of an 18th-century seaport, best showcased in two nationally recognized attractions. The Mystic Seaport delights visitors with maritime exhibits, including tall ships from the 19th century, while neighboring Mystic Aquarium provides a glimpse under the waves, at the region's rich aquatic life.

Even before the arrival of Dutch and then English settlers, the village was an established trading post, used by the far-flung Pequot tribes. According to the Mystic Historical Society, Mystic was a derivation of the Pequot name for the area, "missi-tuk," a word that described "a large river whose waters are driven into waves by tides or wind."

Start: Mystic Aquarium Parking Lot

Length: 29.4 miles

Riding time: 2 hours

Best bike: Road bike or hybrid

Terrain and trail surface: Asphalt

Traffic and hazards: Traffic is busy in downtown Mystic but, otherwise, most of these roads are quiet country lanes. Routes 1 and 184 are fast but are bordered by generous shoulders, making for comfortable riding.

Things to see: Mystic Aquarium and Seaport, downtown Mystic, North Stonington and Stonington, farmland in the north section, several historic cemeteries, and many, many scenic views of harbors, coves, and rivers

Fees: None. Parking is free at Mystic Aquarium.

Getting there: Mystic Aquarium is located just off of I-95. Take exit 90 for CT 27 toward Mystic Aquarium/Mystic Seaport, and follow signs to Frontage Road, and then the parking area.

GPS: 41.37232 / -71.95339

THE RIDE

Mystic is a village of some 5,000, comprising parts of neighboring Groton and Stonington. This ride starts in Mystic near the aquarium, winds through a historic district around the harbor and past the seaport, and follows the river north into a pastoral section of Stonington before returning in a loop through the Stonington Harbor and historic district. Most of the route is flat and easy, but a few miles in the middle, around North Stonington, can be fairly hilly.

Starting on Coogan Boulevard, behind the aquarium, follow a some-times-busy four-lane road past a quaint village pond and turn right when the road ends onto Jerry Browne Road.

This narrow road is bordered by a charming stone wall on either side and wooded views to the left. At the large, ramshackle old estate home on the left, turn right onto Pequotsepos Road, just past the half-mile mark.

This quiet road travels through a lovely area with infrequent houses, passing the Denison Homestead and Nature Center after a half-mile or so, and ending in a T-junction with Mistuxet Avenue, where the route turns right.

Mistuxet is a busier road with more housing and low traffic speeds. Follow the route to a slightly built-up section, at a four-way intersection with Greenmanville Avenue, and turn right for one block, taking the first left onto Holmes Street. This is the closest the ride comes to the Mystic Seaport, which is just a thousand feet up Greenmanville Street.

Holmes is a short side street, through a small commercial district, with views of a pond to the left and Mystic River to the right, ending after a third of a mile at East Main Street.

Turn right onto East Main Street, around an anchor sculpture on the right, and cross the small steel-deck drawbridge over a photogenic section of Mystic River. Turn right shortly after the ice cream shop, at the first turn, onto Gravel Street and out of the bustling downtown area.

Gravel Street is a quiet riverfront street bordered by docks and large single-family homes. Follow it up, curving left away from the water, and then turn right at the end of the road onto Pearl Street at the 3-mile mark.

Pearl Street connects back to the river, with views of the seaport on the opposing bank, and then curves left, up to an intersection with River Road and Grove Avenue.

River Road is the most beautiful section of the route so far, offering nearly 2 miles of unobstructed water views and a municipal open space while following the natural curves of the river. The road ends at a four-way intersection. Carefully cross CT 27 onto North Stonington Road and continue up a quiet neighborhood street past classic saltbox and wood shingle-style homes.

Mystic Seaport near the start of the route.

After a half-mile or so, the route continues left at a fork onto Lantern Hill Road. A short detour to the right is Clyde's Cider Mill, a steam-powered cider mill open seasonally. Visitors can purchase wine, hard cider, and jams, or view the mill in operation during demonstrations of the antique machines.

Continuing on the route, Lantern Hill Road crosses CT 184, followed by a tiny historic cemetery on the left. This winding country road travels past working farms and long fields, over nearly 2 miles, up to a serious climb and the hilly section of the route.

At the four-way stop after a weedy, overgrown field, turn right onto Wolf Neck Road. This quiet stretch heads uphill, starting steep and smoothing out over a 120-foot climb before leveling out and passing a scenic pond before the intersection with North Stonington Road.

Carefully turn left onto North Stonington Road, a sometimes fast main thoroughfare, and ride in the generous shoulder up a gradual climb bordered by low stone walls, tucked-away homes, and open farmland.

After a quick descent, follow a curve in the road to the right, around the St. Thomas More Church, into a more rural area where the road narrows, losing the shoulder, and becomes Mystic Road.

Mystic Road continues through a heavily forested area until reaching the major intersection in North Stonington. Carefully cross CT 2 onto Main Street, passing another picturesque cemetery, and follow the road for a half-mile into the North Stonington Village Historic District.

Turn right, over the lovely stone bridge, and continue on Main Street for a short stretch out of town. When Main Street turns left, stay to the right, onto Rocky Hollow Road.

This road continues for a mile and a half through another quiet neighborhood, ending at a large intersection with CT 184, the Providence–New London Turnpike. Carefully turn right into the shoulder of this busy road, and proceed for the next mile, until reaching Wheeler Road on the left.

When clear, turn left onto Wheeler Road, a quiet country road. Scenery includes a gorgeous panoramic view of nearly a mile of farmland and fields along the right, all part of the Pequot Plant Farm. After a tranquil forest, bear right to continue on Wheeler Road, through a more suburban section with a mix of single-family homes and woods, followed by the Pequot Golf Course property to either side.

The road ends in a T-junction with CT 234, where the route turns left, crossing I-95 on an elevated section of road. After the crossing, turn right onto Flanders Road, another quiet street with views of a historic cemetery. At the three-way intersection, turn left to continue on Flanders, into a suburban neighborhood with denser housing.

In 1 mile, the route crosses Route 1 onto North Water Street, where the road has a small shoulder. This road has a particularly scenic spot on a narrow causeway with cove views to either side, followed by a historic home on the left.

At a stop sign, turn left onto Trumbull Avenue, and then right onto Alpha Avenue just after the athletic field. Alpha Avenue crosses the railroad tracks below and ends in a T-junction with Water Street, where the route turns left past a historic green. The road ahead is bordered by charming local shops and restaurants in tightly packed historic buildings, ending on a point offering the Old Lighthouse Museum and panoramic views of Long Island Sound.

After seeing the sights, turn around, and ride back up the street to Cannon Square, where the route turns right and then left onto Main Street No. 1. Follow Main Street No. 1 back to the town green, primarily past historic homes, and turn left onto Broad Street at the end of the green. Take the next right, back onto Water Street, and then the right onto Alpha Avenue, backtracking via Trumbull Avenue and North Water Street to Route 1.

Turn left onto Route 1, locally named Stonington Road, and ride the wide shoulder on this fast, busy thoroughfare. Views include the picturesque marshy area and historic cemetery, immediately on the left, and water views to either side just before the route turns right onto Cove Road.

Cove Road travels through a quiet neighborhood with occasional water views on the right past houses and ends in a T-junction. Turn right and follow Mistuxet Avenue for less than a quarter of a mile, taking the next left onto Jerry Browne Road.

Turn left onto Coogan Boulevard after a mile on Jerry Browne Road, ending the ride back at the aquarium.

MILES AND DIRECTIONS

0.0 Start at Mystic Aquarium on Coogan Boulevard

0.3 Right onto Jerry Browne Road

0.6 Right onto Pequotsepos Road

1.6 Right onto Mistuxet Avenue

2.2 Right onto Greenmanville Avenue

2.3 Left onto Holmes Street

2.6 Right onto East Main Street

2.7 Continue on West Main Street then right onto Gravel Street

3.0 Right onto Pearl Street

3.3 Continue on Starr Street

3.3 Right onto River Road

5.6 Continue on North Stonington Road

6.2 Continue on Lantern Hill Road

8.2 Right onto Whitford Road

9.2 Left onto North Stonington Road

10.7 Continue on Mystic Road

13.1 Continue on Main Street

13.7 Right onto Main Street and continue on Rocky Hollow Road

15.2 Right onto Providence–New London Turnpike

16.3 Left onto Wheeler Road

19.4 Left onto Pequot Trail

19.6 Right onto Flanders Road

20.5 Left to continue on Flanders Road

21.5 Continue on North Water Street

22.2 Left onto Trumbull Avenue

22.4 Proceed onto Alpha Avenue

22.6 Left onto Water Street

23.5 Right onto Cannon Square, then immediate left onto Main Street

23.7 Continue on Main St. No. 1

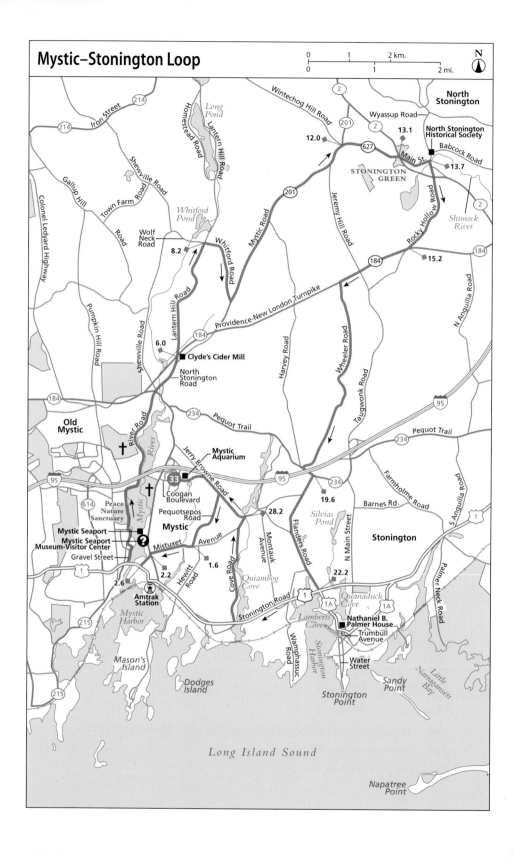

Mystic–Stonington Loop

N

23.9 Left onto Broad Street

24.0 Right onto Water Street/Alpha Avenue

24.2 Left onto Trumbull Avenue

24.4 Right onto North Water Street

25.1 Left onto Stonington Road

26.5 Right onto Cove Road

28.0 Right onto Mistuxet Avenue

28.2 Left onto Jerry Browne Road

29.1 Left onto Coogan Boulevard

29.4 Finish ride at parking lot

RIDE INFORMATION

Bike Shops
Mystic Cycle Centre: 25 Stonington Rd., Mystic; (860) 572-7433; mysticcycle centre.com

Local Events and Attractions
Mystic Seaport: This unique museum consists of a village, ships, and 17 acres of exhibits depicting coastal life in New England in the 19th century.
Mystic Aquarium: This is one of the most famous aquariums in the United States, with notable sea lion, beluga whale, and African penguin exhibits.
Denison Pequotsepos Nature Center and Museum: This nature center offers walks through an ecologically rich preserve and a nature museum.
Stonington's Old Lighthouse Museum: The Stonington Historical Society maintains this preserved lighthouse as a museum.

Restaurants
Engine Room: 14 Holmes St., Mystic; (860) 415-8117; engineroomct.com
The Pita Spot: 45 Williams Ave., Mystic; (860) 415-4656; thepitaspot.com
Oyster Club: 13 Water St., Mystic; (860) 415-9266; oysterclubct.com

Old Lyme: Beach Trip

Old Lyme is a quiet shoreline town with a rich arts heritage, stemming largely from the efforts of Florence Griswold, or "Miss Florence" as the locals call her, an enterprising early-20th-century resident who ran a boarding house for artists and supported the early American impressionism movement.

Start: Morning Glory Cafe parking lot

Length: 14.2 miles

Riding time: 1 hour

Best bike: Road bike

Terrain and trail surface: Asphalt

Traffic and hazards: Route 1 and the roads around it are all fairly high-volume, high-speed, so use caution and stick to the shoulder. If taking the detour to Rocky Neck, be aware that the highway exits right at the beach, and traffic can be a bit hectic there.

Things to see: Beaches, marshland, and art-related attractions in downtown Old Lyme

Fees: None

Getting there: From the west, take I-95 to exit 70 for US 1/CT 156. Turn left onto CT 156W, then immediately right onto US 1N. The parking lot will be on the left. From the east, take I-95 to exit 70 toward CT 156/Old Lyme. Turn left onto US 1, then right to stay on US 1. The parking lot is on the right.

GPS: 41.32375 / -72.33004

THE RIDE

This mostly flat ride starts in a dense part of Old Lyme, by the Morning Glory Cafe. If the parking lot is full, other parking is available at the commuter lot just down the street, off of I-95 exit 70, or at the Old Lyme Shopping Center, a nearby strip mall development. Three optional detours explore wetlands and beaches and, added together, all three detours could increase the ride by nearly 9 miles, for a 23-mile trip.

The route heads west, toward the Connecticut River, on a half-mile stretch of Route 1 past a grocery store and gas stations.

Turn left at the end onto Neck Road and ride under the I-95 overpass, using caution around the highway exit and entrance ramps. Neck Road becomes Shore Road just up ahead, and continues over the Lieutenant River. Road speeds are slightly fast here, but the road is fairly safe, with a wide shoulder and good visibility; the road gently curves left as the route heads toward the beaches.

When Shore Road crosses the Duck River, look to the right for unobstructed views across the Elizabeth B. Karter Watch Rock Preserve, which can

Beaches

Soundview Beach is a popular beach with paid parking and many rental cottages and a quiet residential neighborhood around it. A number of food options include Lenny's on the Beach, a fun bar with a tiki motif and an outdoor patio. The Sugar Shack offers grilled foods and smoothies. For something different, visit the Wäfflebar, a Belgian waffle spot offering a wide selection of savory and sweet waffles. If you're looking for iced desserts, family owned and operated Vecchitto's Italian Ice has been open since 1946.

White Sands is a quiet beach with a boardwalk, trails, and a gazebo for picnicking. Walkers can access Griswold Point Preserve via a trail from the beach. This is a small beach without the many commercial attractions of Soundview.

Rocky Neck is an aptly named stretch of gorgeous beachfront with rock outcroppings and protrusions; the park is more than 700 acres, with extensive walking trails to different natural attractions, including glacially formed caves and stone formations. The unique natural beauty was created by the movement of glaciers into Long Island Sound. The architecture dates back to Depression-era construction; a large timber-and-granite pavilion provides a shaded area to rest and enjoy a picnic.

View of the Elizabeth B. Karter Watch Preserve.

be accessed by turning right at the 2.1-mile mark onto Noyes Road and then right onto Frontage. The detour follows Frontage as it curves left, and then turns right onto Joel Road, which leads directly into the preserve. Riding to and from the parking lot would add just about a half-mile to this route.

Just up the road at the 2.5-mile mark is The Nature Conservancy Great Island Marshes. To detour to this lovely spot take a right onto Smith Neck Road, a narrow, winding country lane that passes stately mansions and classic stone walls for 0.6 mile. This detour would add 1.2 miles to your total route.

Continuing on the mapped route, cross the Black Hall River and make a right in another 0.1 mile onto Old Shore Road. This is a quieter side road through a residential neighborhood with seasonal cottages and rentals and has access to White Sands Beach, following the posted signs.

Old Shore Road is only a mile long before it reconnects to Shore Road. Turn right onto Shore Road, and after 1 mile, take a right onto Hartford Avenue, which leads to Soundview Beach. This is the most commercial of the beaches, with a number of food and entertainment options.

After visiting Soundview, make a U-turn and follow Hartford Avenue back to Shore Road and turn right. Shore Road starts to head more uphill here and after 1.8 miles the mapped route turns left onto Mile Creek Road. For a lengthy detour to visit Rocky Neck State Park, continue following Shore Road, bearing

Women and the Arts

The historical center of the local arts scene, the Florence Griswold Museum, is a restored 19th-century home that once housed the Lyme Art Colony. The property was owned by the aforementioned Miss Florence Griswold, an educator who founded and ran a school with her mother and two sisters. After the death of her mother and a sister, Griswold ran into financial difficulties and began renting rooms to boarders.

Prominent landscape artist Henry Ward Ranger arrived in Old Lyme after a stay in Europe and in 1899 became Griswold's tenant. Ranger invited his artist friends to stay, and they founded the Lyme Art Colony in 1900, inspired by the Barbizon School of France.

The colony is remembered as a crucial place in the development of the American impressionist movement because of the later arrival of Childe Hassam, who shifted the focus away from Tonalism. Ranger moved to Noank within a year and his later work bore traces of Hassam's influence.

The colony expanded to the Lyme Art Association in 1921 and thrived until the 1930s, managed by Griswold. Facing failing health, Griswold sold her home to a local judge in 1936, but he allowed her to stay on. She would die in comfort at her former home the next year. Residents purchased the home in 1941 through "The Florence Griswold Association" and opened the museum to celebrate the memory of their beloved "Miss Florence" and to remember her contributions to the arts. The Lyme Art Association is still open, offering a gallery for sales and viewing in addition to classes, workshops, and lectures.

Farther down the street, the Lyme Academy College of Fine Arts, a nationally accredited university, was also founded by a local woman, one Elisabeth Gordon Chandler. Chandler was a harpist and sculptor who remained active as an artist and professor of sculpture until her death at 93. The college features ongoing exhibits and student galleries across a spectrum of artistic disciplines.

right at a forthcoming fork in the road, then continue along Shore Road until reaching the park. The total mileage added will be 6.4, but the more daunting figure may be the elevation; there is a serious 100-foot climb with grades up to 10 percent right in the middle of the trip. After the climb, it's a fast descent to sea level, so the return trip is also challenging.

To combine this route with Old Lyme: Rogers Lake (Ride 35), follow the detour for Rocky Neck to the fork and bear left onto Fourmile River Road. This road passes under I-95 before ending at Route 1, a busy thoroughfare. Turn left onto Route 1 for a short stretch and then turn right onto Grassy Hill Road to join the Rogers Lake ride.

Back to the mapped route, follow Mile Creek Road, a quiet neighborhood street, which winds and curves through the town for 4.2 miles until ending at Shore Road. Turn right here and then right again in just under a half-mile onto McCurdy Road.

McCurdy Road passes the historic Duck River Cemetery just before curving right and becoming Lyme Street, a quiet street running right through the heart of the arts and cultural attractions. Follow Lyme Street under the highway overpass, turning left just before the Lyme Art Association and Florence Griswold Museum onto Route 1, finishing this trip.

MILES AND DIRECTIONS

- **0.0** Start at Morning Glory Cafe on Halls Road
- **0.5** Left onto Neck Road
- **0.7** Continue on Shore Road
- **2.1** OPTIONAL: Right onto Noyes Road to the Elizabeth B. Karter Watch Rock Preserve detour; Noyes Road to Frontage, right onto Joel Road, adding a total of 0.5 mile round-trip
- **2.5** OPTIONAL: Right onto Smith Neck Road to The Nature Conservancy Marshes, adding a total of 1.2 miles round-trip
- **3.4** Right onto Old Shore Road
- **4.4** Continue on Shore Road
- **5.4** Right onto Hartford Avenue to end, U-turn
- **6.0** Right onto Shore Road
- **7.8** OPTIONAL: Right onto CT 156 to Rocky Neck State Park, turn around and resume normal course, adding 6.4 miles round-trip
- **7.8** Left onto Mile Creek Road
- **12.0** Continue on Smith Neck Road then right onto Shore Road
- **12.4** Right onto McCurdy Road
- **13.3** Right onto Lyme Street
- **14.1** Left onto Halls Road to finish
- **14.2** Finish ride at Morning Glory Cafe

Old Lyme: Beach Trip

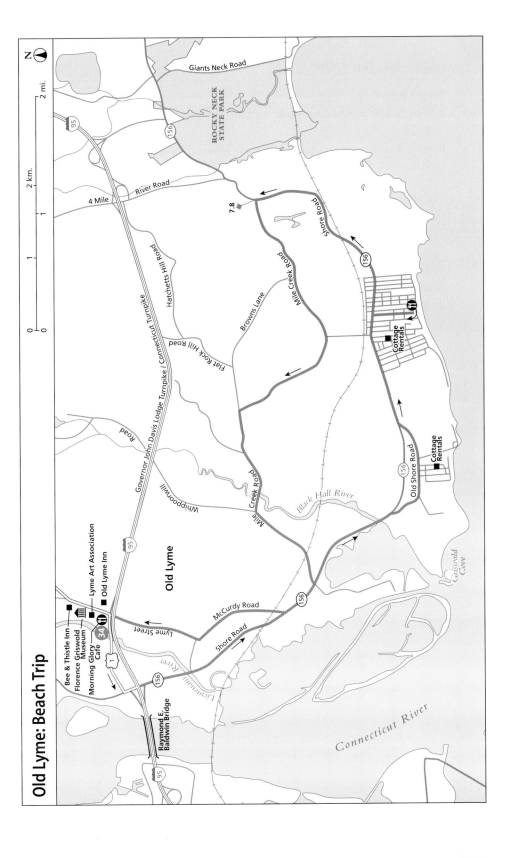

Giants Neck Road

ROCKY NECK STATE PARK

95

156

River Road

4 Mile

7.8

Shore Road

156

Hatchetts Hill Road

Browns Lane

Mile Creek Road

Flat Rock Hill Road

Cottage Rentals

Governor John Davis Lodge Turnpike / Connecticut Turnpike

Whippoorwill Road

Mile Creek Road

Black Hall River

156

Old Shore Road

Cottage Rentals

95

Old Lyme

Lyme Art Association

Old Lyme Inn

Bee & Thistle Inn

Florence Griswold Museum

Morning Glory Cafe

Lyme Street

McCurdy Road

Shore Road

156

1

Griswold Cove

Raymond E. Baldwin Bridge

95

Lieutenant River

Connecticut River

N

0   1   2 km.

0   1   2 mi.

RIDE INFORMATION

Bike Shops
Action Sports of Old Saybrook: 1385 Boston Post Rd., Old Saybrook; (860) 388-1291; actionsportsct.com
Niantic Bay Bicycles: 8 Methodist St. # 1, Niantic; (860) 691-0757; nianticbay bicycles.com

Local Events and Attractions
Florence Griswold Museum: An important landmark in the development of American impressionism
Lyme Art Association: A gallery and class space for artists
Lyme Academy College of Fine Arts: This college hosts student shows.
Studio 80 + Sculpture Grounds: More than 100 sculptures, set into a natural environment on four and a half acres of land, and an indoor exhibition space
Cooley Gallery: This nationally recognized exhibition and sales space shows a wide range of American art.

Restaurants
Morning Glory Cafe: 11 Halls Rd., Old Lyme; (860) 434-0480; morningglory cafeoldlyme.com
Old Lyme Ice Cream Shoppe and Cafe: 34 Lyme St., Old Lyme; (860) 434-6942; oldlymeicecreamshoppe.com
Vecchitto's Italian Ice: 80 Hartford Ave., Old Lyme; (860) 434-9231
Wäfflebar: 65 Hartford Ave., Old Lyme

Restrooms
5.6 Miles: Soundview Beach

Old Lyme: Rogers Lake

Old Lyme is best known as a quaint beach town with an historic arts scene. What is less well known is the impressive cycling pedigree of Old Lyme and the surrounding communities. This route follows the scenic roads that professional racers Tom Danielson and Benjamin Wolfe cut their teeth on. They also are popular group ride destinations for local cycling clubs. Serious hills, scenic ponds, and rural life, just a short distance from downtown Old Lyme and the interstate highway, can make any rider feel like a professional honing their craft.

Start: Morning Glory Cafe parking lot

Length: 17.4 miles

Riding time: 1 hour 30 minutes

Best bike: Road bike

Terrain and trail surface: Asphalt

Traffic and hazards: Use caution when turning onto Hamburg Road, a fast road with no stop for oncoming traffic. Route 1, Lyme Street, is a busy, built-up road, which may have heavy traffic visiting the commercial businesses along the route.

Things to see: Rogers Lake, ponds and a nature preserve, historic cemeteries, and rolling farmland

Fees: None

Getting there: From the west, take I-95 to exit 70 for US 1/CT 156. Turn left onto CT 156W, then immediately right onto US 1N. The parking lot will be on the left. From the east, take I-95 to exit 70 toward CT 156/Old Lyme. Turn left onto US 1, then right to stay on US 1. The parking lot is on the right.

GPS: 41.32375 / -72.33004

THE RIDE

This rolling and sometimes hilly ride starts by the Morning Glory Cafe. If the parking lot is full, other parking is available at the commuter lot just down the street, off of I-95 exit 70, or at the Old Lyme Shopping Center, a nearby strip mall development.

This ride has a mild start up to and past Rogers Lake, before a nearly 2-mile-long climb with an elevation gain of more than 300 feet, all on a beautiful, quiet back road through state forests. Sights include historic cemeteries and Foxglove Farm, a traditional horse farm with a working farrier and carriage rides.

After the climb, the ride visits an easier series of rolling hills, heading through the heart of Beckett Hill State Park Reserve. Through this area you pass farmland and multiple ponds, before one last climb near Ashlawn Farm Coffee and a fast, curvy descent back into Old Lyme.

The ride starts on the sprawling Route 1. There are several surface lots and busy intersections over the next 2.5 miles. Near the end of this stretch, the road passes Coffee's Country Market, a quiet market and coffee stop with a scenic view of Black Hall Pond in the back.

Just ahead, the route passes Rogers Lake, before a left turn onto Grassy Hill Road. The next 2.5-mile stretch affords photographic views of the 260-acre

Old Lyme's Cycling Pedigree

The region has a surprising number of professionals and notable cyclists. Old Lyme native Benjamin Wolfe, an affable young racer, has raced on the US Olympic team and distinguished himself on the UCI (Union Cycliste International) world racing circuit. Neighboring East Lyme was home to professional cyclist Tom Danielson, the top American finisher in the 2012 Tour de France, and record holder for the fastest ascent up New Hampshire's Mt. Washington.

Other notables include a mechanic for the US Olympic Team who works at Niantic Bay Bicycles, and famed frame-builder J. P. Weigle, who builds classic French touring bikes by hand in a small studio in Old Lyme. Weigle has drawn international acclaim for making randonneuring frames for long-distance riding, a skill he learned under master frame-builders in England in the early 1970s. His work is celebrated for the careful attention to details. Like most frame-builders, his lugs are works of beauty, but he also makes fenders, stays, and other parts of the bike to create unique works of art and skill.

Backroad near Rogers Lake.

lake and a quiet, mostly flat road. After a T-junction, continue following Grassy Hill Road, into an even quieter neighborhood and the start of the big climb.

Over the next half-mile, the route ascends more than 200 feet of elevation, in one mostly steady climb, with a quarter-mile recovery downhill before another 130-foot climb of more than a third of a mile. At the crest of the hill, pass Foxglove Farm on the left and then a tiny historic cemetery named after William Gillette, the famous stage actor who portrayed Sherlock Holmes, on the right. From here the ride evens out and eventually heads downhill.

Stay left on Grassy Hill Road and enjoy a fast descent down to an intersection with Beaver Brook Road. Turn left here at the 7.2-mile mark, with Beebee Cemetery on the left, and follow Beaver Brook Road for three-quarters of a mile, passing New Mercies Farm, a small family operated organic farm, and a tiny, beautiful cemetery with an old gate and stone wall on the right.

At the 7.9-mile mark, take a left onto Keeny Road, a beautiful rambling road through an undeveloped forest with very few houses separated by large sections of woods. This road passes through the Beckett Hill State Park Reserve, an undeveloped and unmarked state park abutting the Nehantic State Forest, consisting of hundreds of acres of watersheds and woods. Centerpieces of the area include two fish-stocked ponds, Uncas and Norwich, which only allow fishing from nonmotorized boats and from the shore (fishing license required throughout the state, of course, for anybody 16 or older).

Keeny Road ends at the T-junction with Hamburg Road (CT 156). Use caution and turn left onto busy Hamburg Road. In less than a half-mile, at 13.2, turn left onto Bill Hill Road, another quiet side street, up a last quick climb of nearly 100 feet. As the climb peaks, take note of Ashlawn Farm Coffee on the right; they roast coffee on premises and operate a high-end espresso bar where they serve a variety of baked goods and snacks.

The route continues along Bill Hill Road past the cafe and farm, curving right and then turning left back onto CT 156. Take the first left off 156 onto Saunders Hollow Road.

Saunders Hollow Road curves around through a quiet neighborhood and a quick descent. At the 15.8-mile mark, Sill Lane intersects with Saunders Hollow; continue heading straight as Saunders Hollow becomes Sill Lane.

Sill Lane continues for the next mile, ending when it meets Route 1/Lyme Street. Continue onto Route 1 and follow the road for a half-mile, passing the arts attractions and historic inns, before turning right to stay on Route 1 to finish this ride at Morning Glory Coffee.

MILES AND DIRECTIONS

0.0 Proceed onto Halls Road

0.1 Left onto Lyme Street

0.5 Continue on Boston Post Road

2.6 Left onto Grassy Hill Road

7.2 Left onto Beaver Brook Road

7.9 Left onto Keeny Road

12.7 Left onto Hamburg Road (CT 156)

13.2 Left onto Bill Hill Road

14.7 Left onto Neck Road (CT 156)

14.9 Left onto Saunders Hollow Road

15.8 Continue on Sill Lane

16.9 Continue on Lyme Street

17.3 Right to continue onto Route 1

17.4 Finish the ride back by Morning Glory

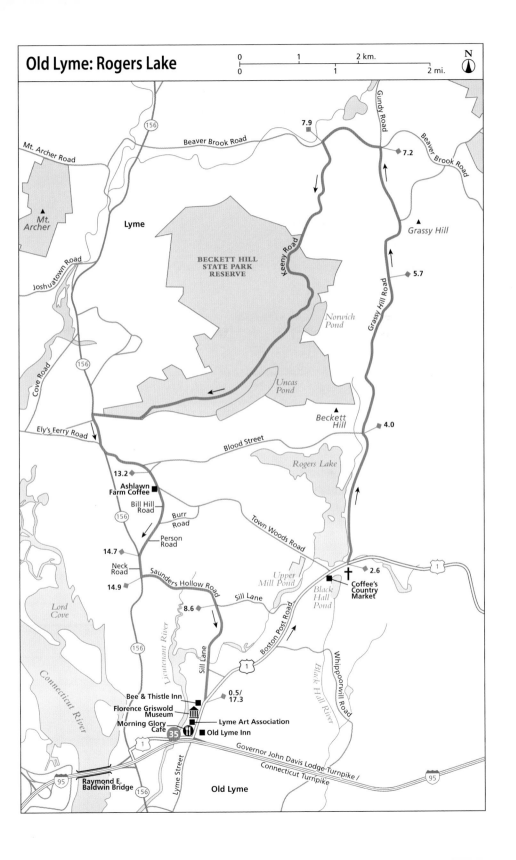

Old Lyme: Rogers Lake

0   1   2 km.
0   1   2 mi.

N

156

Mt. Archer Road

Beaver Brook Road

7.9

Gundy Road

7.2

Beaver Brook Road

Mt. Archer

Lyme

Grassy Hill

Joshuatown Road

Keeny Road

BECKETT HILL STATE PARK RESERVE

Grassy Hill Road

5.7

156

Cove Road

Norwich Pond

Uncas Pond

Beckett Hill

4.0

Ely's Ferry Road

Blood Street

Rogers Lake

13.2

Ashlawn Farm Coffee

Bill Hill Road

Burr Road

156

Person Road

Town Woods Road

14.7

Neck Road

Saunders Hollow Road

2.6

Coffee's Country Market

14.9

Upper Mill Pond

Sill Lane

Black Hall Pond

8.6

1

Lord Cove

Lieutenant River

Sill Lane

Boston Post Road

Whippoorwill Road

Black Hall River

Connecticut River

156

0.5/ 17.3

Bee & Thistle Inn

Florence Griswold Museum

Lyme Art Association

Morning Glory Cafe

35

Old Lyme Inn

Governor John Davis Lodge-Turnpike /

95

Lyme Street

Connecticut Turnpike

95

Raymond E. Baldwin Bridge

156

Old Lyme

Lovely home behind a stone wall.

RIDE INFORMATION

Bike Shops
Action Sports of Old Saybrook: 1385 Boston Post Rd., Old Saybrook; (860) 388-1291; actionsportsct.com
Niantic Bay Bicycles: 8 Methodist St. # 1, Niantic; (860) 691-0757; nianticbay bicycles.com

Local Events and Attractions
The Farmers' Market: This market is held on the grounds next to Ashlawn Farm Coffee, from June to October. Vendors sell prepared food and local produce (farmcoffee.com/about-us/the-farmers-market).

Restaurants
Ashlawn Farm Coffee: 78 Bill Hill Rd., Old Lyme; (860) 434-3636; farmcoffee.com
Morning Glory Cafe: 11 Halls Rd., Old Lyme; (860) 434-0480; morningglory cafeoldlyme.com

Restrooms
13.2 Miles: The Farmers' Market/Ashlawn Farm Coffee

Best Bike Rides Connecticut

The Quiet Corner

The part of Connecticut known as the "Quiet Corner" is a series of scenic villages in the upper northeast characterized by low population density, pastoral landscapes, and winding country roads. The borders are ambiguous, incorporating most of Windham County and parts of Tolland and New London counties. Coventry is the farthest town to the west before reaching denser suburban towns.

Although small, these northeast towns are full of attractions and popular with visitors. Antiques and small, locally owned shops are among the commercial offerings; and no other area has as many major agricultural fairs. Historic museums include the Prudence Crandall House in the Canterbury-Scotland Loop and the Roseland Cottage in Woodstock.

CT 169, a scenic low-volume road through the region, offers excellent motoring and is a popular leaf-peeping route. Many of the towns are easily accessed from this main route, which makes nice connections between many of the following routes for long-distance cyclists looking to extend their ride.

Rides in this section prominently feature the quaint farming villages of the region. Thompson, the most northeastern town in the state, borders Massachusetts and Rhode Island; one of the chief natural attractions is Quaddick Pond, a large body of water surrounded by homes and protected water company land.

Nearby Woodstock and Pomfret have active village greens and several historic inns for overnight visitors. Scotland, settled by immigrant Issac Magoon, celebrates its cultural heritage in the Highland Games each year. And nearby Canterbury was home to Prudence Crandall, a schoolteacher and abolitionist who was arrested for teaching African-American women.

The quietest of the quietest, Union, is a heavily forested town with fewer than 700 residents. The town is home to the Nipmuck State Forest, Bigelow Hollow State Park, the Yale Forest, and a number of other parks and preserves.

36

Bigelow Hollow and Yale Forest

The town of Union is the least populated municipality in Connecticut; fewer than 700 people live in nearly 30 square miles of forested land on the northern border with Massachusetts. Quiet back roads, many of them unpaved, and serious hill climbs make this little region in the "Quiet Corner" a fun challenge for cyclists. The lack of motor vehicle traffic makes for quiet, low-volume roads, through deep forests and past scenic water views. There are few commercial amenities or food stops, but the natural beauty and tricky riding make this a must-ride course.

Start: Bigelow Hollow State Park

Length: 22.4 miles

Riding time: 1 hour 45 minutes to 2 hours

Best bike: Road bike

Terrain and trail surface: Asphalt, some dirt

Traffic and hazards: While the area does have many unpaved roads, this route doesn't require a mountain or cyclocross bike. None of the roads should prove too challenging, but riders who are averse to dirt may want to detour around some of the noted undeveloped roads or try thicker tires for these areas. The climbing is technical, with fast descents over some poorly maintained stretches of pavement, but none of it is outside the comfort level of a regular recreational cyclist.

Things to see: Bigelow Pond, several other smaller ponds and creeks, Yale Forest

Fees: There is a weekend/holidays fee for parking at Bigelow Hollow State Park (higher for non-residents).

Getting there: I-84 to exit 73 or 74, then follow CT 190N to CT 171 east to the park entrance.

GPS: 42.00463 / -72.12882

The pond at Bigelow Hollow.

THE RIDE

This 22.4-mile ride starts in Bigelow Hollow State Park, at the last parking lot, by the boat launch. The slightly downhill park road, Bigelow Brook Road, travels along the eponymous waterway and pond for nearly a mile before ending at CT 197, Bigelow Hollow Road, where you cautiously turn left, mindful of quickly descending traffic coming down the hill.

The road climbs uphill fairly steeply, rising nearly 300 feet in three-quarters of a mile, followed by a short plateau, steep descent, and then rolling terrain over the next several miles.

Bear left at the 2-mile mark, near the end of the first steep climb, onto Old Turnpike Road (CT 197).

CT 197 heads toward Black Pond, where you turn right at the 4.9-mile mark. Use extra caution as you make the hairpin turn to follow Old Turnpike Road; oncoming traffic has no stop.

This road is very scenic, bordered by camps and undeveloped forests. You have more views of Black Pond on your left, then Keach Pond on your right, and Still River on the left just up ahead.

Cross CT 198 to stay on Old Turnpike Road and continue, bearing left to stay on the Old Turnpike again when it intertwines with Taylor Road for a dozen feet or so.

The Still River opens up and provides some excellent marsh views on the left just before Old Turnpike Road becomes Centre Pike, at the 7-mile mark.

Area Parks and Forests

Bigelow Hollow State Park, where the ride begins, adjoins the Nipmuck State Forest. Together, the two parks comprise more than 9,000 acres of forest, trails, and water, including an impressive 18-acre lake intended for slow, recreational use. Jet Skis and other fast boats are prohibited, making it one of the top lakes in Connecticut for fishing, kayaking, and resting. The tranquil setting is perfect for a post-ride picnic.

This ride passes through and along the Nipmuck State Forest, which completely surrounds Bigelow Hollow. The most popular trails lead to Breakneck Pond, a completely undeveloped 92-acre lake that extends into Massachusetts northeast of the ride start. The pond is accessible only from trails and offers seasonal camping. Motorized boats are not permitted. Visitors can also hike or drive up to the Mountain Laurel Sanctuary, a few miles to the west, over I-84. The mountain laurel is the state flower of Connecticut and parks employees here maintain a mile-long stretch of the beautiful light-pink and white blossoms.

The Yale-Myers Forest, the largest forest property owned by the Yale School of Forestry, is a large preserve of mixed hardwoods, hemlock, several white pine stands, and a few red pine plantations, planted in the 1940s. The property contains forests in many towns in the Quiet Corner, and this route heads directly through some of the denser sections, on serene country roads with very rare motorized traffic.

The road continues for less than a half-mile to Union Road (CT 171); turn left and then right again to continue on Centre Pike.

Some unpaved sections of road lie ahead; it is also some of the most beautiful and tranquil riding available in the state. If you can't imagine riding over a well-maintained hard-packed road, you can follow CT 171 into Kenyonville, turning right onto CT 198, and then right again onto Westford Road when you reach the town center of Eastford. Westford Road eventually becomes Eastford Road, then intersects with Boston Hollow Road, where you turn left and resume the mapped route. This detour is not recommended, however. Although it adds nearly 6 miles, it means skipping some incredible back roads riding.

Following the planned route, Centre Pike continues through almost 3 miles of nearly unpopulated woodlands before re-crossing the Bigelow Brook and becoming Boston Hollow Road. Follow this road for almost 2 more miles

A waterfall near the end of the route.

of undeveloped forest, intersected by a hiking trail through Nipmuck Forest, before passing the Westford Cemetery on your left and continuing onto Turnpike Road (CT 89).

In 0.1 mile take the right onto Waterfall Road, for 2.5 miles of scenic hill riding, up to Hillside Road, where you turn left. This should be the 15-mile mark. In less than a half-mile, you cross the Mount Hope River, a narrow little waterway, before the road becomes Ference Road and continues.

Ference Road passes Morey Pond, on the right, and then goes over I-84, becoming Fish Point Road.

In a half-mile, turn right onto Buckley Highway and reach the highest elevation of the ride, at nearly 1,150 feet, and the last real climb of the day. The road descends now before evening out. In about 2 miles it passes back over the highway, in a slightly built-up area with entrance and exit ramps; use caution continuing along this roadway.

Buckley Highway continues until a right-hand turn onto Bigelow Hollow Road, at the 19.5-mile mark, with a slight uphill effort, before a final descent of more than 400 feet down to the park.

Here you have a scenic view of Bigelow Pond on the left on this high-speed, steep road, just before you reach the park road at the 20.8-mile mark. Exercise caution in turning into the park; the road behind you is curvy and steep; motor vehicle traffic can be very fast as it heads downhill here. Bigelow Brook continues for 1 mile into the park, to the lot where you started, finishing this route.

Bigelow Hollow and Yale Forest

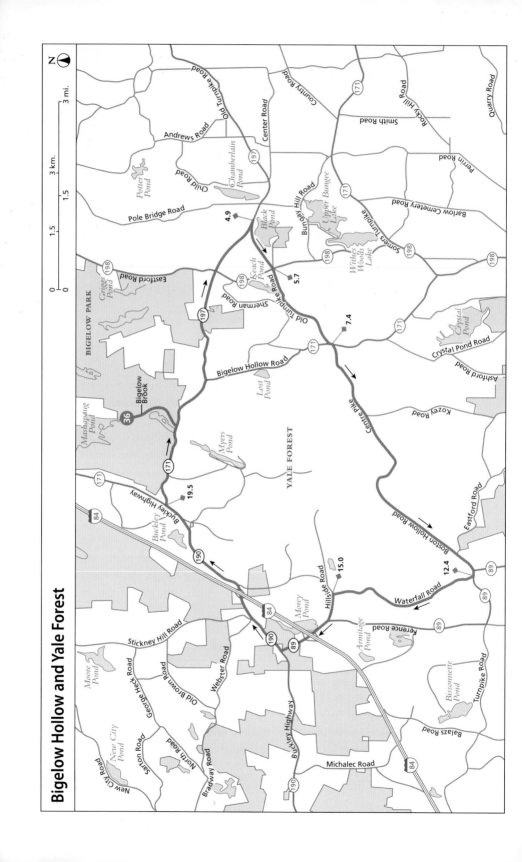

MILES AND DIRECTIONS

0.0 Start on Bigelow Brook

1.1 Left onto CT 197 (Bigelow Hollow Road)

2.9 Continue on Old Turnpike Road

4.9 Right onto Old Turnpike Road

5.7 Cross Route 198 to continue on Old Turnpike Road

7.0 Continue on Centre Pike

7.4 Left onto CT 171 (Union Road) to continue on Centre Pike

10.1 Continue on Boston Hollow Road

12.3 Right onto Turnpike Road

12.4 Right onto Waterfall Road

15.0 Left onto Hillside Road

15.4 Continue on Ference Road

15.8 Continue on Fish Point Road

16.3 Right onto Buckley Highway

19.5 Right onto Bigelow Hollow Road

20.8 Left into Bigelow Hollow Park

22.4 Finish ride at parking lot

RIDE INFORMATION

Local Events and Attractions
Bigelow Hollow State Park: This remote park consists of more than 500 acres of evergreen forest, navigable on 35 miles of trails.
Breakneck Pond: This 92-acre lake is secluded and quiet, accessible only by hiking trails from Bigelow Hollow.

Restaurants
Traveler Restaurant: 1257 Buckley Hwy., Stafford Springs; (860) 684-4920

Restrooms
0.0 Miles: Bigelow Hollow State Park

37

Canterbury-Scotland Loop

Canterbury and Scotland are classic New England villages in the rural, bucolic "Quiet Corner" region of northeastern Connecticut, offering rural charm, an active agricultural economy, and miles of scenic roads. Canterbury developed out of a small homestead, named Kent, when former Plainville residents built their own church and parish. The town was named Canterbury as an allusion to the major cathedral city, located in the county of Kent in the United Kingdom. Canterbury, a town of some 5,000, is larger in land and population than Scotland, its smaller neighbor to the west. Scotland has roughly 1,000 residents on 19 square miles of property, all of which originated from a 5-square-mile property purchased by Isaac Magoon in 1700. Magoon named the area after his ancestral Scotland, and the name stuck. The area has a rich Scottish heritage, celebrated each October during the Highland Games festival. Scotland is especially notable for still maintaining the now-rare town meeting style of government. Every citizen is invited to speak and participate in making decisions about the future of the village.

Start: In downtown Canterbury at the intersection of CT 169 and US 14.

Length: 24.1 miles

Riding time: 1 hour and 45 minutes to 2 hours

Best bike: Road bike

Terrain and trail surface: Asphalt

Traffic and hazards: The intersection of CT 169 and US 14 can be busy. Bennett Pond Road is somewhat choppy, so use caution and watch for potholes.

Things to see: Ponds, stone walls, a historic house museum, and fields and meadows

Fees: None. There should be ample parking in the post office lot and at the nearby little league field.

Getting there: CT 169 is a long north-south road, accessible from US 6 in the north. Take CT 169S into Canterbury, to the intersection with CT 14. From the south, take I-395N to exit 19, onto CT 169N into Canterbury, to the intersection with US 14.

GPS: 41.69837 / -71.97117

THE RIDE

This ride begins west of the Quinebaug River, very near to where the first homestead was built. Cross US 14 to stay on CT 169 (locally South Canterbury Road), passing the Prudence Crandall Museum on the right.

Continue for 0.1 mile, bearing right at the fork in the road onto Elmdale Road by a lovely stone wall. Elmdale is a quiet country road heading mostly downhill. Bear right at another fork ahead to stay on Elmdale, with views of a tranquil pond and open fields to the right, just after the fork.

After another half-mile through sparsely developed neighborhoods, Elmdale Road ends at a T-junction with Bennett Pond Road, where the route turns right.

This is an at-times choppy section of road, through a thickly forested area with infrequent rustic houses. The eponymous pond is visible on the left, after a quarter-mile, through trees bordering the road.

After the pond, ride up a slight hill, past a large working farm on the left, and then turn right onto Tracy Road, just past the 2-mile mark.

Tracy Road is a tiny, narrow road hemmed in by thick vegetation and a variety of hardwood trees. Follow the road up the hill to the stop sign and turn left onto Cross Road for a short stretch connecting back to Bennett Pond Road, where the route turns right.

Bennett Pond Road continues climbing upward, past a lovely field on the right, leveling out and ending at the T-junction with Lisbon Road ahead, just under the 3-mile mark.

Turn left onto Lisbon Road, heading downhill past several homes, leading to another short hill just after a small pond on the right. The road continues along, passing a large, scenic pond on the left, followed by a less pastoral repair yard. In a bit more than a half-mile, at the four-way intersection, turn right onto Bates Pond Road, a slightly choppy, rough section of road through another beautiful wooded area. Note the classic stone walls along most of the route, a quintessentially New England sight, as the road climbs along, opening up in an area of beautiful farmland, just before a stop sign at the intersection with Water Street.

View of Prudence Crandall House Museum from the road.

Cross Water Street onto Woodchuck Hill Road, continuing to head uphill, past more fields and a second farmhouse. The hill evens out as the route passes another bucolic pond on the right, followed by a fast, steep descent, with a quick switchback at the end, over a small bridge on Hanover Road. Hanover Road curves here, heading straight ahead and to the left.

Continue straight on Hanover Road for a mile and a half, past an area with more homes than the previous roads, past a number of planted fields and some open space. After spotting two ponds and then a field on the right, take the left turn onto Cemetery Road near the 10-mile mark.

Cemetery Road is a short stretch of road with several scenic farms. The road ends at a T-junction with CT 97, known locally as Devotion Road. Devotion Road is a slightly busier, faster road, with a comfortable shoulder for cyclists.

Turn right onto Devotion Road and note the picturesque historic cemetery on the right, behind a low stone wall and extending up a short hill. Following the cemetery, the road passes modern suburban houses and more farmland.

Bear right at the fork onto Center Street, past a charming town green with a gazebo and history plaque and cross CT 14, turning left and then immediately right onto Brook Road, passing a congregational church with a tiny historic cemetery in the backyard.

This narrow road passes a series of municipal buildings, in a quiet, scenic section of town. Shortly after the elementary school, the steadily uphill road passes more farms, followed by picturesque meadows overgrown with wildflowers.

After a small green, cross Brooklyn Turnpike at the four-way intersection, continuing up Brook Road until it ends in a T-junction with Kemp Road. Turn right onto one of the steeper climbs of this route, riding a quaint bridge over a tiny brook, until Kemp ends at the next junction with the Brooklyn Turnpike.

Turn left onto Brooklyn Turnpike for 0.1 mile, crossing CT 97 and continuing as the road becomes Windham Road.

Windham heads back uphill for another long, sometimes steep climb, with views of a gorgeous meadow and a tranquil river crossing near the 16-mile mark. In another mile and a quarter, Windham becomes Raymond Schoolhouse Road, at a section bordered by more low stone walls.

At the intersection with Brooklyn Road, with a no outlet sign ahead, turn left, heading briefly uphill along another quiet stretch of road bordered by stone walls, before the road heads downhill to an intersection where you bear slightly right to continue onto Windham Road for less than a half-mile. At that point, the route turns right onto Grass Road, a connection to North Society Road, less than a quarter-mile ahead.

Turn right onto North Society Road, at what should be the 19-mile mark, and head mostly downhill through more forests and country homes for

Prudence Crandall House Museum

This historic house museum honors Prudence Crandall, a schoolteacher who opened an academy here in 1831 aiming to educate wealthy local women. She was successful but local families withdrew their daughters after she admitted Sarah Harris, a 20-year-old black woman who wanted to become a teacher herself.

Crandall actively began seeking other black women for her school, at which time the state passed what was known as "the Black Law," making Crandall's school illegal. Crandall was arrested, but was found not guilty and released.

Violent acts of vandalism escalated, ultimately to a life-threatening act of arson, causing Crandall to close the school. She left the area, married, and lived out the rest of her life in Kansas. Connecticut repealed the law by 1838, but only recognized Crandall as a state hero 4 years before her death, in an 1886 bill supported by Mark Twain. The act made Crandall the State Heroine of Connecticut, granting a small pension.

The house museum is open for seasonal tours. A ticket from this museum grants half-off admittance to the three other state museums, including the Sloane-Stanley in Kent and the Henry Whitfield in Guilford, covered in Ride 18 and 25, respectively.

another 4.5 miles. Just after the 20-mile mark, Ledgebrook Farm provides a particularly scenic view, followed by an open meadow on the left.

After a traditional red barn on the right, the road ends in a T-junction with North Canterbury Road, where the route turns right, leading back toward the start. Canterbury Cones, immediately on the left, is a popular local ice cream joint in a park-like setting that serves homemade ice cream and grill fare.

Just a little bit farther down the road, note the very old cemetery on the right, followed by a particularly lovely old home on a large estate with a scenic pond.

The route continues on for a short distance, ending back at the start, where North Canterbury Road and South Canterbury Road intersect with CT 14.

MILES AND DIRECTIONS

0.0   Start at South Canterbury Road

0.1   Continue on Elmdale Road

1.4   Right onto Bennett Pond Road

2.1   Right onto Tracy Road

2.4   Left onto Cross Road

2.7   Right onto Bennett Pond Road

2.9   Left onto Lisbon Road

5.5   Right onto Bates Pond Road

6.7   Continue on Woodchuck Hill Road

8.2   Left on Hanover Road

9.8   Left onto Cemetery Road

10.7   Right onto Devotion Road

11.4   Bear right on Center Street

11.5   Cross CT 14 (turning left and then immediately right onto Brook Road).

13.8   Right onto Kemp Road

14.7   Continue on Brooklyn Turnpike

14.8   Continue on Windham Road

15.9   Right onto Windham Road, crossing over Reilly Road, then left back onto Windham Road

17.2   Continue on Raymond Schoolhouse Road

17.8   Left onto Brooklyn Road

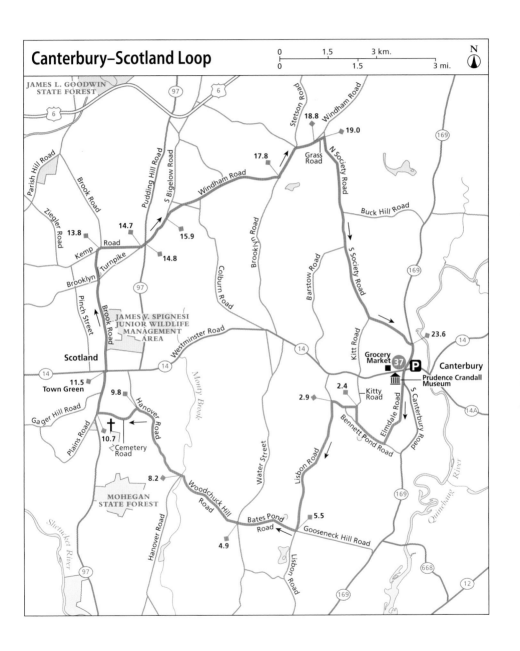

Canterbury–Scotland Loop

0   1.5   3 km.
0   1.5   3 mi.

N

JAMES L. GOODWIN
STATE FOREST

97   6

6

Stetson Road

18.8   Windham Road
19.0

17.8   Grass
Road

N Society Road

169

Parish Hill Road

Brook Road

Pudding Hill Road

S Bigelow Road

Windham Road

Ziegler Road

13.8   14.7   Road

15.9

Kemp   Brooklyn Turnpike

14.8

Brooklyn Road

Buck Hill Road

Barstow Road

S Society Road

169

Pinch Street

Brook Road

97

JAMES V. SPIGNESI
JUNIOR WILDLIFE
MANAGEMENT
AREA

Colburn Road

Westminster Road

14

Kitt Road

23.6   14

Scotland

14   14

11.5
Town Green

9.8

Gager Hill Road

Plains Road

Hanover Road

10.7   Cemetery
Road

Monty Brook

Water Street

Lisbon Road

2.9   2.4   Kitty
Road

Grocery
Market   37   P

Prudence Crandall
Museum   Canterbury

Bennett Pond Road

Elmdale Road

S Canterbury Road

14A

Quinebaug River

MOHEGAN
STATE FOREST

8.2

Woodchuck Hill Road

Bates Pond
Road

5.5

Gooseneck Hill Road

169

668

Hanover Road

4.9

Lisbon Road

Shetucket River

97

169

12

The Scotland Town Green, with historic buildings, is ahead.

18.4 Continue on Windham Road

18.8 Continue on Grass Road

19.0 Right onto North Society Road

23.6 Right onto North Canterbury Road

24.1 Finish ride

RIDE INFORMATION

Bike Shops
Danielson Adventure Sports: 21 Furnace St., Danielson; (860) 774-6010; bikect.com

Local Events and Attractions
Prudence Crandall House Museum: This Connecticut State house museum honors the work of Prudence Crandall, a 19th century educator who fought racism.

Haul of Fame Museum: This unusual museum offers a look into the history of commercial trucking.

Scotland Connecticut Highland Games: This annual competition includes harp playing, dancing, and piping and drumming. scotlandgames.org

Restaurants
Canterbury Cones: 57 N Canterbury Rd., Canterbury; (860) 617-4441

D and G Pizza and Pub: 200 Westminster Rd., Canterbury; (860) 546-6007

Pomfret-Woodstock Loop

A charming town in the northeast "Quiet Corner," Pomfret is often described as "vintage" New England. This community of more than 4,000 is a popular destination for cyclists from across the state who come for the winding country roads and organized charity rides in the region. The town was once the site of an ashram, or Hindu religious center, founded by Woodstock opening speaker Satchidananda Saraswati, in 1980.

North of Pomfret is Woodstock, an 8,000 person village and the second largest town in Connecticut, geographically. Woodstock is a lovely pastoral community with the largest concentration of dairy farms in the state and an economy shared between light manufacturing, agriculture, and tourism. Made up of six distinct villages, Woodstock has several charming commercial districts with boutiques and bed-and-breakfast style accommodations.

Start: Municipal lot in Pomfret, by the Vanilla Bean Cafe, on Route 97.

Length: 16.2 miles

Riding Time: 1.5 hours

Best bike: Road bike

Terrain and trail surface: Asphalt

Traffic and hazards: This route forms a rectangle, following Route 169 on either side, which can be a fast, sometimes narrow road. It is a popular cycling road, with few reported accidents, but use caution and pay attention to surroundings.

Things to see: Natural beauty, farmlands, Roseland Cottage, Roseland Park, Woodstock Fairgrounds, historic mansions in Woodstock, some lovely ponds and brooks

Fees: There is no fee to park in the small municipal lot. If it's full, look for other spots to park on-street nearby. Do not park in the Vanilla Bean Cafe's lot to ride; they are a busy spot and run out of parking quickly.

THE RIDE

This 16.2-mile route offers excellent tempo riding on long, mostly unobstructed main roads. The route out has only one intersection on the outbound trip, in Woodstock, and very few on the return leg.

Starting on West Road, CT 97, proceed toward the intersection with CT 169, keeping the Vanilla Bean Cafe to the left. Turn left onto CT 169, also called Pomfret Street, for an exhilarating, mostly downhill ride of more than 2.5 miles. The road passes a series of lovely old homes, then heads downhill on a steeper stretch past a rustic wood fence and an expansive meadow.

The rest of the road is equally beautiful. Note the transition to old stone walls ahead in an area surrounded by open space, then a second transition to more modern stone walls as the route approaches the campuses of Woodstock Middle School and Hyde School, a boarding school for college preparatory students.

On the right is a cheerful red building, part of the florist on the street corner, just before the intersection with CT 171.

Carefully turn left to continue on CT 169, into the village of South Woodstock. To the left are the fairgrounds where the Woodstock Fair is held each year.

After the fairgrounds, turn right onto Roseland Park Road, noting the cracked and irregularly maintained asphalt. This rural country road proceeds over 2 miles, passing through Roseland Park, situated around a scenic natural lake.

A mile or so after the park, the road approaches a fork; bear left, onto Dugg Hill Road, for a mile-long ride past some modern homes and more scenic farmland. Ride up a short climb, past an open field to the left, and turn left at the intersection onto Woodstock Road.

Woodstock Road is another quiet rural path, traveling through the tiny village of East Woodstock and ending at North Woodstock. East Woodstock features a collection of farms and the Rogers Corporation, a manufacturer of specialty materials like computer circuit boards.

After passing through East Woodstock, bear right on Woodstock Road, past a farm and a pastoral pond, heading mostly uphill on a rolling section of

Farm view from CT 169.

road. At the end of the road, turn left, around a lovely old saltbox house, onto CT 169, into the most challenging climb of the day.

This 200-foot climb is a manageable steady effort, sustained over the next mile and a half. The climb peaks just after a lovely red barn on the left, and then heads downhill, past suburban homes that resemble renovated farmhouses and barns, most bordered by more rustic wooden fences.

Near the base of this slope, the road becomes more scenic. Note North Running Brook, to the right, behind Sweet Evalina's Stand, a classic roadside diner serving sandwiches, celebrated pizzas, and other traditional fare in an agricultural setting.

Keep watching for more scenic overlooks after the stand, with one particularly photogenic spot just up the road on the right.

The road curves and twists a bit, passing through a small intersection, and then past the misleadingly named Roseland Cottage on the right. This was the summer home of abolitionist Henry C. Bowen, who also donated the Roseland Park grounds. It is open year-round for tours on the hour. The distinctive Gothic Revival property is also known as "the Pink House" for its cheerfully painted vertical siding. The interior, largely unchanged since the late 19th century, provides a window into life in the Victorian era.

After the Cottage, the road curves along a lovely green, entering the village of Woodstock and passing a tall-steepled Congregational church on the left. The road is bordered by magnificent historic homes over the next quarter-mile, showcasing a variety of architectural styles.

Near the 11.5-mile mark, shortly after passing the Woodstock Historical Society building on the left, bear right onto Plaine Hill Road, past the Inn at Woodstock Hill.

The road continues downhill over the next half-mile, with lovely views of fields on the right, past the Mansion at Bald Hill, a traditional bed-and-breakfast. Turn right onto Somers Turnpike when the road ends, then onto a slightly fast road bordered by pastureland on the right and modest homes on the left.

Carefully turn left at the second road, East Quasset Road, watching for oncoming vehicles and fast-moving traffic from behind. This quiet side road passes farmlands, modern homes, and has some views of the Quasset Pond on the right before continuing onto Quasset Road, just after the 14-mile mark.

Cross Fox Hill and Tyott Road to stay on Quasset into a more scenic area with more water views to the right and farmhouses on either side. Near the end, the road passes a manufacturing company and ends in a T-junction with CT 97 (Deerfield Road).

Carefully turn left onto CT 97. This is the busiest and narrowest section of the ride, with fast-moving traffic and only a narrow shoulder, but some lovely views on the right over the short half-mile to the finish in Pomfret.

To extend the ride with the Natchaug State Forest Loop (Ride 39), turn right instead, then take a left onto Peterson Road in a mile and a half and follow the other route as if it began at that point. After finishing the loop, continue along CT 97 back into Pomfret to end the ride.

There are a few food options in Woodstock, such as the aforementioned Sweet Evalina's. The Vanilla Bean Cafe at the ride start is highly recommended for a post-ride break on their outdoor patio or inside a comfortable interior space decorated with local art and antique bicycles. The cafe serves espresso, coffee, baked goods, and a full menu of sandwiches and traditional breakfast and grill foods.

MILES AND DIRECTIONS

0.0 Start on CT 97 (Deerfield Road) and turn left onto CT 169 (Pomfret Street)

2.5 Left to continue on CT 169

2.9 Right onto Roseland Park Road

5.2 Continue on Dugg Hill Road

6.2 Left onto Woodstock Road

7.9 Left onto Norwich Worcester Turnpike

11.4 Continue on Plaine Hill Road

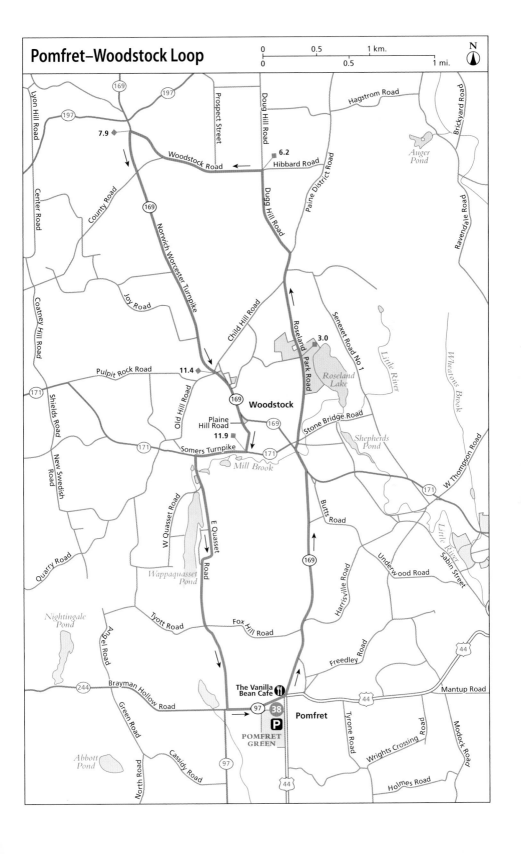

Pomfret–Woodstock Loop

N

0   0.5   1 km.
0   0.5   1 mi.

169
197
197
7.9
Lyon Hill Road
Prospect Street
Doug Hill Road
Hagstrom Road
Brickyard Road
Auger Pond
Woodstock Road
6.2
Hibbard Road
Paine District Road
Ravendale Road
Center Road
County Road
169
Norwich Worcester Turnpike
Dugg Hill Road
Joy Road
Coatney Hill Road
Child Hill Road
Roseland Park Road
Seneket Road No 1
3.0
Roseland Lake
Little River
Wheatons Brook
Pulpit Rock Road
11.4
171
Old Hill Road
169
Woodstock
Shields Road
Stone Bridge Road
Shepherds Pond
Plaine Hill Road
11.9
169
New Swedish Road
171
Somers Turnpike
171
W Thompson Road
171
Mill Brook
Little River
Sabin Street
Quarry Road
W Quasset Road
E Quasset Road
Wappaquasset Pond
Butts Road
Underwood Road
169
Nightingale Pond
Tyott Road
Fox Hill Road
Harrisville Road
44
Angel Road
Freedley Road
Mantup Road
244
Brayman Hollow Road
The Vanilla Bean Cafe
44
Green Road
97
38
Pomfret
Tyrone Road
Wrights Crossing Road
Modock Road
Abbott Pond
Cassidy Road
POMFRET GREEN
97
North Road
44
Holmes Road

11.9 Right onto Somers Turnpike

12.5 Left onto East Quasset Road

14.1 Continue on Quasset Road

15.6 Left onto CT 97 (Deerfield Road)

16.2 Arrive at finish

RIDE INFORMATION

Bike Shops
Danielson Adventure Sports: 21 Furnace St., Danielson; (860) 774-6010; bikect.com

Local Events and Attractions
Roseland Park: This park has been open to the public since 1876. The land was set aside for the people of Woodstock by notable local Henry C. Bowen, a famous abolitionist who was born in Woodstock and later, as a successful New York City merchant, spent his summers in his beloved hometown. The park has public restrooms.

Roseland Cottage: This historic property provides tours and a glimpse into the Victorian era in America.

Woodstock Fair: This large agricultural exhibition has been held in the region continuously since 1859, originating from a multi-town exhibition first held in 1809. The Woodstock Fair is a 4-day event held every year on the Labor Day weekend, starting on the Friday preceding, and running all weekend, ending on Monday.

Airline State Park Trail: There are a number of ways to get onto the Airline Trail nearby. Visit the CT DEEP website (www.ct.gov/deep) and search for the Airline Trail.

Restaurants
Sweet Evalina's Stand: 688 CT 169, Woodstock; (860) 928-4029
Vanilla Bean Cafe: 450 West Rd., Pomfret; (860) 928-1562; thevanillabean cafe.com
Sharpe Hill Vineyard: 108 Wade Rd., Pomfret; (860) 974-3549; sharpehill.com

Restrooms
3.0 Miles: Roseland Park

Natchaug State Forest Loop

Hampton is a small rural community near Pomfret, surrounded by beautiful country roads. Part of the Quinebaug and Shetucket Rivers Valley National Heritage Corridor, the area is characterized by rolling hills, farmland, and New England village charm. Hampton's residential town center, full of historic homes on large setbacks and anchored by the Hampton General Store, is a perfect staging point for a ride through nearby Natchaug State Forest and neighboring villages.

Start: Hampton General Store on Main Street

Length: 23.9 miles

Riding time: 1 hour 45 minutes to 2 hours

Best bike: Road bike

Terrain and trail surface: Asphalt

Traffic and hazards: This ride follows bucolic country roads, many of which are in low-volume areas. A few sections are on noticeably faster roads with generous shoulders. Use caution and ride in the shoulder on these sections.

Things to see: Natchaug State Forest, farmlands, historic homes in downtown Hampton, and some lovely ponds

Fees: None. Parking at the Hampton General Store should be no problem for customers looking to enjoy riding the area, but check with the employees before leaving your car. There is curbside parking just north of the ride start at the town open space, on the route, if needed.

Getting there: The Hampton General Store is on CT 97, near US 6. From due south or north, follow CT 97 to the store. From US 6, turn onto CT 97 for Thompson and head north a short distance. The store is on the right.

GPS: 41.78486 / -72.05511

THE RIDE

This ride is somewhat hilly, with a total elevation gain of 1,843 feet over 23.9 miles of riding. The start point is at the Hampton General Store, which at the time of this writing opens seasonally. The historic building houses a grocery store and deli, serving a variety of sandwiches, pizza, and prepared foods and groceries, with picnic tables for outdoor seating.

Follow Main Street, bordered by lovely old homes, past the elementary school and a town open space on the right. After three-quarters of a mile, bear left onto Station Road, carefully crossing a sometimes-fast section of CT 97.

Station Road is a lovely country road with minimal traffic volumes through pastoral farmland, intersecting the Airline State Park Trail, and skirting along the Natchaug State Forest.

The Airline State Park Trail is a linear trail converted from an old rail line, which once provided train access between New York City and Boston. The project consists of three separate sections. This route crosses the 22-mile North section, from Windham to Putnam. The other two sections are the 21-mile South section, from East Hampton to Windham, and the Thompson Addition, a 6.5-mile spur trail into Massachusetts. This trail provides scenic off-road riding through particularly beautiful scenery on this section.

After more than 2.5 miles, Station Road becomes Morey Road, curving right and continuing for another mile on another section of tree-shaded country road. Morey Road provides a steep 300-foot descent over a mile of road, ending at a T-junction with CT 198 (Phoenixville Road).

Turn right onto CT 198, a slightly busier, faster road with a comfortable shoulder, and head up a short hill into a section of rolling road bordered by thick woods and overgrown meadows.

The road name changes to Chaplin Road just ahead, by a lovely stone wall and the town limit sign for Eastford, and continues for another 3 miles, bearing left to stay on Chaplin at the fork with General Lyon Road, named for the Civil War hero born nearby.

Continue on for another half-mile, into Phoenixville, a small community of Eastford. Carefully cross the intersection with US 44, staying on CT 198 where it is locally named Eastford Road, and note the colorful directional sign pointing out area attractions to westbound drivers on US 44, just to the left.

The road mostly heads uphill over the next several miles, past an old mechanic garage and along open fields and modest, spaced-out suburban homes. After crossing CT 244, near the 8.75-mile mark, the road passes a lovely cornfield, followed by a scenic historic cemetery bordered by a lovely wall of old fieldstones.

View of old church from Hampton General Store.

The route continues on past another expansive field, past the Eastford town limit sign, then into downtown Eastford. This slightly built-up section has a car dealership, the Coriander Cafe, and a number of small businesses, all at the intersection of multiple roads.

Turn right at the intersection, keeping the car dealership on the right, onto Old Colony Road, and up a particularly steep 40-foot climb. Continue on Old Colony Road for a mile, over a scenic brook and through open farmland, until the route turns right onto Schoolhouse Hill Road, for an equally steep climb of more than 200 feet.

After the climb, the road descends for a brief respite, ending at Boston Turnpike. Turn left and continue through a neighborhood of modest homes separated by forested yards and greenways. After a more gradual climb of 100 feet, you see a scenic pond on the right and continue down Boston Turnpike on a fast, steep descent, past an even more impressive pond view on the left, and into the next climb, a short, punchy hill.

At the peak of the hill, you can continue forward to add the Pomfret-Woodstock Loop (Ride 38). Follow the road to the Pomfret Green and then use the route from that section.

Continuing on the mapped course, turn right onto Peterson Road into a fast downhill ride through expansive farmland and fields bordering either side of the road. At a fork in the road, bear right onto North Road, for a faster, steeper descent through a mile of farms and forest.

Half-Moon Farm on route around Natchaug State Forest.

Turn right when the road ends, onto CT 97, Hampton Road, for a fairly steep section of road that curves out and around a beautiful cleared pond on the left, before a steeply rolling section that leads down into the village of Abington.

On the right, you pass Rucki's Abington Store, another quaint country market with a deli and packaged food. The building is adorned with kitschy signs and knick-knacks harkening back to a simpler time.

The road continues through a mix of modern suburban homes and older farmhouse-style buildings. On the left, near the 18.5-mile mark, the route passes the We-Li-Kit Farm, a sixth-generation family farm that has been making and selling homemade ice cream for 25 years. Just ahead, the road intersects with another section of the Airline Trail and then continues downhill through another section of well-spaced housing.

Up another hill, the route passes a horse-boarding farm, and the local name for the road becomes Pomfret Road, at the 19.75-mile mark.

Continue following the road over the next 3.5 miles, past a sanctuary on the right and through more scenic forests. Bear left onto Main Street, and ride three-quarters of a mile to the Hampton General Store to finish the ride.

Rucki's General Store in Abington.

MILES AND DIRECTIONS

0.0 Start by the Hampton General Store on Main Street

0.7 Left onto Station Road

3.3 Continue on Morey Road

4.3 Continue on Phoenixville Road

4.6 Continue on Chaplin Road

7.9 Continue on Eastford Road

9.7 Right onto Old Colony Road

10.6 Continue on Schoolhouse Hill Road

11.3 Left onto Boston Turnpike

14.3 Right onto Peterson Road

15.1 Continue on North Road

16.1 Continue on Hampton Road

19.7 Continue on Pomfret Road

23.2 Left on Main Street

23.9 Arrive at finish

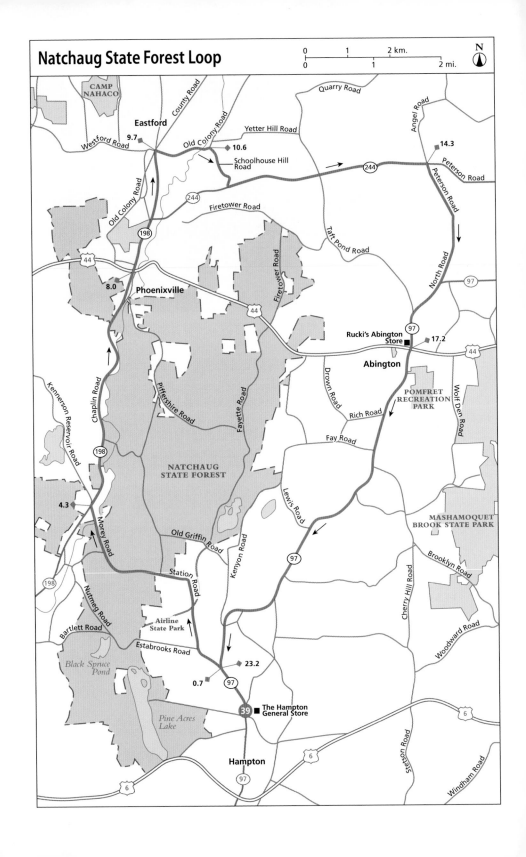

Natchaug State Forest Loop

0   1   2 km.

0   1   2 mi.

N

CAMP NAHACO

Quarry Road

Angel Road

Eastford

9.7

Westford Road

Old Colony Road

County Road

Yetter Hill Road

10.6

Schoolhouse Hill Road

14.3

Peterson Road

Peterson Road

244

244

Old Colony Road

198

Firetower Road

Firetower Road

Taft Pond Road

North Road

97

44

8.0

Phoenixville

44

Rucki's Abington Store

97

17.2

44

Abington

Chaplin Road

Kennerson Reservoir Road

198

Piffershire Road

Fayette Road

Drown Road

Rich Road

POMFRET RECREATION PARK

Wolf Den Road

Fay Road

NATCHAUG STATE FOREST

Lewis Road

MASHAMOQUET BROOK STATE PARK

4.3

Morey Road

Old Griffin Road

Kenyon Road

97

Brooklyn Road

Station Road

198

Nutmeg Road

Cherry Hill Road

Woodward Road

Bartlett Road

Airline State Park

Estabrooks Road

Black Spruce Pond

23.2

0.7

97

39

The Hampton General Store

6

Pine Acres Lake

Stetson Road

Hampton

6

97

6

Windham Road

RIDE INFORMATION

Bike Shops
Danielson Adventure Sports: 21 Furnace St., Danielson; (860) 774-6010; bikect.com

Local Events and Attractions
Natchaug State Forest: The forest is a 13,438-acre parcel, popular for horseback riding on miles of dedicated trails, backpack camping, hiking, and mountain biking. The park also has a historic site consisting of a large stone fireplace and chimney. These structures are all that remain of the birthplace of General Nathaniel Lyon, the first Union general killed in the Civil War.

The Airline Trail: This area is covered by a 22-mile section of the trail. Access it in Hampton at Potter Road, 0.6 mile north of its intersection with US 6 in Goodwin State Forest.

Restaurants
We-Li-Kit Ice Cream: 728 Hampton Rd., Pomfret Center; (860) 974-1095
Rucki's Abington Store: 489 Hampton Rd., Pomfret Center; (860) 974-0746
Coriander Cafe: 192 Eastford Rd., Eastford; (860) 315-7691; coriandercafe eastford.com

Restrooms
7.1 Miles: Natchaug State Forest

40

Thompson: Quaddick Pond

Thompson is the most northeastern town of both the state and the "Quiet Corner," bordered by neighboring Massachusetts and Rhode Island. This quiet town is notable for a number of natural features, including the 200-million-year-old Wilsonville Fault, created during the breakup of Pangea, and chiefly, Quaddick Pond and State Forest, both located in Quaddick, a small village community of Thompson.

Start: Quaddick Pond parking lot

Length: 10.6 miles

Riding time: 45 to 60 minutes

Best bike: Road bike

Terrain and trail surface: Asphalt

Traffic and hazards: Most of these roads are quiet country roads through scenic neighborhoods. East Thompson Road is an important local route into Massachusetts, so use caution and good judgment.

Things to see: Quaddick Reservoir, quiet back roads, several water crossings, the "Hermit Cave" in East Thompson

Fees: Quaddick State Park charges in-season parking fees (non-residents pay more).

Getting there: From US 44, turn onto Town Farm Road in East Putnam and follow the road north for 2.7 miles until the park entrance. From I-395N, take exit 97 to US 44 and follow the steps above. From I-395S, take exit 99 onto Quaddick Road and proceed south for 3.2 miles to Town Farm Road. Head left onto Town Farm Road and proceed north for 1.4 miles to the park entrance on the left.

GPS: 41.95579 / -71.81175

Quaddick Pond State Park.

THE RIDE

Quaddick Reservoir is a man-made body of water originating with the creation of a dam on the Five Mile River in 1865. The reservoir consists of three sections: Upper, Middle, and Lower. Quaddick State Park is on the Middle Reservoir, on a quiet section of road, and includes a sandy beach and cool, clear water for swimming and human-powered boating.

From the parking lot, turn right onto Quaddick Town Farm Road, a narrow country road with a wide shoulder just ahead. The route follows this largely quiet road for three-quarters of a mile and then makes a hairpin turn, right, onto Brandy Hill Road.

Brandy Hill Road is a short descent on a sometimes-choppy section of road. After a small neighborhood of waterfront cottages, the road approaches a narrow causeway and crosses the Quaddick Pond at a particularly scenic spot. Look to the left for an unobstructed view of two islands; the right-side island is smaller and wild, and the left island much larger and inhabited.

Brandy Hill Road continues on through another tiny neighborhood and then along a small bay, with two more islands, both inhabited. The farthest island, harder to spot, is larger and once operated a private seaplane base. The road continues on through a mix of low, modern homes and older saltboxes before a particularly scenic section of thick, towering woods and old stone walls to either side. As the road starts to climb a steep 80-foot hill, the trees clear, affording views of peaceful meadows and open fields.

After a half-mile respite on flatter ground, the route passes through the Thompson Rod and Gun Club property and turns left to stay on Brandy Hill Road up an even steeper climb, gaining nearly 60 feet of elevation over sections nearing a 15 percent grade.

The hill ends by a small green and a fork in the road. Bear right up to East Thompson Road and take a hard right turn. This slightly fast road heads downhill through an American Legion forest and then levels out with a pastoral pond view on the left. Just ahead is the Thompson Speedway, an internationally known racetrack that hosts a number of races each year. The grounds are an open green space, bordered with a low post fence.

After the park, the route passes a tiny pond on the left and an open field to the right, followed by a long, historic cemetery of faded memorials built right up to the road.

After the scenic cemetery, Sunny Croft Equestrian Center provides a more cheerful view; the farm provides instruction in jumping, running, and showmanship, in a track visible on the left.

The road continues over varied terrain into East Thompson, passing over an unremarkable portion of the Five Mile River used to create the reservoir passed on the first leg of the ride. In East Thompson, note the Southern New England Trunkline Trail that runs parallel to East Thompson Road. This is part of the Massachusetts off-road trail that connects to Connecticut's Airline Linear Trail. The Airline is a rails-to-trails project, starting in East Hampton and connecting to Massachusetts, currently existing in three separate segments. The section nearby, the Thompson Addition, is the shortest at 6.1 miles. The other two portions are roughly 21 miles each.

East Thompson is a quiet, rural residential area without a commercial center. Of interest however is the Corbeled Chamber, colloquially referred to

History of Quaddick Pond

Quaddick Pond was a fishing spot for the Nipmuc, a tribal group devastated by smallpox and early encounters with European settlers in Massachusetts. A century later, the area was established as an early elderly community for European settlers, then an industrial site in the late 19th century, and finally a residential neighborhood until the early 20th century. The artificial pond was prone to flooding, and the state eventually purchased the land in lieu of building flood control structures, turning it into a reserve and park.

View north from the causeway.

as the "Hermit Cave" by locals. No one knows who built this little cave a few hundred yards into the woods. The cave was built through a technique called corbelling, popular with the ancient Celtics. In this technique, stones are stacked atop each other, making a strong and enduring structure. Nearby, a historic plank bridge that was once a major thoroughfare still stands, although in great disrepair and no longer safe. This small oddity can be found off the New England Trunk Trail, preferably on foot, about 1,200 feet to the northeast.

Local journalist Kent Spottswood has shared the known history of the cave and bridge, and the fascinating history of early East Thompson Road, once an important transportation corridor, in a post on his Stone Wings blog (http://stonewings.wordpress.com). In addition to likely origin stories behind the cave, Spottswood recounts the life-threatening journey of an early president over the rough roads, and one of the worst train accidents in US history, involving a collision of four trains.

Thompson has a rich treasure trove of historical artifacts, photographs, and documents, including several well-researched history books. If interested, contact the Thompson Historical Society (www.thompsonhistorical.org/) to learn more.

Turn right onto New Road, a quiet little back road bordered by heavy woods and forest, and continue for a mile until the road ends in a T-junction with Quaddick Town Farm Road.

Turn left onto Quaddick Farm Road, just before reaching the 7.5-mile mark, and follow this tranquil back road as it slopes gently along through the

View south from the causeway.

Quaddick State Forest. These woods are owned by the state and used to provide a natural buffer for the northernmost section of the Quaddick Reservoir.

As the forests thin and houses become more numerous, the road approaches the parking lot for Quaddick State Park, where you finish the ride.

This is a very quiet and scenic area, with few options for food. The Quaddick Country Store is a surprising treat, with highly regarded pizza and even Irish pub fare like fish 'n' chips with hand-cut fries, all in an unremarkable building resembling a small convenience store.

MILES AND DIRECTIONS

0.0   Start at Quaddick State Park on Quaddick Town Farm Road

0.7   Right onto Brandy Hill Road

3.4   Right onto East Thompson Road

6.5   Right onto New Road

7.4   Left onto Quaddick Town Farm Road

10.6   Finish at park

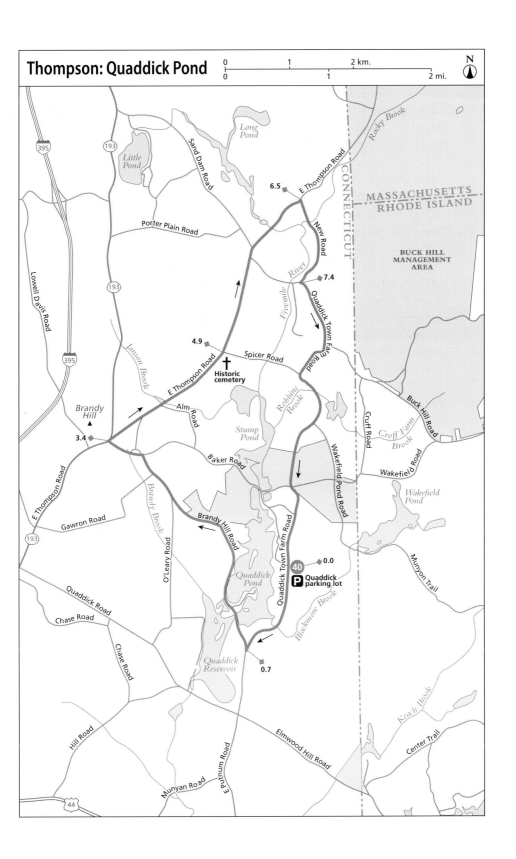

Thompson: Quaddick Pond

0   1   2 km.
0   1   2 mi.

N

395

193

Long
Pond

Little
Pond

Sand Dam Road

Porter Plain Road

Rocky Brook

CONNECTICUT

MASSACHUSETTS
RHODE ISLAND

BUCK HILL
MANAGEMENT
AREA

6.5

E Thompson Road

New Road

Fivemile River

7.4

Quaddick Town Farm Road

193

Lowell Davis Road

Ianson Brook

4.9

E Thompson Road

Spicer Road

✝
Historic
cemetery

Robbins Brook

Buck Hill Road

Cruff Road

Croff Farm Brook

Wakefield Road

395

Brandy
Hill ▲

3.4

Alm Road

Stump
Pond

Baker Road

Wakefield Pond Road

Wakefield
Pond

E Thompson Road

Gawron Road

Brandy Brook

O'Leary Road

Brandy Hill Road

Quaddick Town Farm Road

40

0.0

P Quaddick
parking lot

Munyon Trail

193

Quaddick
Pond

Blackmore Brook

Quaddick Road

Chase Road

Chase Road

Quaddick
Reservoir

0.7

Hill Road

Munyan Road

E Putnum Road

Elmwood Hill Road

Keach Brook

Center Trail

44

RIDE INFORMATION

Bike Shops
Danielson Adventure Sports: 21 Furnace St., Danielson; (860) 774-6010; bikect.com

Local Events and Attractions
Southern New England Trunkline Trail: This hiking trail comes from Massachusetts and connects with the nearby Airline Trail.

Thompson Historical Society: The society maintains a museum and gift shop in the old town hall (thompsonhistorical.org).

Restaurants
Monte Bianco: 1097 Thompson Rd., Thompson; (860) 923-0202; montebianco restaurant.com

Cakettes Coffee Shop: 773 Quinebaug Rd., Quinebaug; (860) 497-0011

Raceway Restaurant: 205 E Thompson Rd., Thompson; (860) 923-9591; racewayrestaurant.com

Restrooms
Miles: Quaddick Pond State Park

References

This is a very incomplete list of additional resources and where to find out more about the places these rides visit. Nearly every town in this guide has a historical society website, for further research.

BOOKS

Diana Muir. *Reflections in Bullough's Pond*. Hanover, NH: University Press of New England, 2000.

Dr. Lucianne Lavin. *Connecticut's Indigenous Peoples*. Yale University, 2013.

Chard Powers Smith. *The Housatonic: Puritan River*. Rinehart, 1946.

John Mason. *A Brief History of the Pequot War*. Thomas Prince, 1736.

Rachel Carley. *Building Greenwich: Architecture and Design, 1640 to the Present*. The Historical Society of the Town of Greenwich, 2005.

Douglas W. Rae. *City: Urbanism and Its End*. Yale University Press, 2005.

Hon. Ralph D. Smith. *The History of Guilford, Connecticut, from Its First Settlement in 1639*. Albany, NY: J. Munsell, Printer, 1877.

Ross King. *Defiant Spirits: The Modernist Revolution of the Group of Seven*. Vancouver, B.C., Canada: Douglas & McIntyre, 2011.

WEBSITES

Post on Stone Wings, Kent Spottswood's blog, about the hermit cave and Thompson
https://stonewings.wordpress.com/2012/03/14/the-hermit-cave-hot-house-cold-house-or-something-in-between/

Website for the Glass House in New Canaan
http://theglasshouse.org/

The Florence Griswold Museum site
https://florencegriswoldmuseum.org/

Weir Farm Art Center
http://www.weirfarmartcenter.org/

LaChat Town Farm in Weston
http://www.lachattownfarm.org/

Sound Cyclists Bike Club
http://www.soundcyclists.com/

Elm City Cycling, New Haven bike club and advocacy
https://elmcitycycling.org/

Bike Walk CT, advocacy and events group based in Hartford County
http://www.bikewalkct.org/

Pequot Cyclists in New London County
http://pequotcyclists.com/

The Bicycling Committee of the Connecticut Chapter of the Appalachian Mountain Club
http://ct-amc.org/cycling/index.shtm

The Southern Connecticut Cycle Club
http://www.ctcycle.org/

Eastern Bloc Cycle Club in the Simsbury/Avon/Canton area
http://www.easternbloc.net/

Bike races throughout the Northeast
http://carpediemracing.org/

Expo Wheelmen cycling club in Manchester
http://www.expowheelmen.com/

Laurel Bicycle Club, based out of Woodbridge, CT
http://www.laurelbicycleclub.org/Home.html

Triathlons and other competitions, primarily in southwest CT
http://www.teammossman.com/

The biggest metric century ride in Connecticut, held every spring
http://www.bloominmetric.com/

The Two Ferry Ride, starting in Glastonbury and covering Middletown, Haddam, East Haddam, and Manchester
http://www.cyclingconcepts.com/two-ferry-ride-time/

About the Author

David Streever is a writer and cyclist originally from the shores of the Connect-icut River. He started out recreationally riding in his hilly hometown of East Haddam and became a dedicated road cyclist and advocate with the help of his New Haven community. David is a professional writer who covered the 2015 UCI bike race in Richmond. In addition to cycling, he also writes essays about ethics, religion, and social issues.

He now lives in Richmond, Virginia, in a rambling home in the city's historic Fan District, with his Virginian wife and their bike-hating dog and disinterested cat.